Funding Virtue

GLOBAL POLICY BOOKS
FROM THE CARNEGIE ENDOWMENT

Africa's New Leaders: Democracy or State Reconstruction?
Marina Ottaway

Aiding Democracy Abroad: The Learning Curve
Thomas Carothers

From Migrants to Citizens: Membership in a Changing World
T. Alexander Aleinikoff and Douglas Klusmeyer, Editors

New Markets, New Opportunities? Economic and Social Mobility in a Changing World
Copublished with Brookings Institution Press
Nancy Birdsall and Carol Graham, Editors

Repairing the Regime: Preventing the Spread of Weapons of Mass Destruction
Copublished with Routledge
Joseph Cirincione, Editor

The Third Force: The Rise of Transnational Civil Society
Ann M. Florini, Editor

Funding Virtue

Civil Society Aid and Democracy Promotion

Marina Ottaway
Thomas Carothers
Editors

CARNEGIE ENDOWMENT FOR INTERNATIONAL PEACE
Washington, D.C.

To order, contact Carnegie's distributor:
The Brookings Institution Press
Department 029, Washington, D.C. 20042-0029, USA
1-800-275-1447 or 1-202-797-6258
Fax 202-797-2960, Email bibooks@brook.edu

Printed in the United States of America on acid-free, recycled paper with
vegetable oil based inks by Malloy Lithographing, Ann Arbor, Mich.

Typesetting by AlphaWebTech, Mechanicsville, Md.

Library of Congress Cataloging-in-Publication Data

Funding virtue : civil society aid and democracy promotion /
 Marina Ottaway, Thomas Carothers, editors.
  p. cm.
 Includes bibliographical references and index.
 ISBN 0-87003-181-3 (alk. paper) — ISBN 0-87003-178-3 (pbk. : alk.
paper)
 1. Civil society. 2. Democratization. 3. Economic assistance. I.
Ottaway, Marina, 1943- . II. Carothers, Thomas, 1956- .
 JC337 .F85 2000
 327.1'11—dc21

                                                              00-010804

 06 05 04 03 02 01 00 5 4 3 2 1   1st Printing 2000

Contents

Foreword

TODAY'S RAPIDLY EXPANDING ROLE of civil society in political, economic, and social life, both within and across borders, commands attention in many quarters. Some people invest great hopes in civil society, holding it out as a unique repository of values, virtue, and voluntarism. Others worry about the effects of proliferating nongovernmental organizations, arguing that governments are still the only legitimate source of order and authority and that too much of a good thing on the side of citizen empowerment could turn out to be a source of domestic political gridlock and international impotence.

Debate and discussion over civil society are especially prevalent in the domain of democratization. After the heroic dissidents of Eastern Europe adopted the mantle of civil society in the 1980s, the concept suddenly caught on as a key element in the "Third Wave" of democracy that was spreading around the world in those years. Assistance programs aimed at fostering civil society became a major part of the democracy promotion efforts of Western aid agencies, private foundations, and international nongovernmental organizations. Under the rubric of such assistance, thousands of nongovernmental organizations in the developing world and the post-communist societies of Eastern Europe and the former Soviet Union now receive training, advice, and financial support.

Knowing how much a vibrant civil society has contributed to America throughout its history, it is hard not to believe that promoting civil society abroad is a worthwhile endeavor. At the same time, it is natural to ask how much the aid in this field is actually accomplishing. This timely book addresses precisely that question. The book's editors, two leading experts in democracy promotion, have assembled a talented group of authors, each of whom has had hands-on practical experience with civil society aid at either the giving or receiving end. The editors asked them to address a challenging set of questions: What conceptions of civil society do aid providers employ, and how do these conceptions relate to local realities in the recipient countries? Where do the programs make a difference, and where do they fall short? How can civil society aid be improved? The result is an unusually frank collection of essays, with case studies from Asia, Latin America, the Middle East, Africa, and Eastern Europe, that goes a long way to answering basic questions about this still rapidly growing area of international assistance.

The diversity of the authors leads to contending perspectives that enrich the book. At the same time, several common conclusions stand out. Most generally, the authors agree that civil society development is a valuable, even essential area of focus for Western public and private aid. They also raise significant questions about the limited focus of most civil society aid, in particular the concentration of aid to Westernized nongovernmental organizations engaged in public interest advocacy, and they urge donors to cast a wider net. They also highlight the many sticky political choices inherent in civil society aid and pop the bubble of the idea that civil society development is somehow a safely apolitical domain. Finally, they find many shortcomings in the day-to-day methods of implementation of such aid and usefully point to some remedies.

Civil society aid clearly is a field with a future. This book helps chart the path for that future and will, I believe, be an important part of it. I am proud that the Carnegie Endowment has undertaken this research project and am delighted to offer you the results.

JESSICA T. MATHEWS
President, Carnegie Endowment for International Peace

Acknowledgments

WE WOULD LIKE TO THANK Michael Foley for his insightful comments on a draft of the manuscript and Will Barndt for his research help throughout. Dianna Christenson handled the preparation of the manuscript with consistent good cheer and competence. Alice Phillips and Lynn Whittaker contributed much in editing and copyediting. Trish Reynolds and Sherry Pettie of the Carnegie Endowment publications department smoothly guided the process of going from manuscript to book. We are greatly indebted to the Ford Foundation, especially Mahnaz Ispahani, for financial support that made the whole project possible.

Introduction

The Burgeoning World of Civil Society Aid

Thomas Carothers and Marina Ottaway

U.S. AID AIMED AT PROMOTING the development of civil society in other countries has increased dramatically in the past ten years. In the nearly one hundred countries in Latin America, Africa, Asia, the Middle East, Eastern Europe, and the former Soviet Union where the U.S. government is engaged in democracy assistance, civil society aid is almost everywhere part of the portfolio. The rise of civil society assistance is by no means strictly a U.S. government phenomenon. Many of the major private American, European, and Japanese foundations are deeply involved in this arena. In addition, all of the major bilateral donors engaged in democracy and governance work have begun to give attention to civil society development. A number of international institutions have taken up the topic as well. All around the world, one hears aid officials and aid recipients talking about civil society and its importance for democratization. Aid officials happily report that they have "got civil society talking to the government" or "developed civil society considerably." Some aid recipients feel compelled to assure foreign visitors that they are "civil society representatives" and that the basic goal of their efforts is to "make civil society strong and independent." A term that was scarcely used within the aid community ten years ago has become a ubiquitous concept in discussions and documents about democracy promotion worldwide.

At the same time, articles and books pour forth in great numbers from academia on the theory of civil society and the nature of its development. Definitional analysis dominates the discussion although more work

3

is now appearing on patterns of civil society development in transitional countries in different parts of the world, especially Eastern Europe and Latin America.

In the eyes of many donors and recipients, and even of many democratic theorists, the idea that civil society is always a positive force for democracy, indeed even the most important one, is unassailable. An active—"vibrant" is the adjective of choice—civil society is both the force that can hold governments accountable and the base upon which a truly democratic political culture can be built. There follows from this assumption the related idea that promoting civil society development is key to democracy-building.

This book takes a hard look at these assumptions about civil society and the burgeoning universe of civil society assistance. It very much accepts the idea that democracy requires continuous, active participation in public affairs by citizens organized in a great variety of interest groups, rather than simply the periodic casting of votes by unorganized individuals. It also shares the common assumption that democracy requires civically aware citizens who combine understanding of and confidence in the political system with a healthy skepticism about the performance and good faith of politicians. And it proceeds from the belief that it is valuable and important for democracy promoters to work from the bottom-up rather than just the top-down in developing and transitional societies. What some of the authors question is the assumption that the activities that go under the rubric of "civil society assistance" produce the kinds of far-reaching results that donors implicitly or explicitly promise by framing their aid in such sweeping terms. The problem is not simply that donors' efforts are limited in scope and thus can have only a limited impact—this is unavoidable with any assistance program. Rather, the problem resides both in the conception of civil society that donors build into their assistance programs and the methods by which they implement such aid.

The Rise of Democracy Assistance

In the mid-1980s, the United States and many other wealthy, established democracies started sponsoring increasing amounts of what has come to be known as "democracy assistance": aid programs specifically designed either to help nondemocratic countries become democratic or to help countries that have initiated democratic transitions consolidate their democratic systems. The U.S. government currently devotes more than $500 million annually to such activities, with a number of U.S. agencies (primarily the U.S. Agency for International Development—USAID) and U.S.-funded nongovernmental organizations (such as the National Endowment for Democracy, the Asia Foundation, and the Eurasia Foundation) responsible for developing and implementing suitable programs. Many other bilateral donors, including most of the major European countries as well as Canada, Australia, Japan, and others, have also moved into the democracy aid arena. A number of international institutions have followed suit, among them the United Nations, the Organization of American States, the Organization for Security and Cooperation in Europe, and others. In a relatively short period of time, democracy assistance has become an important part of development cooperation and of international relations generally.

Two main factors have prompted the democracy aid boom. The first is the global democratic trend itself. As democratic openings spread through Latin America and parts of Asia in the 1980s and then surged in Eastern Europe, the former Soviet Union, and sub-Saharan Africa at the start of the 1990s, the established democracies have sought to respond positively. Although the United States and most other OECD countries frequently maintain friendly relations with nondemocratic regimes, once a nondemocratic country experiences a democratic opening, the established democracies are inclined to support it. They do so out of both a generalized idealistic sense that democracy is the best political system and the belief that democratic regimes are likely to make better political and economic partners over the long run.

The second factor is the end of the Cold War. During the Cold War, efforts by the United States and other powerful democracies to influence the internal political evolution of other countries were often linked to security objectives. Aid agencies within the major Western donors shied away from politically oriented work, seeing it as a potentially dangerous domain for developmentalists. Within most developing countries, skepticism and resistance to externally sponsored political programs were understandably high, providing little fertile ground for such work. The end of the Cold War substantially lowered ideological tensions and barriers in many parts of the world and dramatically reduced the assumption that any politically oriented aid was driven by underlying security concerns. Combined with the rapid increase in the number of democratic openings, the end of the Cold War thus greatly facilitated the rise of explicitly democracy-oriented aid efforts.

Civil society assistance was not a major component of democracy aid at the outset. In the first phase, which unfolded primarily from the mid-1980s to the early 1990s, donors concentrated on elections. The United States and other aid-giving countries underwrote countless election observer missions and election administration projects to support the many transitional elections occurring in the developing world and the former communist countries of Eastern Europe and the Soviet Union. In the second phase, donors added to their portfolio of democracy assistance the reform of major state institutions, especially judiciaries and legislatures, to help render them more competent, accountable, and representative. In the third phase, which arose in the mid-1990s, they began to focus on strengthening civil society. In the past five to seven years, civil society programs have mushroomed. In most countries attempting transitions to democracy, numerous donors are sponsoring programs explicitly labeled as "civil society assistance" with pro-democratic objectives. More broadly, the general notion that civil society development is critical to democratization has become a new mantra in both aid and diplomatic circles.

Why Civil Society Assistance?

What accounts for the burgeoning interest in civil society assistance as a way to promote democracy? Americans often explain their enthusiasm for the subject as a logical outcome of America's own Tocquevillian tradition. With the long history of grassroots activism that so impressed the French visitor more than 150 years ago and continues to distinguish American democracy from that of Western European countries, Americans, it is argued, are naturally inclined to focus on civil society when they seek to promote democracy abroad. For the United States at least, civil society assistance is explained as a natural extrapolation of domestic experience.

Unfortunately, however, the facts do not support this explanation. Throughout the Cold War, American aid providers and policy-makers were habitually averse to the idea of bottom-up development, fearing that grassroots political activity would veer into leftist political movements. In many countries the United States supported anticommunist "friendly tyrants" who harshly repressed populist movements. To the extent that the United States did try to encourage democratization in other countries, it was through the indirect method of promoting economic development, in the hope that economic growth would produce democratic change; or it was by supporting moderate political parties against the political extremes in highly polarized societies, such as in Central America in the 1980s.

The exception was in the communist world, where political activists were bound to oppose rather than to support leftist ideologies. In the 1980s in Poland, Czechoslovakia, Hungary, and to a lesser extent the Soviet Union, East Germany, and Bulgaria, emergent civil society groups heroically challenged communist rule. The United States backed such groups, sometimes financially and sometimes diplomatically. When the revolutions of 1989 arrived, civil society suddenly gained cachet in Eastern Europe as the key to democratization. The "lesson" of the fall of the Berlin Wall—that civil society could be a major force for democracy—was incorporated during the 1990s in the democratization programs implemented in many other parts of the world. U.S. civil society assistance should thus be seen as the product of particular historical developments and circumstances, rather than as an inevitable extension of America's Tocquevillian tradition. The fact that many West European donors, who do not draw upon American-style Tocquevillian traditions, have gravitated to very much the same sort of civil society aid programs as the United States further casts doubt on the Tocqueville factor as a determining causal explanation.

In addition, initial experiences with other types of democracy aid and the political shortcomings of many unfolding democratic transitions also encouraged the United States and other donors to turn to civil society strengthening as a means of promoting democracy. Aid providers were able to help produce elections in transitional countries, but they soon found that elections in and of themselves were at most only a very preliminary step toward genuinely democratic societies. When they turned their attention to the reform of state institutions as a way to deepen fledgling democratic systems, they found such efforts much more daunting than anticipated. Will to reform was often lacking at the top of such institutions among incumbents whose power was directly threatened. Even personnel at the middle and lower levels, ensconced in comfortable routines, often displayed little enthusiasm for change. More fundamentally, reform of government institutions was a large-scale undertaking that did not dovetail well with the limited funds available, an issue of particular importance to U.S. aid providers given the sharp cutbacks in U.S. foreign aid in the 1990s. A comprehensive program of judicial reform, for example, was far more than any donor could think of financing in any country. The assistance that USAID and most other donors were in a position to offer was often too modest to make a fundamental difference with major state institutions in transitional countries.

Civil society assistance appeared to address all these problems at the same time. As new organizations within transitional countries, civil society groups did not have interests vested in the old system and thus appeared to be by nature genuinely reform-oriented. They also seemed to be a potential source of pressure for reform that could reach entrenched power holders. The icing on the cake was that these organizations were also small enough that modest amounts of aid were significant to them. A $20,000 grant, ridiculously small if applied to judicial reform, could make all the difference for a struggling civil society organization in a poor country. Civil society assistance made a virtue out of necessity by providing a theoretical justification for the small-scale assistance dictated by many donor budgets.

In the United States, the arrival to power of the Clinton administration in early 1993, with a new set of political appointments to the senior ranks of USAID and the State Department, confirmed the emphasis on civil society. Although both the Reagan and Bush administrations had stressed at the rhetorical level that nongovernmental organizations (NGOs) were better vehicles than government agencies to tackle social and economic problems, when it came to democracy promotion they put the emphasis on government agencies. The political appointees who had occupied high positions within USAID before 1993 were not generally inclined toward a bottom-up approach to democratization, or to development generally. The Clinton appointees, in contrast, often came to government from the world of NGOs, were much less affected by the lingering wariness of citizen movements, and changed the emphasis of democracy assistance accordingly.

What Is Civil Society?

Although "civil society" has become a very familiar term, its meaning is still often elusive. Among political scientists and philosophers, an active debate has emerged in recent years over the definition of the term. These debates are not purely academic. On the contrary, each definition implies a different course donors should pursue in order to promote civil society and, through it, democracy. It is thus worth briefly reviewing some of the major points of the scholarly debate before turning to what aid providers and democracy promoters mean when they talk of civil society.

There exists a fair amount of scholarly consensus around a broad view of civil society as one of the basic elements of a society, alongside the state and the market. In this account, civil society is:

> an intermediate associational realm between state and family populated by organizations which are separate from the state, enjoy autonomy in relation to the state and are formed voluntarily by members of the society to protect or extend their interests or values.[1]

This associational realm is highly varied in most societies, being made up of groups that vary:

> between "modern" interest groups such as trade unions or professional associations and "traditional" ascriptive organizations based on kinship, ethnicity, culture or region; between formal organizations and informal social networks based on patrimonial or clientelistic allegiances; between those institutions with specifically political roles as pressure or advocacy groups and those whose activities remain largely outside the political system; between legal or open associations and secret or illegal organizations such as the Freemasons, the Mafia or the Triads; between associations which accept the political status quo or those who seek to transform it by changing the political regime.[2]

In this view, civil society is not a normative concept: "there is no teleological virtue in the notion of civil society."[3] Moreover, civil society does not play any simple well-defined role or maintain any one relationship with the state. It is largely autonomous of the state but may in parts overlap with or depend upon the state. Although parts of civil society may interact regularly with the state, others are remote from it. Understandably, this broad view of civil society has little appeal for donors, given that it points to an entity or sector too encompassing and inchoate, and insufficiently democratic to boot, for them to consider supporting.

Another influential alternative conception of civil society focuses less on the importance of specific types of organizations or associations than on the role that certain associations play in fostering norms of reciprocity and trust, or what Robert Putnam calls "social capital." These norms provide the cultural pedestal on which democratic institutions are built. Putnam argues that citizen participation in chorus groups, bowling leagues, parent-teacher associations, and other civic groups generates "mutual reciprocity, the resolution of dilemmas of collective action, and the broadening of social identities," all of which contribute directly and indirectly to social cohesion and democratization.[4] This view of civil society also held little appeal for donors, particularly for USAID: with a limited amount of money, the need to produce visible results in a short time, and a critical press and an even more critical Congress ever alert to denounce waste of taxpayer money, USAID could hardly get in the business of setting up bowling leagues in the name of democracy.

A further issue that provokes disagreement in scholarly debates on civil society is the relationship of civil society to political society. A majority of writers hold that political society—that is, political parties and other groups that explicitly seek to gain political control of the state—is separate from civil society. Some, however, assert that the line between the two concepts is often not clear. Michael Foley and Bob Edwards argue, for example, that social movements and other explicitly political groups effectively play the pro-democratic role that civil society is thought to perform. "In short," they assert, "decidedly political associations may play the roles attributed to civil associations in the civil society argument, and may play them better."[5] Some authors writing about non-Western societies have argued for the inclusion of political parties in civil society. Donors have chosen to consider civil and political society as separate realms because, as we shall see later, doing so helps defend the claim that it is possible to support democracy without becoming involved in partisan politics or otherwise interfering unduly in the domestic politics of another country.

The view that has most influenced donors, especially in the U.S. government, is one according to which civil society consists only of voluntary associations that directly foster democracy and promote democratic consolidation. These are associations that specifically seek interaction with the state, whether to advocate interests of the citizens, to oppose nondemocratic behavior of the state, or to hold states accountable to citizens for their actions. Donors favor groups that interact with the state through advocacy work and those that do not explicitly compete for political office. In its purest form, this normative conception also insists that not only must a group actively promote democracy to be part of civil society but must also follow internal democratic procedures.

Promoting Civil Society in Practice

When they attempt to strengthen civil society as a means of promoting democracy, aid providers from the United States and most donor countries end up concentrating on a very narrow set of organizations: professionalized NGOs dedicated to advocacy or civic education work on public interest issues directly relating to democratization, such as election monitoring, voter education, governmental transparency, and political and civil rights generally. These are organizations set up along the lines of advocacy NGOs in the United States and other established democracies, with designated management, full-time staff, an office, and a charter or statement of mission. Some U.S. aid providers have taken to calling such organizations "democracy groups," a term that rarely has much currency in the recipient countries themselves.

Many of these groups, though by no means all, have very small memberships and thus speak in the name of constituencies that have given them no mandate. Absent from most civil society assistance programs is the wide range of other types of organizations that typically make up civil society in most countries, from sports clubs and cultural associations to religious organizations and less formalized social networks. Such groups, which would undoubtedly be difficult to assist, often play important roles in political transitions. Media and trade unions do frequently receive support through democracy programs, but outside of the efforts specifically designated as civil society aid.

Following their initial surge of interest in this very narrow band of advocacy and civic education NGOs, donors have started broadening the scope of civil society programs that have a democratic focus. They increasingly reach NGOs whose advocacy work aims at social and economic issues rather than specifically political ones. These may include environmental groups, women's organizations, indigenous people's groups, tenants' associations, business associations, and others. Additionally, they are shifting emphasis away from groups based in the capital cities of the recipient countries—which typically received much of the donors' attention in the initial phase of civil society assistance—to more local groups operating in smaller cities, towns, or villages. But this broadening process has been slow and cautious, and in their democracy-oriented programs, donors continue supporting above all urban-based advocacy and civic education NGOs.

There are several reasons for this emphasis. To start with, advocacy and civic education are activities that seek to have a direct impact on political development. It is through advocacy work that NGOs perform some of the key pro-democratic roles of civil society—articulating citizens' interests and disciplining the state. Civic education, usually involving efforts to teach people the basic principles and procedures of democracy, similarly connects directly to donors' democratic goals. In addition, democracy promoters are attracted by the idea of nonpartisan civic engagement as a means of producing political change. This idea has appeal as a technocratic, peaceful, rationalistic mode of activity that permits external actors to have influence on the political life of other countries without explicitly "playing politics." NGOs are attractive because they seek to perform many of the same roles as political parties—representing interests, building participation, and checking the state—not through ideological appeals and organized competition among different political groupings, but on the basis of nonpartisan civic engagement. Civil society actors, which supposedly seek to make their countries better by influencing government policies but not by seeking power, can thus appear to make up an antipolitical domain, a pristine realm in which a commitment to civic values and the public interest rules in place of traditional divisions, beliefs, and interests.

There is also a more mundane reason for donors' preference for professionalized NGOs. These groups have, or can be trained to have, the administrative capabilities donors need for their own bureaucratic requirements. They can produce grant proposals (usually in English), budgets, accounting reports, project reports, and all the other documents donors ask of beneficiaries. In contrast, many other types of organizations within the civil societies of developing countries, especially informal associations, social movements, and other kinds of networks, are not set up to be administratively responsive to donor needs.

It should be noted that the civil society programs that are part of democracy aid are by no means the only donor-supported programs channeled through NGOs or civil society more broadly. Since the 1980s, donors have spent an increasing proportion of social and economic aid—in the areas of public health, population control, agriculture, poverty reduction, and small business development—through NGOs in the recipient countries. Such programs clearly have effects on the development of civil society in those countries, even though the programs are not designed explicitly with civil society development as an objective. As a result, there is considerable debate in the field whether NGOs whose work focuses mainly on economic development and social issues make as much a contribution to democracy as those that focus specifically on democracy. According to this argument, all NGOs promote participation, and thus empowerment, and this is the basis on which democracy can be built. We do not reject the idea that all activities that entail citizen participation help build social capital and thus have an indirect impact on democracy. Analytically, however, we find it more useful to differentiate between those NGOs donors treat as being directly engaged in democracy work and those that donors consider to be contributing only indirectly to democratization. In this book we thus focus on the civil society aid that is carried out explicitly as democracy-building work. We do not attempt a study of Western aid to NGOs generally. Nor do we try to assess the overall contribution that NGOs make in developing countries.

Taking Stock

This burgeoning world of civil society aid under the democracy rubric is freighted with high expectations. Democracy promoters wax enthusiastic about civil society, conveying a heady sense that they are "onto something" and that civil society is the key that will unlock the door to democratic consolidation in the many countries that have embarked upon democratic transitions. But the modest level of funding for civil society assistance, the inherent difficulty of intervening in countries that donors only partially understand and of changing the fabric of the society, and the continuing skepticism of even democratizing governments that NGOs have a legitimate role alongside elected officials all suggest that civil society assistance may not always live up to claims made about it. With the 1990s now over, and an increasing number of questions being raised about the health and the future of the "Third Wave" of democracy, it is a natural time to step back and take stock of this domain. This book seeks to do that. It aims to illuminate the underlying assumptions and expectations that donors bring to civil society assistance, the basic methods and forms of the aid programs themselves, and the kinds of impact they do and do not have.

The world of civil society aid has become too large to permit a systematic examination of the whole realm. Our approach instead is that of selective sampling, based on a regional comparative framework. We focus on five of the main regions that are recipients of civil society aid—the Middle East, Africa, Asia, Eastern Europe, and Latin America. For each region we present two chapters: a broad-ranging study of civil society aid to that region, written by a U.S. or West European researcher with hands-on experience in that region; and a country-specific study of civil society aid, written by a citizen of that country who has extensive experience as a civil society activist, a scholar of civil society development, or both.

The primary focus of the studies is U.S. government-funded civil society aid, the main source of which is USAID. Some of the chapters also examine European aid. Although we focus on U.S. aid, we do so because it is the most accessible to us, not because we believe it is unique or uniquely important. In fact the studies in this volume largely confirm our belief going in that the basic issues of conception, design, implementation, and impact relating to U.S. civil society aid are largely similar for almost all Western aid efforts explicitly directed at civil society development.

The chapters in this volume show that while USAID and other donors basically follow the same approach to civil society assistance everywhere, civil society develops different characteristics in the various regions. History and culture, the characteristics of civil society organizations that existed before donors started their programs, and the presence or absence of civil society organizations other than those assisted by the donors create a context for donor programs that influence their outcome. Writing about Latin America, Michael Shifter refers to this phenomenon as the "civil society puzzle"—the challenge for the donors to reconcile a region's tradition of civil society, the organizations that have emerged more recently to press for political change, and their own views of an effective, democratic civil society. The puzzle is solved relatively easily in Eastern Europe, where communist governments eliminated independent organizations and almost all civil society groups are new, as Kevin Quigley and Dan Petrescu show. But the puzzle is proving very difficult in other regions: in the Middle East, for example, donor-supported civil society organizations coexist uneasily with a vast array of Islamist organizations that are anathema to donors but enjoy a high level of popular support, as Mustapha Kamel Al-Sayyid and Imco Brouwer argue.

Another issue highlighted by a number of chapters is the fact that civil society assistance risks undermining the legitimacy of the very organizations it seeks to promote. Al-Sayyid, Christopher Landsberg, Marina Ottaway, and Carlos Basombrío point out that civil society organizations that accept donor support often come under suspicion or are seen as less legitimate and authentic than organizations that receive no external support. But such support can also play a critical role, as Basombrío and Landsberg argue, when government repression closes the political space and threatens the survival of independent organizations. Many of the studies also show that donors confront a challenge in adapting to the changing requirements of civil society as political circumstances change—both Eastern Europe and Africa provide interesting examples.

Several chapters, but above all those by Mary Racelis and Stephen Golub on Asia, raise the important issue of the contribution to democracy made by civil society organizations whose primary focus is socioeconomic development. This is particularly evident in the Philippines, where development NGOs have a presence everywhere, from Manila to the villages. These organizations have created a tradition of participation and activism that helped put an end to the Marcos regime and bring Corazon Aquino to power long before donors formally conceived of civil society assistance as a means of promoting democracy. But Racelis also shows the limits of the political role of development NGOs, which have encountered scant success when they have deliberately sought to sway their members to vote for pro-democracy candidates. Development NGOs appear to create ample social capital that does not translate directly into political clout.

Several chapters also show the limitations of even pro-democracy NGOs as instruments for political change. Civil society organizations of the type favored by democracy promoters may be very important at times—Basombrío argues they are a last resort when political space is closing down—but they are no substitute for political parties or social movements. Organizations of civil society, Basombrío and Ottaway argue, are not representative organizations, so they can speak on behalf of people, but not for them. Petrescu also raises the issue whether the attempt to influence legislation by nonrepresentative advocacy organizations—an approach favored by USAID—is really democratic or is simply an imitation of a questionable U.S. practice that gives special interest groups the possibility of exercising inordinate influence.

In addition to these and other problems emerging from the concept of civil society that underlies assistance programs, all authors also point to numerous shortcomings of implementation. Quigley summarizes these problems well when he contrasts the lofty goals of the donors to the meager results they frequently achieve. Many of the authors denounce the slowness of the planning process, the excessive and at times arcane controls, the narrow conditions for eligibility that make it difficult in some countries to find suitable recipients, and the onerous reporting requirements. Several point to the donors' facile assumption that their programs are encouraging political pluralism when in reality they are simply creating a plurality of organizations. Many of the articles also call for a rethinking of the relation between donor governments and organizations and the recipient NGOs, with the aim of increasing the autonomy of the latter.

This brief summary does not do justice to the array of issues raised by the individual chapters or to the range of attitudes toward civil society assistance on the part of the authors. We thus turn to the regional and country studies before returning to some more general issues in the concluding chapter of this volume.

Notes

1. Gordon White, "Civil Society, Democratization and Development (I): Clearing the Analytical Ground," *Democratization,* vol. 1, no. 3 (Autumn 1994), p. 379.

2. Ibid. at 379–80.

3. Jean-François Bayart, "Civil Society in Africa," in Patrick Chabal, ed., *Political Domination in Africa* (Cambridge, UK: Cambridge University Press, 1986), p. 118.

4. Robert D. Putnam, "Bowling Alone: America's Declining Social Capital," *Journal of Democracy,* vol. 6, no. 1 (January 1995), p. 76.

5. Michael W. Foley and Bob Edwards, "The Paradox of Civil Society," *Journal of Democracy,* vol. 7, no. 3 (July 1996), p. 48.

Part One

Middle East

1

Weak Democracy and Civil Society Promotion: The Cases of Egypt and Palestine

Imco Brouwer

IF THERE IS ONE REGION of the globe in which democracy is deemed extremely weak and difficult or impossible to develop in the near future, it is the Arab world. At the beginning of twenty-first century, none of the twenty-two members of the Arab League has a democratic system of government or can be said to be democratizing, and only nine—Algeria, Egypt, Jordan, Kuwait, Lebanon, Morocco, the Palestinian proto-state, Tunisia, and Yemen—have experienced a degree of liberalization.[1] Even the more liberal regimes, furthermore, allow some political freedom and political competition not because they are committed to democratic change but because they have concluded that limited reform is less costly than social crisis. Essentially conservative and monolithic, Arab ruling elites have introduced political reform as a means to manage crisis and preempt protest. Thus, formally democratic institutions coexist with fundamentally nondemocratic practices.

The weakness of democracy in the Arab world leads many Westerners to believe that civil society does not exist there, or at least is weak. They assume that Islamic culture and the authoritarianism of Arab regimes conspire to prevent the development of anything similar to Western civil society. But general overviews and in-depth studies show that there have been civil society organizations in Arab countries for decades, in some cases for more than a century.[2]

Civil society in the Arab world shares some features with Western civil society. Most organizations are based entirely on voluntary participation, and many are inspired by religious beliefs. They are often divided along ideological lines, and they are sometimes used or even set up by governmental and opposition political parties to help further their political goals. In addition, new kinds of civil society organizations are emerging that appear to be identical to Western ones—professional non-governmental organizations (NGOs), for example.

But in other respects, civil society organizations in the Arab world are very different from their counterparts in the West. Governments of Arab nations have often brought civil society organizations—for example, trade unions—under their direct control. In other cases, the state has set up and runs organizations that in the West operate independently of the state—for example, agricultural cooperatives. In addition, legislation regulating civil society organizations in Arab countries is extremely restrictive compared to the West, making it difficult for them to operate. Finally, a certain number of civil society organizations in the Arab world are only minimally "civil"—for instance, in their toleration of identities and opinions that diverge from their own.

The nine Arab countries in which some political liberalization has occurred over the last two decades have a wide variety of active civil society organizations. These groups constitute a civil society, albeit a weak one, on the basis of two important criteria: they represent a space where citizens organize themselves voluntarily and their organizations are not government-controlled; and they engage with and challenge the state.

Assisting Two Societies

This chapter focuses on efforts by the United States, and to a lesser extent other Western countries, to help civil society in Egypt and Palestine grow and become stronger as part of a broader effort to promote democracy.

I chose Egypt for a number of reasons. First, it receives a significant amount of civil society assistance from Washington. Second, it provides a test of the effectiveness of civil society assistance in a climate of limited and diminishing political liberalization: after periods of relaxing its hold in the 1970s and 1980s, the Egyptian government in the 1990s became increasingly restrictive. Third, Egypt illustrates how the donors' goal of democracy promotion is balanced against—or outweighed by—their desire for political stability in a country and a region. Moderate Islamist forces have been important social and political actors in Egypt for many decades, and radical Islamist forces that espouse the use of violence have put the regime under strong pressure in the 1980s and 1990s. The regime has adopted a hard line against moderate and radical Islamist activists alike, and most donors, including governments, intergovernmental organizations, and to a lesser degree NGOs, accept or even sympathize with Cairo's policy. The reason for this acquiescence is that they consider stability in Egypt crucial for maintaining and furthering peace with Israel.

I chose Palestine because it is in many ways a contrasting case. It is not a state but a state in the making, and the struggle against Israel for independence, now moved to the negotiating table, has a negative influence on the process of political liberalization. In Palestine, most institutions must be built from scratch, whereas Egyptian institutions are old and considered almost impossible to reform. Palestine is a small society, especially compared to Egypt, the most populous Arab country. Total democracy assistance to Palestine is modest in absolute terms but possibly among the largest in the world in per capita terms. Egypt receives a much larger total amount, but much less on a per capita basis. Finally, external donors have a great deal of leverage over the Palestinian authorities because of the Palestinians' need for international recognition and their lack of resources, while Egypt can draw on more resources when confronting foreign actors pushing their own agendas.

The two cases also share a few characteristics. An important one is the donors' perceived need to balance democracy promotion and stability, in both instances to help guarantee the Middle East peace process and Israeli security. And in both Palestine and Egypt the political opposition is largely made up of moderate and radical Islamist forces. In sum, the analysis of these two rather different cases will shed some light on the dynamics of democracy assistance in general and civil society assistance in particular in the Arab world.

Conditions in Egypt and Palestine

Egypt and the Shell of Democracy

Egypt today is governed by a more authoritarian regime than in the mid-1980s, although major institutions generally associated with democracy remain in place. In Egypt, however, these institutions do not function along democratic lines. For example, there are regular elections, with many parties (there are thirteen registered ones, but not all choose to compete in elections) and a slew of candidates participating. However, elections are not free or fair. The dominant National Democratic Party takes a variety of steps to hinder opposition parties and regularly wins at least two-thirds of the seats in parliament—a crucial margin, since parliament proposes by a two-thirds majority the sole presidential candidate, who must then be confirmed by referendum.

Within these clear limits, there is some room for opposition parties. The liberal New Wafd Party, the leftist Tagammu Party, and the Socialist Labor Party, which has acquired an Islamic identity, have some visibility because of their newspapers but win few votes in elections. The group that is potentially the most representative political force in Egypt, the Muslim Brotherhood, is not allowed to register as a party or to compete in elections. The government has blocked all attempts to form an alternative party—the Wasat Party—that would allow Muslim Brothers to run. On occasion, members of the Muslim Brotherhood have attempted to run as independents or as candidates on other parties' lists, but the government is making it increasingly difficult for them to do so. One of the results of unfree and unfair elections is that the Egyptian parliament, the oldest in the region, carries little weight.

The political system is dominated by the president, who has strong legislative powers and can dissolve parliament. If national elections are at least held regularly, balloting for other public positions, such as mayor, has been abolished "to reduce conflict." The judiciary, especially the Supreme Constitutional Court, is relatively independent, and has ruled against the executive branch several times. In two cases, it ruled the election laws were unconstitutional, forcing them to be amended and new elections to be held. The independence of this court, however, is not sufficient to guarantee the fairness of the election process.

The Egyptian military does not have a direct say in decisions about who is allowed or not allowed to run in elections (unlike, for example, the military in Turkey), but its role in Egyptian politics and society can hardly be overstated. President Hosni Mubarak is a former military officer, like all previous presidents. The ministers of defense and many other ministers have also been regularly selected from the ranks of the military. The military establishment is large and its role in both the economy and the society is enormous, but it cannot be discussed, let alone challenged, in public.

Since the electoral path to political change has been blocked, political and social forces have attempted to gain political influence by other means. The relatively free print media offers a channel through which political groups can disseminate their ideas, but radio and television are under strict government control. Most importantly, since the 1980s, opposition groups have devoted much effort to gain control over the professional syndicates—notably those of engineers, lawyers, and physicians. Fierce competition for control has taken place in these organizations, and Islamist groups have won majorities in many. Although the political power of these syndicates is limited—they do not serve as full alternatives for political parties—the government could not tolerate their domination by the Islamists, adopted a more restrictive law on the syndicates, and placed them under direct state control by appointing bureaucrats to their boards. This closed yet another venue for the expression of political views different from those of the ruling coalition.

Another means of expressing political opposition has been the use of violence, a method used predominantly by radical Islamist organizations. In the 1990s, especially between 1992 and 1994, Islamist groups challenged the state by attacking and sometimes killing major politicians, other public figures, and tourists, creating fear among the political incumbents and causing revenues from tourism to plunge. Eventually, the state won the battle—though not necessarily the war—by resorting to force. Egyptian officials justified their use of repression by citing the example of Algeria, where democratization almost resulted in the Islamists gaining power. Egyptian intellectuals and many foreign observers argue that Egypt is too different from Algeria for Islamists ever to gain power through elections, but the international community, including donors of civil society assistance, has been receptive to the regime's arguments and policies. As a result, the government has been able to further restrict political activity without incurring much international criticism.

A Vibrant but Harassed Civil Society

Egypt has a vibrant civil society. About thirteen thousand legal civil society organizations are registered with the Ministry of Social Affairs, virtually all of them in the service-delivery category. But there are also organizations representing interest groups, including twenty-three official labor unions (plus some illegal ones), twenty-six chambers of commerce, a dozen business and bankers' associations, and twenty-one professional associations.[3] Then there are the thirteen legal political parties, but only a few of them have members, with the rest consisting simply of a few leaders. The Muslim Brotherhood is the major social organization with a large membership and a strong potential for political mobilization and representation. As for advocacy NGOs, their numbers have burgeoned over the past two decades. Egypt has more than a dozen human rights groups and about a dozen organizations that monitor state policies and provide civic education. The print media, as has been mentioned, are still relatively free, although the government has recently attempted to curb it by adopting a more restrictive press law.

The organizations mentioned above are those that Western donors consider most important. But the extent and vitality of Egyptian civil society cannot be captured without including the hundreds or even thousands of private voluntary associations that assist citizens whom the state is unable or unwilling to reach. Frequently these associations are affiliated with mosques (less often with the Coptic Church), are run by professionals volunteering their time, and are financed by the collection of *zakat* (alms). Notwithstanding the dominant interpretation in the West, the Islamic identity of most of these associations has few political implications. The organizations do not seem to be channels for recruiting cadres, organizing citizens for political action, or promoting violence.[4] Nor would it be easy to rally Egyptians around the idea of establishing an Islamic state. It is true that most Egyptians (excluding the 10 percent who are Copts) have a strong Islamic identity and follow Islamic traditions faithfully—witness the huge number that observe Ramadan. At the same time, however, Egyptians are secular in many ways. One can compare them with Catholics who observe the main holidays but do not follow many of the other prescriptions of Catholicism and above all have no desire to establish a Catholic state.

The Egyptian state has long been paranoid about civil society and has sought to control it. After the revolution against the monarchy broke out in 1952, the state took over most independent organizations—chambers of commerce, trade unions, and the federation of industries, among others—and it has never given up control. A number of organizations that in other countries would have been established by citizens, such as agricultural cooperatives, have been set up and are controlled by the government in Egypt. The Mubarak regime shares this fear of civil society. As already mentioned, stricter controls were imposed on the professional syndicates under a law adopted in 1993. A new Law on Associations and Civil Institutions, adopted in May 1999 after a long debate in the Egyptian People's Assembly and notwithstanding opposition from civil society organizations and some Western donors, is as restrictive as the infamous Law No. 32 of 1964 it replaced. Among other provisions, it allows the state to intervene in the administrative and financial affairs of civil society organizations. The regime can dismiss board members, appoint government representatives, and prevent organizations from receiving foreign funds. The ruling party's fear of civil society and determination to keep it under control have been well expressed by the Minister of Insurance and Social Affairs, who oversees civil society organizations: "I am not allowing this [new] law for the creation of 14,000 political parties."[5] Among other things, the government is highly sensitive to the foreign funding of civil society organizations and seeks to curb it. In the winter of 1998–99 the issue again came to the fore with the arrest of the secretary-general of the Egyptian Organization for Human Rights on charges that his group had received financing from the British Parliament for a report on human rights abuses against Copts and Muslims. He, his organization, and the British government were accused of stirring up religious strife and damaging Egypt's image abroad. The subsequent debate in the Egyptian press showed clearly that the issue of foreign funding remains extremely sensitive, that the NGOs receiving such funding are open to government reprisal, and that the Egyptian government is unwilling to remove the uncertainty surrounding the legality of foreign financing of civil society, while receiving billions of dollars of foreign assistance itself.

In summary, Egypt has a vibrant but heavily controlled civil society in which groups with an Islamic identity play an important role. The vast majority of these cannot be said to pose major threats to political liberalization or democratization. On the rare occasions when they have been allowed to participate in elections for parliament, such as in 1987, or to be active in civil society without some kind of state intervention, they have adhered to the rules. A few relatively small Islamist groups have espoused violence and used it effectively to attract attention and create fear, but moderate Islamic actors should not be lumped with the radical ones, as Cairo has done.[6] The regime has also used all possible means to cripple and control other segments of civil society—making it difficult for Egyptians to operate organizations of civil society effectively and for donors to assist them.

Palestine: Authoritarianism in a Proto-State

After twenty-seven years of Israeli occupation of the West Bank, in 1994 the Palestinian Authority was established for direct rule over Gaza and Jericho, with other areas to follow. Six years later, the authority was still an inefficient apparatus with a great many people working for it and few institutionalized mechanisms for decision-making and control. Because it was established without an independent Palestinian state being created, and because it is uncertain what such a state will look like and when it will come into existence, a great deal of ambiguity is built into the Palestinian Authority. With the peace process sometimes stalled and sometimes proceeding very slowly and with great uncertainty concerning the final status of the area, the struggle against Israel for independence continues in the Palestinian territory. The governments of Israel, the United States, and some other Western countries encourage Palestinian Authority Chairman Yasir Arafat to take a tough stance against those who resort to violence in their opposition to peace with Israel. As a result, major violations of human rights and undemocratic rule are tolerated in Palestine. The situation has allowed Arafat to establish personal rule and to keep power from becoming institutionalized.

Arafat's governing style is less the result of an Arab authoritarian mentality than of pure calculation. After living outside the territories for decades, Arafat has attempted to gain control over the Palestinian polity and society by replacing or coopting the leaders of the *intifada*—the popular revolt against the Israeli occupation of the West Bank—and substituting for a decentralized power structure one that centralizes power in his hands. He appears to consider the negotiating of a good final agreement with Israel as a secondary goal and to have little or no interest in establishing a democratic and efficient government in Palestine. In pursuing his main objective, Arafat employs an enormous number of security personnel organized in nine different bodies, all reporting directly to him.[7] He also relies heavily on patronage, distributing government jobs and other material and nonmaterial rewards to supporters.

In January 1996, the first elections were held for the presidency of the Palestinian Authority and for the Palestinian Legislative Council. Arafat won the presidency with 88.2 percent of the vote. An impressive total of 676 candidates ran for the eighty-eight council seats, but the district-based, winner-take-all system gave Arafat's Fatah faction of the Palestine Liberation Organization (PLO) fifty seats, a number that increased to fifty-five when some council members who were elected as independents joined Fatah. Arafat thus enjoys a comfortable majority of close to two-thirds. The legislative council, which negotiators of the Oslo Agreements designed as a central decision-making body and as a check on the executive, is not yet fulfilling its envisioned role. Arafat has been relatively successful in preventing the council from gaining more power, although on several occasions its members (including a number of Fatah members) have openly challenged the chairman's way of governing.

Arafat's most assertive opposition has come from Islamist organizations. The most important is Hamas, the more radical and political offshoot of the Muslim Brotherhood, which strongly opposes the peace process and has a fairly large following, especially in Gaza. In the complex relationship between Arafat's Fatah faction and Hamas, neither is able or willing to destroy the other, because both represent large portions of the population. Moreover, they have the same external enemy. Like Fatah, Hamas is not monolithic. Its ranks include supporters as well as opponents of self-rule. Among the latter, one finds those who approve the use of violence as well as those favoring other forms of opposition.[8] Often, Solomonic solutions are found. For example, Hamas boycotted the 1996 elections, but some of its members ran as independents, winning four seats on the legislative council.[9]

The presence of Hamas, a significant and legitimate component of the Palestinian polity and society, has not contributed to the democratization of Palestinian politics, but has had the opposite effect. Hamas is strongly rooted at the local level; thus Fatah continuously postpones local elections to avoid a Hamas victory. But the PLO has much more support at the national level, since the majority of Palestinians are secular and less socially conservative than members of Hamas; so Hamas refused to take part in the 1996 elections. Democracy would be best promoted, and the violent elements in Hamas isolated, if the organization was allowed to operate freely and encouraged to engage in the formal political process. Unless this happens, the existence of Hamas, and of other smaller nationalist and leftist groups opposed to the Oslo Agreement, only contributes to the authoritarianism of Palestinian politics.

Despite these problems, some political liberalization has taken place in Palestine but even when Palestine becomes independent, the odds of a democratic transition are not good. Any democratic government would face great challenges. First, the territory of a Palestinian state will be extremely fragmented because of the continuing presence of a large number of Jewish settlements. Second, a Palestinian state will not be economically viable. It will long remain dependent on foreign aid, possibly leading to a *rentier* state structure in which significant benefits are distributed to the people as long as they keep quiet and make no political demands. The Palestinian state will be accountable exclusively to foreign donors, who are likely to go on closing their eyes to undemocratic practices so as to ensure political stability and the implementation of economic reform.

Civil Society Demobilized

Palestinian civil society grew extremely vibrant in the late 1970s and early 1980s. Recovering from the state of shock caused by Israel's occupation of the West Bank in 1967, Palestinians began to organize themselves to resist occupation, to ensure the survival of their society, and to prepare for an eventual state.[10] After long gestation, the *intifada* broke out in December 1987. Organizations combining the delivery of services with grassroots political activity increased sharply in number. These politicized service-delivery organizations included health and agricultural relief committees, women's and workers' organizations, student organizations, human rights groups, and trade unions formed before the occupation. Charitable societies with no political agenda, run by notable figures in the community, continued to do their work. The highly decentralized new organizations and networks caught up tens of thousands of Palestinians in a political experience both civic and democratic. Islamic charities were financed by the *zakat* and by other Arab countries, while secular Palestinian organizations depended on foreign funding from both Arab and Western sources.

During the *intifada*, Palestinians bridged most ideological differences for the sake of the national cause. All the new organizations of civil society were affiliated with—in some cases established by—one of the five main PLO factions: Fatah, the Popular Front for the Liberation of Palestine, the Democratic Front for the Liberation of Palestine, the Palestinian Communist Party (which joined the PLO in 1987), and Hamas. The *intifada*'s leaders were a new elite—professionals formed in Palestinian universities and Israeli jails—radically different from the notables of an earlier period.[11] Factional rivalry, along with the donors' agenda for a peace settlement, helped shape both the Palestinian government and civil society.

Eventually, the *intifada* made the occupation too costly for Israel and prepared the ground for the Oslo Agreements. But after the establishment of the Palestinian Authority in 1994, many civil society organizations and networks demobilized. To some extent, this was natural: although the Palestinian Authority was not yet a state structure in the strict sense of the term, it was designed to assume some of the roles previously filled by civil society organizations and networks. In addition, foreign donors were sensitive to Palestinian Authority officials' arguments that aid for those organizations and networks should be redirected to the authority. In particular, they argued, it could not go to organizations that opposed the Oslo Agreements. Finally, Arafat deliberately tried to curb the power of the new elites and their organizations by proposing a restrictive law regulating Palestine's approximately 1,500 civil society organizations, based upon the Egyptian law of 1964.[12] Protest by civil society organizations and pressure by foreign donors eventually convinced Arafat to desist. A less restrictive law was adopted in the summer of 1999.

Foreign aid to Palestinian NGOs, which had declined after 1990 because of Palestinian support for Iraq in the Persian Gulf War, dropped even more after 1994, from approximately $140–$220 million in 1990 to $60 million in 1996.[13] Service-oriented organizations of civil society were particularly affected as donors switched their focus to human rights organizations and advocacy groups. But autonomy has affected most grassroots organizations. Political parties, trade unions, and service-delivery organizations have lost much of their strength. Palestinian civil society seems less vibrant than five or ten years ago. The strongest groups today are the service-delivery organizations—most of them Islamic—

and Western-style advocacy groups, including human rights organizations. But these have not been strong enough to fully resist Arafat's imposition of authoritarian government.

What Donors Have Done

Strategies

The literature on democratic transitions stresses that they are the result of power struggles between actors—elite and/or mass groups—over alternative political programs and world views. Such struggles can be more or less peaceful and can be resolved in various ways: through a pact, imposition, reform, or revolution.[14] In short, regime transitions are political processes.

Foreign democracy promoters, however, shy away from that idea, putting their faith instead in a "nonpolitical," technical, incremental path to democracy. In their Western-liberal view, democracy is the natural endpoint of a line of social and political development that donors can speed up even when all socioeconomic prerequisites have not been met. Foreign donors have thus intervened in many transitional countries with expensive programs that seek to promote democracy through technical assistance.

These supposedly nonpolitical forms of democracy promotion basically involve creating or reinforcing democratic institutions (parliaments, judiciaries), civil society organizations (interest groups, NGOs), and civic-minded citizens. Donors, on the other hand, stay away from political forms of democracy promotion—ones intended to assist actors and organizations that work openly and directly for the democratization of the political regime. Such organizations are typically political parties, social movements, interest groups that act as political movements, or informal networks (for instance, Solidarity in Poland and the African National Congress in South Africa). Donors argue that assistance to such groups would amount to interference in the political life of the target country and in any case would be too politically sensitive. In reality, even the supposedly nonpolitical programs have political implications, and governments and political factions in target countries often criticize this form of democracy promotion for their own political ends. Nevertheless, donors favor the so-called apolitical programs because predictable, slow political transitions appeal to them much more than unpredictable, more rapid ones. Stability is always a major concern of donors, as this chapter's final section will show. That is certainly true of programs in Egypt and Palestine.

Some Quantification of Democracy Aid

The amount of money spent on democracy assistance is a crude indicator of the importance of such assistance for the donors but does not give any indication of its impact on the recipient country. It should also be kept in mind that large amounts of money are never spent in the recipient country but are usually paid to expatriate consultants. In addition, a large portion of U.S. assistance is spent for administrative overhead. Finally, data is often imprecise or incomplete. The figures below must be considered with these caveats in mind.

The Civil Society Assistance program of the United States Agency for International Development (USAID) in Egypt is one of three components of its effort to promote democracy in Egypt, along with assistance to the legislature and to the judiciary. Civil society assistance is by far the largest component, amounting in 1999 to $25 million, or 81 percent of the total democracy assistance budget of $30 million. The total cumulative budget for projects active in January 1998 (some of which began as early as 1993 and one of which will stretch on until September 2004) was $137.4 million. Of that, $104.4 million, or 76 percent, went to only six civil society projects. Compared to the U.S. budget for civil society assistance in most countries, these amounts are large. They represent, however, only a small fraction of total U.S. assistance to Egypt: in 1988, civil society assistance represented less than 4 percent of the $815 million in economic support and only 1 percent of the $2.3 billion in combined economic and military aid.[15]

U.S. assistance to Palestinian civil society is much more modest in absolute terms, just $5 million from 1996 to 1998, of which $2.2 million went to a single civic education program. This represents less than a third of the total democracy assistance of $16 million for the period, with $6.5 million going to the Palestinian legislature, $3.5 million to electoral assistance, and $1 million to the executive branch.[16] As in the case of

Egypt, civil society assistance to Palestine is only a small part of the total aid flow from America, which has amounted to about $100 million annually since 1993. On a per capita basis, however, U.S assistance to civil society is high.

"Nonpolitical" Programs and Projects

U.S. civil society assistance in Egypt and Palestine has four major components:

- civic education;
- assistance to private voluntary organizations (PVOs), which focus on service delivery and community development;
- nongovernmental organizations (NGOs), which focus predominantly on advocacy and issues of public interest; and
- interest groups, which pursue the specific interests of their members.

CIVIC EDUCATION. Civic education programs attempt to do one or more of the following: 1) increase knowledge of Western liberal democratic principles and institutions; 2) socialize people in recipient countries to Western civic values; and 3) stimulate them to become politically active citizens who vote in elections, write petitions to their representatives, and eventually become members or founders of civil society organizations. The programs assume that the targeted individuals lack knowledge, are not sufficiently civic-minded, or are politically passive—sometimes all three. While civic education possibly has a strong, positive effect on the recipients' formal knowledge of democratic institutions, its effect on values and behavior is much less certain and has been shown to diminish rapidly after a program ends.

Nevertheless, large-scale civic education programs have been financed and implemented in both Egypt and Palestine. Civic education was used to provide information and motivate citizens to participate in the 1996 elections in Palestine and the 1997 local elections in Egypt. The election in Palestine was the first held after the territories had become autonomous and was expected to be relatively free and fair. Civic education seems to have had a positive effect on voters' turnout and on the proportion of valid votes cast.[17] But the local elections in Egypt were not expected to be either free or fair, and the civic education programs—implemented by the newly established Group for Democratic Development and by Hoda, the Association of Egyptian Women Voters—were useless. Citizens who had been led to believe that their vote was important discovered otherwise, and possibly this increased political pessimism and passivity. Under such conditions, citizens probably should not be taught how to vote, but be assisted in organizing against the regime.

A second form of civic education, unrelated to a specific election, was provided in Palestine by a U.S. organization, the National Democratic Institute for International Affairs (NDI). NDI set up Civic Forum in 1995 with the aim of increasing citizens' understanding of democratic concepts, developing community leaders, and encouraging local organizations to play a role in decision-making. NDI trained about twenty Palestinians as moderators for the forum and held some three hundred educational sessions. Those sessions, held every six weeks on a different topic, were hosted by civil society organizations that encouraged their members to take part. Civic Forum claimed to reach some 6,000 Palestinians every six weeks; since 1995, about 25,000 people have participated in at least one session. Topics have included elections, the judiciary, the role of NGOs, general budgetary practices, political parties, local governments, and the media in democratic regimes. Civic Forum became a Palestinian NGO in June 1998, but NDI has continued to support it with funds provided by USAID. An independent assessment by a Canadian consultant found that participants were extremely satisfied with the program, finding the sessions useful.[18]

Despite the favorable assessment, Civic Forum has some problems. It reaches only citizens who are already members of civil society organizations and who can be expected to be better informed and more active than most. Moreover, the program's content is rather theoretical and there is little evidence that it has helped participants get concrete results by compelling local authorities to be more transparent and accountable. The study mentioned earlier could only find three examples in the experience of several thousand participants of how lessons learned in the program led participants to find solutions to concrete problems. Finally, the program seems culturally biased in implying that one cannot be politically aware and active if one has a "traditional" outlook based on Islamic political philosophy.

PRIVATE VOLUNTARY ORGANIZATIONS. Donors have for decades financed private voluntary organizations, defined here as a subset of civil society organizations that focus on service delivery and economic development. Since the early 1990s, with the growth of democracy assistance, donors have tried to tap the PVOs' potential for increasing democratic participation and advocacy. In rural Egypt, USAID's longstanding PVO project, which focused on participatory development to increase living standards, was expanded to include training in how to get services delivered by local authorities and how to make those authorities more accountable and transparent. Since the introduction of the advocacy component, USAID lists the project under its democracy promotion activities in Egypt. In this project, USAID works with many PVOs, including Islamic groups.

The underlying assumptions are that such projects increase participation at the local level, and that such participation in turn contributes to the democratization of the entire political system. While local participation may affect the functioning of local government, the notion that it makes the political system more democratic at the national level is wishful thinking. Projects that link advocacy to concrete problems of the local community are more likely to positively affect living standards and group empowerment than democracy at the center.

Programs encouraging local participation usually encourage organizations to cooperate with the authorities. This is the case, for example, in a World Bank project with the goal of transforming Palestinian PVOs into more efficient service providers. The bank helped set up a $20 million trust fund for the project, contributing half the money. Bank officials invited existing NGO networks to get involved in project planning and execution. In order for the Palestinian Authority to be included in the planning and execution, it quickly established two new NGO networks. As a result of this, the bank dropped consultations with all NGO networks, and the project was placed under the management of the largest Palestinian charity (the Welfare Association, based in Jordan and the U.K.), the British Council, and the Charities Aid Foundation of the U.K. Its goal is to reinvigorate Palestinian "not-for-profit public service organizations of a charitable or developmental nature" that deliver economic and social services to needy Palestinians—help for the handicapped, low-cost housing, women's health and development, and preschool education.[19] Organizations receiving funds are expected to pursue strictly humanitarian and development agendas and to design projects that do not "have as principal objective the promotion of any particular political or religious viewpoint."[20] They are also expected to establish cooperative relations with the Palestinian Authority.

NONGOVERNMENTAL ORGANIZATIONS. NGOs that monitor, document, and investigate the effect of government policies on their societies, as well as denounce inefficiencies and violations of human rights, have become the major focus of foreign donors in both Palestine and Egypt. Donor-funded organizations are characterized by a well-educated, professional staff; minimal or no membership; financial dependence on foreign donors; and no formal links to political parties. In other words, they are similar to those in established Western democracies, although they operate in an authoritarian context.

Western donors support these NGOs because they seem to offer a technical, nonpolitical way to promote democratization, or at least to prepare personnel and organizations to play a useful role once more overtly political groups push the regime into democratizing. The NGOs can also help make the existing regimes less authoritarian and, especially, more efficient, even if the upshot still falls short of democracy. Finally, they are easy to assist: such NGOs understand what donors want and speak the same language, literally (their officials usually speak English) and figuratively.

Private and public research institutions and think tanks receive significant foreign funding—some rely on it exclusively—to prepare documentation, do research, publish reports, and organize conferences on current political and economic issues. USAID and U.S. democracy promotion NGOs such as NDI, the International Republican Institute (IRI), and the National Endowment for Democracy (NED) support such institutions, along with the Ford Foundation, the German party foundations, and such intergovernmental organizations as the European Union (EU), the United Nations Development Programme (UNDP), and the United Nations Educational, Scientific, and Cultural Organization (UNESCO). In Egypt, the Ibn Khaldoun Center for Development Studies is probably the leading recipient. Other institutions receiving assistance include the New Civic Forum, established with UNDP funds to promote political and economic reform, and the prestigious semigovernmental al-Ahram Center for Political and Strategic Studies. Egyptian university institutes also receive foreign aid—for example, the Center for Political Research and Studies and the Center for the Study

of Developing Countries, both at Cairo University. In Palestine, the
Center for Palestinian Research and Studies, the Jerusalem Media and
Communication Center, the Palestinian Academic Society for the Study
of International Affairs, al-Muwatin, Arab Thought Forum, and the universities of Birzeit and al-Quds are important recipients of foreign aid.
Most of these organizations receive support from more than one foreign donor; some of them favor support from European nongovernmental donors over support from U.S. governmental and nongovernmental donors.

In the NGO sector, the NGO Service Center in Egypt is the leading
recipient of USAID funds, having taken in around $40 million. The cen-
ter aims to help civil society organizations to better represent and articulate the needs of their constituencies. It offers business center facilities
and staff support and, most important, a place to network and exchange
information; eventually it will award grants. But the center reveals the
limits of USAID assistance to civil society in Egypt. First, it shows the
agency's preference for large projects and its reluctance to directly support NGOs. Second, it gives the Egyptian government a large voice in
the choice of recipients. The 1978 Camp David agreement provides for
Cairo's approval of all USAID projects—hence the government is represented on the center's board of directors, along with USAID and the
Egyptian NGO community. The result is that only NGOs registered under the restrictive Egyptian law may use the center.

Human rights groups have long been a focus of foreign funding. In
Palestine in the late 1970s and the 1980s, European donors supported
them because they documented and denounced Israeli human rights
violations and assisted victims. The activities of human rights groups
have since been extended. In Palestine, organizations that had concentrated on abuses of the Israeli occupiers began examining the human
rights violations of the Palestinian Authority. As the 1990s ended, both
Egypt and Palestine had at least a dozen human rights groups financed
by U.S. and European donors. The NED, for example, supports since
1994 the Egyptian Organization for Human Rights to monitor human
rights abuses and issue reports, newsletters, statements, and appeals on
specific human rights issues and cases. It is not a coincidence that the
NED and not USAID funds human rights groups because of the sensitivity of the issue and the fact that the NED is formally independent from
the U.S. government.

There are a number of reasons for this proliferation of human rights groups. The need for intervention on issues ranging from torture to women's rights, from labor rights to freedom of expression, has led organizations to specialize. The different kinds of tasks human rights organizations must perform—reporting, campaigning to stop abuses, assisting victims, educating the public—were also an incentive for specialization and multiplication of organizations. Then, too, diverging political views have split human rights movements. The large donor community with its large pool of funds to give away has also encouraged, indirectly or directly, the creation of new groups.

A final, and highly important, issue that donors have taken up is NGO legislation. In Egypt and Palestine, foreign donors have worked to avert the introduction of restrictive laws by which the state would exercise control over NGOs. Donors seem to have been successful in Palestine but to have failed in Egypt. Despite their efforts to persuade Cairo to lift restrictions on NGOs—USAID, for example, invested much money in studies on possible alternatives—a new restrictive law was introduced in parliament and approved. That same day, the U.S. State Department spokesman said the legislation was "the wrong direction to go if Egypt wants to energize civil society and promote development."[21]

INTEREST GROUPS. Interest groups, especially ones representing labor, can become important forces for political liberalization and eventual democratization. This can happen when an interest group insists that specific government policies be implemented or withdrawn, resists a repressive state response, and manages to create a crisis situation. In such a scenario, liberalization and democratization are the by-products of collective efforts to attain other goals. By mobilizing to defend its own interests in the matter of specific government policies, an organization can split the leadership and spearhead protest against the regime.

In Egypt, the state controls all trade unions. Strikes are forbidden, and the frequent wildcat strikes are systematically crushed. In Palestine, the labor movement was a major force in the *intifada* but followed the general trend toward demobilization after the establishment of the Palestinian Authority.[22] Neither Palestinian nor Egyptian trade unions receive more than minimal support from donors. The International Labor Organization, however, has been advising the Egyptian state, trade unions, and business associations on the drafting of a new labor law, which should for the first time formally allow workers the right to strike "in exchange" for employers' right to hire, and especially fire, at will.

Business associations have received, directly or through their members, substantial technical assistance designed to make them more efficient and get them incorporated into international business networks. On the other hand, professional associations in Egypt get no aid from foreign donors since many are or have been controlled by Islamist forces. In any case, the Egyptian government would probably block them from accepting Western aid were any offered, and the groups' members would bridle at being supported by Western donors. However, officials of the Palestinian Bar Association have received training through AMIDEAST, an American educational organization, as well as funds from the U.S. Information Service.

Assessing Civil Society Assistance

U.S. civil society assistance in Egypt and Palestine has multiple goals: developing civil society organizations; contributing to political liberalization and democratization, as well as to economic development and social change; and ensuring Palestinian support for the peace process and Egypt's continuing commitment to peace with Israel.

Those goals are not necessarily compatible and, as a result, U.S. policy has not been consistent, sending contradictory messages to authoritarian incumbents and ordinary citizens alike. A stronger civil society could hamper the peace process, for one thing. Furthermore, the opposition to existing authoritarian regimes in both Egypt and Palestine is made up of Islamists, nationalists, and leftists who—for their different reasons and with their different demands—have a political agenda at odds with donors'. Sometimes opposition groups are simply anti-Western and against liberal democracy. It is thus difficult for donors to support such forces, but turning away from them means turning away from the authoritarian regimes' most effective opponents and running the risk of supporting actors that will not make a difference.

Measuring the impact of civil society assistance on the Middle East peace process, or even on political change under authoritarian regimes, is an arduous task. I will reformulate the problem as three somewhat tentative questions: What impact has civil society assistance had at the micro level, on individuals or specific organizations? What impact has it had on the meso level, that is, on the development of an active civil society? And finally, what impact could it possibly have had at the macro level—on political regimes?[23]

At the meso and micro levels, donors prefer to assess impact by measuring output rather than outcome, and go so far as to consider the two synonymous. The difference, however, is fundamental. For example, the output of a civic education project can be the training of two hundred individuals for ten hours each. The outcome of the same project can be an increase in knowledge, a change in values, a change in the behavior of the participants—or none of the above. Output is easy to measure; outcome is much harder. Outcome, however, is what actually matters.

The Micro Level

The impact at the micro level—on single organizations and individuals that received assistance—has been the strongest. There can be no doubt that external support for Egyptian and Palestinian civil society organizations has allowed weak and often ailing organizations to survive, others to expand, and new ones to be created. A substantial number of civil society organizations, including advocacy NGOs and service-delivery PVOs, particularly in Palestine, rely almost exclusively on foreign aid. Advocacy NGOs receive assistance only from Western countries, whereas service-delivery PVOs receive it both from Western and from Arab countries.

Donors appear satisfied with the impact of their funding. Advocacy NGOs (including human rights associations) have turned into relatively efficient, transparent, and accountable organizations and generally do what they are expected to do: publish reports, provide legal assistance, conduct public opinion polls, etc. Service-delivery private voluntary organizations also seem generally to satisfy donors' expectations. Civic education projects are increasing the knowledge and possibly changing the values of participants, although only rarely affecting their behavior. A more profound longer-term effect on the individual level is that staff of civil society organizations, in general, and of NGOs in particular, have become more skilled thanks to donor-supported training. In some future, more democratic context, they would be much more capable of playing a constructive role.

The Meso Level

Assessing the impact of civil society assistance at the meso level is not an easy task. A relatively simple but also very approximate way is to count the organizations and the people they reach, thus equating civil society with the presence of organizations.

The number of civil society organizations has risen in both Palestine and Egypt since the 1970s and 1980s, when donors started their programs there, although not in a dramatic fashion or without reversals. In Palestine, for example, many organizations disappeared after the *intifada* ended and the Palestinian Authority began operating.

But the tally of organizations is not an accurate gauge of political pluralism. For example, as the number of organizations increases, the average size of their membership falls, indicating that the number of activists has not increased significantly, but that they are now spread among more organizations. Furthermore, organizations of civil society now represent a more limited range of viewpoints; in Palestine, many groups that oppose the peace process have disbanded because they cannot obtain donor funding. Another indicator of limited pluralism is a tendency for directors to sit on several boards, especially when it comes to advocacy NGOs.

In Palestine—and to some extent in Egypt too—professional advocacy NGOs have become the main employers for people formerly active in leftist social movements and political parties, leading some to conclude that these organizations, with their relatively high salaries, have depoliticized the society, making liberalization and democratization less likely.[24] This is difficult to prove: the decline of leftist movements and parties may be unrelated to the proliferation of advocacy NGOs. With the end of the *intifada*, well-educated, middle-class Palestinians who had been politically active would probably have joined the bureaucracy of the Palestinian Authority or found employment in the private sector; advocacy NGOs at least provide them with an opportunity to continue serving the Palestinian people.

There are two other ways of assessing the impact of civil society assistance at the meso level. First is to rely on opinion polls and discourse analysis, thereby defining civil society in terms of the civic-mindedness of its citizens. Second is to assess the effectiveness of civil society to influence specific government policies. There are no studies, either by academics or by donors, that provide information on civic-mindedness. Regarding the policy impact, there are indications that in Egypt the government occasionally listens to actors outside the government, especially businessmen. However, business influence is generally exercised not through business associations that lobby openly for specific policies but through personal connections between individual businessmen and the government. Nevertheless, in Egypt civil society associations most often are not successful at all in changing government policies (consider, for example, the law on the professional syndicates, the law on associations and civil institutions, or human rights abuses by the government).

The Macro Level

At the macro level, foreign donors, especially the United States, continue to announce ambitious and manifestly unrealistic goals. It is doubtful that funding a handful of civil society assistance projects can bring about regime change. The real goals of donors—governments especially—are different. More often than not, they support such programs in order to maintain stability, save the peace process, keep labor under control during privatization, or obtain high-quality socioeconomic and political data on a previously inaccessible society. If they achieve one or more of those goals, donors may consider civil society assistance successful even if democratization does not occur, although they would not admit it publicly.

Regarding democratization, Palestine and Egypt present contrasting pictures at the macro level. Overall, Egypt has gone backward: the regime in Cairo is more restrictive today in 2000 than it was fifteen years ago. The balance for Palestine seems more positive: the regime is less restrictive than it was a few years ago. Neither outcome appears related to democracy assistance.

Neither in Egypt nor Palestine—nor in any other Arab country—have civil society assistance and other forms of democracy promotion brought about political liberalization or democratization. In Palestine and Egypt, human rights organizations have advanced some specific human rights but have made no progress on others. In Palestine, advocacy NGOs have been successful in a small way in making the Palestinian Authority and the Palestinian Legislative Council more accountable and transparent.

The same cannot be said of NGOs and government institutions in Egypt. At most, assistance has been instrumental in limiting the authoritarian character of both regimes. It has not mobilized a strong opposition, which could have been a more effective champion of liberalization and democracy. It should be said, however, that such was never the intention of donors or of most of the organizations they sponsored.

Shelving the Blueprints

Civil society assistance has not been decisive for democratization in Palestine or Egypt, nor is it likely to become a force in the foreseeable future. Civil society, however, could work more effectively toward democracy if donors made some changes.

First, donors should be more honest about their goals in Palestine and Egypt. The priorities of donor governments and multilateral organizations are safeguarding Israel, providing a solution acceptable to most Palestinians, and promoting economic reform, in that order, while democratization is lower on the list. Donors need to be more open about their own objectives, particularly since they preach transparency. International NGOs theoretically place more emphasis on democracy, but their financial dependence on governments and intergovernmental organizations constrains them; despite their need for funds, they should more actively resist the funders' narrow interpretation of democracy promotion in Palestine and Egypt.

Second, donors must invest more time and effort in strategizing. They need to develop clearer and less contradictory goals and sharpen their understanding of the processes of political liberalization and democratization—for example, they should become aware that setting up and sponsoring NGOs does not necessarily help transform a nondemocratic regime into a democracy. Most important, they should think beyond single programs or projects, asking how any effort contributes to the attainment of comprehensive, intermediate (meso) objectives. For instance, creating a better environment for NGOs would achieve more than supporting individual groups. Donors should coordinate civil society assistance with other forms of democracy promotion, and use rewards like increased development assistance and punishments like sanctions to ensure compliance. Finally, donors should focus their efforts on actors that can mobilize large numbers of people, including those whose values donors do not fully share—for example, organizations with a moderate Islamic outlook or with nationalist ideologies that lead them to oppose the Oslo Agreements.

Third, donors should be flexible when it comes to translating their strategies into programs and projects. They should not show up with the blueprint of what a partner organization must look like; instead, they should be guided by local individuals and organizations. Donors need to employ personnel who are knowledgeable about the target society and able to reach out to new organizations beyond the narrow circle of those formed to take advantage of foreign grants. Donors should give preference to organizations that are truly representative of their society and possibly have grassroots membership.

Fourth, donors need to decrease external control on civil society assistance projects and reduce the sums that return to the donor country in the form of field officers' salaries, consultants' fees, and purchased equipment. The Dutch Foreign Ministry has shown how overhead can be reduced and programs improved by relying on local experts. Dutch funds are administered by the major development aid organization Dutch Organization for International Development Cooperation (Nederlandse Organisatie Voor Internationale Ontwikkelingssamenwerking, NOVIB), which has no field office in Cairo and allocates all funds to organizations chosen by local experts. An even better solution might be to establish endowments in recipient countries, administered mainly or exclusively by local citizens, making foreigners' roles as small as possible.

Whatever one thinks of civil society assistance (and democracy assistance as whole), in an increasingly interdependent world it can only be avoided by the most restrictive authoritarian regimes. Civil society assistance is not inherently good or bad. In some cases, it can be instrumental in improving the lives of citizens and can have a positive impact on sections of societies and on polities. In other cases, it only enriches a few individuals and has no impact on society and polity. The main questions that should be asked over and over again about any civil society assistance project include: Whose agenda does the project support? Is it exclusively a Western donor agenda or is it also the agenda of the recipient countries' citizens?[25] Are the donors doing what they are preaching? Are they managing their projects in the best way?

Notes

Together with Philippe C. Schmitter, I was a recipient of a United States Institute for Peace grant to study "Western Democracies and the Promotion of Democracy in the Arab World." The opinions, findings, and conclusions expressed in this publication are my own and do not necessarily reflect the views of the United States Institute for Peace.

I would like to thank the numerous persons in donor and aid recipient organizations (they are too numerous to be mentioned individually) who provided me with insights and information regarding the practices of democracy assistance in Egypt and Palestine. Christine Abele, Bernard Gbikpi, Brad Glasser, Nicolas Guilhot, and especially Philippe C. Schmitter provided very useful feedback. In addition, the comments and suggestions of Marina Ottaway and Thomas Carothers were fundamental in improving this contribution. Of course, the responsibility for the result is exclusively mine.

1. I define democratization as a process whereby, in a significant and substantial way, rules and procedures of citizenship are applied to institutions previously governed by other principles, or are expanded to include people who have not previously possessed citizens' rights and obligations, or are extended to cover issues and institutions not previously subject to citizen participation. Political liberalization is a process whereby political freedom is increased and, in a minimal and more formal than substantial way, rules and procedures of citizenship are applied and expanded. These definitions rely heavily on Guillermo O'Donnell and Philippe C. Schmitter, *Transitions from Authoritarian Rule: Tentative Conclusions about Uncertain Democracies* (Baltimore: Johns Hopkins University Press, 1986), pp. 7–8.

2. See Augustus Richard Norton, ed., *Civil Society in the Middle East*, Vol. I and II (Leiden: E. J. Brill, 1995, 1996).

3. See Mustapha Kamel Al-Sayyid, "A Civil Society in Egypt," in ibid.

4. See Vickie Langohr, "Do Clients of Clinics Become Cadres? Critiquing Some Assumptions About Islamist Social Welfare" (Paper presented at the Middle East Studies Association Annual Conference, San Francisco, November 22–24, 1997).

5. Quoted in "Middle Eastern NGOs Strain at the Bonds of Authoritarian Government," *Financial Times*, June 10, 1999, p. 5.

6. See one of the many who have made this point: Fawaz A. Gerges, *America and Political Islam: Clash of Cultures or Clash of Interests?* (Cambridge: Cambridge University Press, 1999). See especially the chapter on Egypt, pp. 171–91.

7. Glenn Robinson, "Authoritarianism with a Palestinian Face," *Current History* (January 1998), p. 15.

8. See, for example, Jean-François Legrain, "Hamas: Legitimate Heir of Palestinian Nationalism," in John L. Esposito, ed., *Revolution, Radicalism, or Reform?* (Cairo: The American University in Cairo Press, 1997), pp. 159–78.

9. See Ziad Abu Amr, *Islamic Fundamentalism in the West Bank and Gaza: Muslim Brotherhood and Islamic Jihad* (Bloomington: Indiana University Press, 1994).

10. See Joost R. Hiltermann, *Behind the Intifada: Labor and Women's Movements in the Occupied Territories* (Princeton: Princeton University Press, 1991), which shows Palestinians starting to organize intensively before the *intifada* began.

11. See Glenn Robinson, *Building a Palestinian State: The Incomplete Revolution* (Bloomington: Indiana University Press, 1997).

12. Denis Sullivan, "NGOs in Palestine: Agents of Development and Foundation of Civil Society," *Journal of Palestine Studies*, vol. 25, no. 3 (Spring 1996), p. 94.

13. See Robinson, *Building a Palestinian State*, p. 45, and Sullivan, "NGOs in Palestine," p. 96.

14. Terry L. Karl and Philippe C. Schmitter, "Modes of Transition in Latin America, Southern and Eastern Europe," *International Social Science Journal*, vol. 128, no. 2 (May 1991), pp. 269–84.

15. Besides USAID Egypt's projects, other U.S. projects are funded from Washington—for example by the National Endowment for Democracy (NED)—and implemented by such organizations as the National Democratic Institute for International Affairs. Thus U.S. democracy assistance to Egypt (and Palestine) is slightly higher than the figures listed.

16. Besides the official publications of USAID to map democracy assistance to the Palestinians, the following sources are also important: UN Special Coordinator in the Occupied Territories (UNSCO), "Rule of Law Development in the West Bank and Gaza: Survey and Status of Development Effort" (July 1997); Palestinian National Authority Core Group on Rule of Law and Legal Institution Building, "Human Rights, Democracy and Rule of Law: Submission to the Palestinian Development Plan for the Years 1998-2000" (April 1997); Jerusalem Media and Communication Centre, "Foreign Aid and Development of Palestine" (June 1997), and "Mortgaging Self-Reliance: Foreign Aid and Development in Palestine" (November 1997).

17. For example, Friedrich Ebert Stiftung, "Civic Education Measures in Preparation for the Palestinian Elections, 1995-1996" (Jerusalem, 1997).

18. Viewpoints Research Ltd., "Independent Evaluation of Civic Education and Civic Forum in the West Bank, Gaza Strip and East Jerusalem: Report on Qualitative Research," (February 9, 1998). Eighteen focus groups in eleven communities—162 respondents in all—participated. Eight groups had taken part in Civic Forum sessions; ten had not.

19. This is the official definition of the target groups in World Bank, "The Palestinian NGO Project: Public Discussion Paper" (al-Ram, West Bank, July 15, 1997), p. 2. It explicitly excludes organizations such as trade unions, professional associations, and commercial cooperatives.

20. Ibid., p. 10.

21. Quoted in Steve Negus, "NGO Law Controversy," *Middle East International*, June 4, 1999, p. 18.

22. See Hiltermann, *Behind the Intifada*.

23. For a more in-depth discussion of this issue, see Philippe C. Schmitter and Imco Brouwer, "Conceptualizing, Researching and Evaluating Democracy Promotion and Protection," Working Papers in Political and Social Sciences no. 99/9 (Florence: European University Institute, 1999). Available at www.iue.it/PUB/sps_fm.html.

24. Azmi Bishara, "The Civil Society Debate" (Paper presented in the framework of the program "Europe and the Middle East: A Dialogue of Cultures" at the Van Leer Jerusalem Institute, Jerusalem 1997).

25. The author, in the framework of a larger research project on "Democracy Promotion and Protection in Central and Eastern Europe and the Middle East and North Africa," directed by Clause Offe and Philippe C. Schmitter and generously supported by the Volkswagen Foundation, will focus especially on the micro level of civil society assistance, which should allow recipients' perspectives to be more fully explored than they are in this essay. For more detailed information on civil society assistance in Egypt and Palestine, see Imco Brouwer, "U.S. Civil-Society Assistance to the Arab World: The Cases of Egypt and Palestine," Working Paper no. 2000/5 (Florence: Robert Schuman Centre for Advanced Studies, European University Institute, 2000).

2

A Clash of Values: U.S. Civil Society Aid and Islam in Egypt

Mustapha Kamel Al-Sayyid

A MAJOR PARADOX OF U.S. FOREIGN POLICY lies in its proclaimed commitment to support the transition to democracy and consolidation of civil society in countries of the South and of the former socialist bloc on the one hand and its open hostility to certain types of political movements that have become major actors of those countries' incipient civil societies on the other. Washington's hostility stems not from the fear that these movements will turn on the rest of civil society once they gain a measure of power, but from the fact that the organizations that make up the movements oppose some aspects of U.S. foreign policy. The U.S. posture toward Islamist movements in Arab countries illustrates this paradox and eloquently demonstrates the far from total commitment of post-Cold War U.S. administrations to supporting the development of civil society everywhere. Islamist organizations in Arab countries are among the staunchest defenders of civil and political liberties, including freedom of association, without which civil society cannot survive. Nevertheless, the U.S. government withholds supports from them, even as it seeks to assist the incipient civil society.

The United States' attitude toward emerging civil societies is particularly inconsistent in countries with friendly governments. This explains the suspicion with which some segments of the public in those countries greet any form of U.S. assistance to their country's civil society. They do not see the aid as a sign of Washington's commitment to promote democracy. Rather, they look at it as an instrument for furthering U.S. foreign policy goals and for engineering the evolution of other societies along the lines of the American ideal of a free market economic system combined with liberal democracy, regardless of the traditions and preferences of the citizens of those societies. Such so-called assistance not only constitutes unacceptable interference in other countries' internal affairs but disregards other people's right to self-determination, which includes the right to choose the socioeconomic system under which they want to live and the model of economic development they prefer.

U.S. assistance to civil society in other countries is thus riddled with ironies and inconsistencies: it excludes groups of which the United States does not approve, even when they are the best defenders of civil liberties; it constitutes interference in the domestic affairs of the recipient countries, although the United States is always quick to condemn such interference on the part of other governments, particularly those inspired by a different ideology; and finally, such assistance disregards the historical record, which suggests that the emergence of civil society is a function of a country's internal dynamics, not of the actions of any foreign power, however wealthy and mighty.

This chapter strives to illustrate the above points through an assessment of U.S. assistance to civil society in Egypt. It explores the necessary conditions for the birth and growth of civil society in any country and the possible contributions of a variety of actors to it, distinguishing between direct and indirect outside influences. It goes on to examine how the United States tried, in different ways, to encourage the evolution of the emerging civil society in Egypt. Finally, it discusses the limited impact on Egypt of U.S. policies, at the same time suggesting ways in which the United States could positively influence the evolution of civil society there. The sources are writings on civil society in Egypt, interviews with officials of U.S. government agencies directly involved in the country, and my own observations as an active member of some of the organizations of the emerging Egyptian civil society.

Conditions for the Rise of Civil Society

The term "civil society" was coined in the late eighteenth century at a moment of profound socioeconomic and political change in western Europe and later acquired different meanings in the hands of Western philosophers.[1] Some Egyptian and Arab writers have questioned the appropriateness of Western definitions of civil society for the Arab context, arguing that they exclude both religious institutions and tribal or communal entities, although they are principal pillars of civil society in non-Western countries.[2] However, U.S. policy-makers appeared to have no doubts about the universal relevance of the civil society concept when they initiated and expanded programs specifically intended to encourage the growth of civil society organizations in former communist countries and, later, some countries of the South.

Western writings on civil society agree neither on the nature of the phenomenon nor on its significance. However, liberal authors like Adam Ferguson, Adam Smith, John Locke, and Georg Friedrich Hegel, as well as Marxist writers inspired by the Hegelian dialectical method even when they turn it upside down, agree on several basic conditions for the rise of such a sector. Those conditions include: advanced social differentiation, with a multiplicity of social classes and professional groups, or, in the language of classical economists, highly specialized division of labor; a certain degree of autonomy for nonstate organizations vis-à-vis the state; and an ethic of tolerance and acceptance of dissent. Such conditions facilitate adherence by the state to a set of rational rules in its dealings with citizens, including recognition of freedom of association and the right to peaceful dissent, which in turn depend on freedom of conscience, opinion, and expression.[3]

Such conditions developed in Western societies, particularly in Great Britain, France, and the United States, as the result of long processes of domestic socioeconomic and political change, accelerated by revolutions against authorities and institutions that might have impeded or prevented the blossoming of civil society. Although it would be incorrect to deny the influence of external actors on the rise of a civil society in these countries and the diffusion of ideas from one to the other, the conditions favorable to the rise of civil society were largely the outcome of internal social evolution.[4]

One should not conclude from these observations that outside actors do not influence at all the emergence of civil society in other countries. On the contrary, they often do so, both indirectly and directly. External influence, however, is constrained by two factors: first, internal and external variables interact, and the former tend to produce stronger effects; second, external variables only have an impact if they strengthen and lead to maturation of already emerging features of a civil society, such as social differentiation, organizational independence, and tolerance of dissent.

External actors can indirectly stimulate the birth of civil society through their example and their actions. Such indirect influence can be exerted through different mechanisms. One is the demonstration effect of a powerful civil society in one country, which can capture hearts and minds of political elites elsewhere and inspire them to build a civil society at home. For example, many Arab intellectuals have been impressed by the power of both print and electronic media in the West, particularly the United States, and wish that the media in their countries would acquire the same degree of autonomy vis-à-vis the government. Another mechanism that indirectly influences the strengthening of civil society is foreign investment, which can stimulate social differentiation by leading to the creation of a working class and the expansion of the middle class—both important constituencies for civil society organizations. The foreign policy of a great power or neighboring country can also have an impact on the development of civil society, either by contributing to a relaxed political atmosphere conducive to the blossoming of autonomous organizations or by creating great tension and thus encouraging government repression.

But not all influences are indirect. Great powers nowadays deliberately adopt a policy of promoting the emergence of civil society in other countries, particularly in the less powerful ones. Through pressure or encouragement they strive to induce governments to lift restrictions on the establishment and functioning of civil society organizations. They lend moral support to civil society leaders when they are subject to persecution from their own governments. They offer technical and financial assistance to civil society organizations through governmental or nongovernmental agencies, which could work in concert with recipient governments or act on the basis of tacit agreement with them.

Civil Society in Egypt

Conditions favorable to the rise of civil society existed in Egypt long before the United States became deeply involved with the country as a result of President Anwar al-Sadat's signing of the 1979 peace treaty with Israel and the launching of a U.S. military and economic assistance program that has provided Egypt with more than $36 billion in aid since 1978. The social differentiation and the emergence of a middle and a working class began nearly two centuries ago in the reign of Muhammed Ali (1805–48) and have accelerated in the twentieth century because of Cairo's education policies and its encouragement of industrialization, as well as its push for foreign investment. Although a few civil society organizations were established in the nineteenth century; professional associations and trade unions emerged in the twentieth century as the backbone of Egyptian civil society.

Professional associations in particular have played a very important role in Egypt since their formation, establishing close links to the nationalist movements and later to political parties. Two prominent leaders of the nationalist movement—Mohammed Fareed, who became leader of the National Party in 1908, and Sa'ad Zaghloul, leader of the Wafd Party, champion of Egypt's struggle for independence and the first prime minister of an elected government in 1924—encouraged the establishment of the Egyptian Bar Association (Niquabat al-Muhameen) in 1912. Presidents of the bar association during this period (1919–52) were close to leaders of the Wafd Party or even party leaders themselves—Makram Ebeid, for example, was Wafd secretary-general and president of the bar association in the early 1940s. The Syndicate of Journalists (Niquabat al-Sahafeyyeen) was frequently the battleground for political struggles between the country's major political forces. Groups that could not gain legal recognition as political parties found in these two professional associations, and also in those of medical doctors and engineers, an open forum in which they could make their voices heard and their presence on the political scene felt. Communists and Nasserites were prominent in both the bar and the journalists syndicate during the 1970s, while the Muslim Brothers had a strong presence in most syndicates during the 1980s and the 1990s. The politicization of the syndicates has created tensions with all governments since the end of the monarchy in 1952. These governments did not necessarily oppose a national role for syndicates and labor unions, but wanted that role to conform to official foreign and domestic policies.[5]

Egyptian governments have all acted quite autonomously in their dealings with society, and arbitrariness has marked their attitude toward civil liberties. There were, however, short spells of political liberalization under Wafdist governments in the monarchical period (1924–52) as well as under President Anwar al-Sadat (1970–81) and his successor and the current leader, President Hosni Mubarak (1981–). The autonomy of the state has always been a major feature of politics in Egypt whether under the monarchy or a republican regime.[6] The few spells of liberalization were due either to ideological stances, as was the case of the Wafd Party which championed the cause of liberal nationalism, or to the initiative of the head of state, taken as a measure to balance the political weight of the armed forces.[7] Egyptians enjoyed some freedom of expression during these periods, but people asserting views perceived as different from the common beliefs of Egyptian Muslims (who make up no less than 88 percent of the population) faced negative reactions. Such views were unpopular with the conservative sections of the political elite supported by the religious establishment. In such situations, it would have been extremely embarrassing for the government to take sides, although it tended to be more sympathetic towards those conservative forces.[8]

Signs of the development of civil society increased from the 1970s on. Social differentiation became more accentuated under President Sadat's Open Door or "Infitah" policy, which encouraged private sector and foreign investment. The Infitah was also accompanied by the departure of millions of Egyptians for work in Persian Gulf countries; many who went abroad made their fortunes, small ones for the majority but quite large for some. This contributed to the diversification of the society. Authorization of a multiparty system and the end of the control over all associational life by the Arab Socialist Union, the single party under the Nasser regime, paved the way for the expression of varied and sometimes opposing intellectual and political currents within associations. Businessmen established a host of organizations, while the trade union movement ceased to be the department of the ruling party it had become under Nasser. A vocal human rights movement arose in the 1980s and despite legal restrictions on its activity soon acquired respectability and prestige at home and abroad.[9]

The government, however, remained adamantly opposed to any real autonomy for such organizations, whether their ideology was political Islam or yet more freedom for the private sector. This opposition set off a crisis in the relationship between the nascent civil society and Egyptian leaders, which in the 1990s turned virtually into a government siege of many civil society organizations. The Islamists were the first to feel the government's suspicion and repression, since they could easily be accused of threatening the political order. After some of the armed opposition groups raised the banner of Islam, it became convenient for the government to accuse of being a terrorist anyone who proclaimed that Islam can be the source of inspiration for socioeconomic, political, and moral reform in Egypt. In reality, many Islamic NGOs are apolitical, engaged mainly in charitable activities, or led by government sympathizers. Decisions about who should be considered a terrorist thus came to be based on one issue only—criticism of government policies.

The government's wrath fell predominantly on Islamist activists presumed to be members, or at least supporters, of the Muslim Brotherhood. The organization was denied legal recognition not only as an association—a status it held from 1928 until outlawed by President Gamal Abdel Nasser in 1954 after an attempt on his life allegedly perpetrated by one of its members—but also as a political party, because a law banned the establishment of religion-based parties. As a result, the brotherhood's sympathizers found no other channels for making their presence felt and publicizing their ideas than the professional syndicates, which in the 1980s were relatively free from government interference, and some opposition newspapers. Under these new conditions, opposition groups that could not get the right to establish legally recognized political parties managed to win seats on the national boards of several syndicates. The Muslim Brothers in particular were the most successful as they ended up winning the vast majority of seats on the board of a number of major professional associations, including university professors' clubs, syndicates of engineers, medical doctors, and scientists, and finally the bar association, a stronghold of the liberal Wafdist current. In 1984 and 1987 the government finally allowed the Muslim Brothers to participate in the parliamentary elections in alliance with legally recognized parties, such as the Socialist Labor Party and the Socialist Liberal Party, which came to proclaim Islamist stances on several domestic and foreign policy issues. The organization's considerable success in all these elections led some observers to conclude that it had converted to peaceful methods of political action—a stance condemned by the more radical Islamist groups, which continued to espouse armed struggle.

However, the Muslim Brotherhood's success aroused government fears that the group might defeat its supporters in a free general election, if one were ever held in Egypt. To eliminate this perceived threat to its power, the government began in 1992 to introduce a variety of legal provisions intended to make instigation to armed opposition a criminal offense, and to place stringent controls on the internal elections of the professional associations. When those measures failed to decrease the influence of the Muslim Brotherhood, the government took the direct approach, putting professional associations under the administration of its own appointees, indefinitely suspending internal elections in most of them, and harassing and intimidating Islamist activists and even rigging parliamentary elections in constituencies where they might possibly win, as demonstrated by many court orders nullifying such elections.[10]

Even business associations did not escape the government's anger when their leaders showed signs of asserting their autonomy. Mohammed Fareed Khamis, president of the Federation of Egyptian Industries, who had been chosen by the minister of industry to be president of the Federation of Egyptian Engineers after chapter elections in the federation, was suddenly replaced by a more pliant businessman from the private sector after he called for a new law that would possibly have given the federation the character of a negotiating body.

The United States and Civil Society in Egypt

In order to understand U.S. policy toward civil society in Egypt, it is important to keep in mind the close relationship between the governments of the United States and Egypt since the mid-1970s as well as the role Egypt plays in the politics of the region. Although there have been tensions in relations between the two countries, more particularly under President Hosni Mubarak, the two governments have tried to solve their differences and maintain a dialogue on strategic matters. The relationship with Egypt is important to Washington because of Egypt's pace-setting 1979 peace treaty with Israel and its status as the most populous and industrialized Arab country and a historical leader in the Arab world. U.S. administrations regard a stable pro-Western and above all pro-American government in Egypt as vital to their strategy in the region, and they rely on Cairo to ensure support for U.S. policies. The Persian Gulf War of January-February 1991 illustrates such support rendered at a crucial moment. Egypt sided with the United States against Iraq, offering what seemed to some to be an Arab blessing for the U.S.-led military operations in Kuwait and Iraq. The United States seized on Iraqi President Saddam Hussein's grave miscalculation in invading Kuwait to squelch the potential threat Iraq posed to U.S.-backed conservative regimes in the region.

With its ancient history extending over several millennia and with its cultural influence in the Arab region, Egypt has often been seen as a model for all Arab, and sometimes even for many Afro-Asian, countries. After nationalist army officers took power in Egypt in the 1950s, those in other Arab countries—Syria, Iraq, Yemen, Sudan, and Libya—followed suit. They emulated many of Nasser's domestic and foreign policies, such as reliance on state-owned enterprises to lead economic development and maintenance of good relations with the Soviet Union. When Egypt changed course under President Sadat in the mid-1970s, Open Door liberal economic policies became the norm in the Arab region.

For all these reasons, it is important for the United States to keep Egypt within its sphere of influence. To ensure that the model Egypt sets for other Arab countries does not jeopardize U.S. interests, successive U.S. administrations have thus shown much concern for the stability of what they perceive to be a moderate government. A tangible expression of this concern is the large foreign assistance program that since 1979 has made the United States the largest donor to Egypt. Total U.S. economic assistance to the country throughout the period 1975–2000 amounted to $24.46 billion, far larger than what has been offered by any other country. Military assistance was considerably higher, rising to $27.3 billion during the same period.

The web site of USAID Egypt gave the following breakdown of U.S. economic assistance during the period 1979–96 as follows:

- $5.4 billion (25.47%) for physical infrastructure, mostly water and wastewater systems and power generation;
- $3.6 billion (16.98%) for basic services including health, family planning, education, agriculture, and the environment;
- $5.8 billion (27.35%) for commodity imports;
- $2.5 billion (11.79%) cash transfers used to support economic policy reform and structural adjustment; and
- $3.9 billion (18.39%) for food aid imports.[11]

In trying to understand what impact U.S. assistance has had on the development of civil society in Egypt, one has to take into consideration the conflicting pressures that guide U.S. decisions as well as the delicate relationship between the two countries. U.S. policy is influenced by several and contradictory concerns. One is the emphasis on political liberalization and democratization that is part of the policies of all Western countries in the post-Cold War era. Political liberalization has become a major concern for aid donors as seen in the reports of the Development Assistance Committee of the Organization of Economic Cooperation and Development (OECD). In fact, that committee formed an Ad Hoc Working Group on Participatory Development and Good Governance in 1996 to examine practices and policies in two areas, namely human rights and democratic local government. The report of the committee of 1996 noted that:

> Donors can help promote human rights essentially in two ways: through support of the reform of legal systems (in particular by supporting an independent judiciary and professional law enforcement agencies) and contributing to activities of civil society (including non-governmental human rights and advocacy groups, both local and international). Some aid agencies systematically include human rights issues in their regular policy dialogue with partner countries.[12]

USAID in particular has adopted the promotion of democracy worldwide as one of its objectives. Its activities in this respect cover four major areas, namely "rule of law, elections and political processes, civil society, and governance." It has moreover established a Center for Democracy and Governance to help in offering guidance to these activities.[13]

In the particular case of Egypt, U.S. policy is also guided by the necessity to maintain good relations with the Egyptian government and to avoid being seen as interfering in the internal affairs of the country. American officials, aware of the great sensitivity of people of the South in general and Egyptians in particular to superpower involvement in their domestic affairs, initially refrained from making comments on political liberalization and civil society or launching programs that could be seen as political; they then proceeded, quite cautiously in some countries, less so in others, to undertake those actions that they think could promote democracy and civil society in the long term.

Thus, the reluctance to undertake actions that could be interpreted by Egyptians to be undue interference in their internal politics gave way in the 1990s to calculated though very mild efforts to facilitate what could be termed a process of political liberalization. The United States Agency for International Development started its "Promoting Democracy" program for this specific purpose. The program has three components:

1. cooperating in a five-year program with Egypt's national legislature, the People's Assembly, to expand its information data base and provide its members with the needed level of research and analysis skills";

2. providing training and technical assistance to targeted civil society organizations to help them gain skills of leadership, planning, management, and team building, with this assistance expanding later to special interest groups "engaged in lobbying and advocacy"; and

3. "increasing devolution of authority to local government and local government participation in the rural development process."[14]

A new organization known as the NGO Service Center was established in 1999 for the specific purpose of helping civil society organizations in Egypt as understood by U.S. officials. The center is described in its brochure as "a developmental activity aiming to increase the participation of citizens and non-governmental organizations in public decision making."[15]

In order to overcome opposition by the Egyptian government, the center, which is funded by USAID, is sponsored by the Egyptian Ministry of Insurance and Social Affairs. USAID has earmarked $27.3 million over five years for this center, or close to $5.5 million annually. After the five-year period, the center is to become a permanent Egyptian entity. The brochure of the center adds that, in the interim, the center will be managed by "Save The Children in partnership with America's Development Foundation and Infonex Corporation, under the guidance of a Steering Committee and an NGO Advisory Board. The center's operations will be managed from its Cairo office and two regional offices in Upper and Lower Egypt."[16]

The center offers four types of assistance, described in its brochure in the following manner:

- networking and information exchange, in order to promote ties among the principal actors of civil society;
- training, to build NGO capacity in the areas of governance, management, community empowerment, and civic action;
- financial assistance, including civic action micro-grants, institutional development grants, civic action partnership grants, and civil society support organizations institutional support grants; and
- operational support for smaller NGOs by the center itself or an intermediary NGO.[17]

Only NGOs registered with the Ministry of Insurance and Social Affairs under the new Associations Law 153 of 1999 can be clients of the center. Many important organizations are thus not eligible for the center's assistance. For example, the Egyptian Human Rights Organization was denied registration under the old law and is so critical of the new law that it does not even contemplate seeking registration under its provisions, although other human rights organizations decided to do so. Professional associations, which have been among the most dynamic actors of a nascent civil society in Egypt, are not governed by the Law of Associations and thus are not eligible to receive support from this center. The NGO project is focusing therefore on preparing Egyptian NGOs to participate in development efforts rather than democratization, while steering them away from the welfare activities that had been, and still are, a major thrust of many.

The United States also supports civil society at a more local level through a well-known international NGO, CARE. That aid targets community-initiated development activities, as well as small businesses and microenterprises.

Egyptian NGOs also benefit from USAID activities that aim to support the private sector. USAID-funded projects in areas ranging from agriculture to health, from education to sewerage, are implemented by both private firms and NGOs. The private sector is particularly well placed to participate in these projects, as the USAID budget includes a program that provides loans to private sector firms. The NGOs can also participate in and thus benefit from these projects, although I could not determine to what extent they have taken advantage of the opportunity. NGOs sometimes also benefit from funds USAID provides to Egyptian ministries or other government agencies. The Associations of Irrigation Users, which cooperates closely with the Ministry of Irrigation, and the youth centers supervised by the National Youth Authority receive money through projects that USAID funds in their respective areas of interest.[18]

It should be clear by now that neither professional associations nor human rights groups in Egypt benefit directly from U.S. assistance, although some of them are among the most active organizations of the incipient civil society; in fact, an increase in their autonomy and an expansion of their activities would signal the rise of civil society. The United States keeps its distance from both kinds of groups because professional associations are not considered NGOs under the prevailing American definition of the term, and because USAID in Egypt, reluctant to upset or anger Cairo, deals only with NGOs recognized by the Egyptian government under the former Law of Associations 32 for 1964 or the new Law 153 of 1999, which has replaced it.

In this respect it should be stressed that USAID tried to get the Egyptian government to clear away the legal hurdles that stand in the way of NGOs, going as far as asking for the amendment of Law 32 of 1964. When the government finally began discussing an amended law, USAID proffered help, but Egyptian government representatives turned it down. Nevertheless, the agency did provide documentation about different laws on associations to the ministries concerned and to members of the committee drafting the new bill. A USAID official even attended one of the meetings that Mrs. Mervat al-Talawi, then-Minister of Insurance and Social Affairs, held in 1998 and 1999 with representatives of NGOs to discuss the draft law.[19]

But the law that was finally adopted in May 1999 was even more restrictive than Law 32 of 1964. That law had at least left the door open for the establishment of human rights groups and did not require them to obtain the approval of the Ministry of Social Affairs in order to receive foreign funding. Nevertheless, the U.S. government did not take any steps. When Richard Brown, director of USAID in Egypt, was asked, on the eve of the adoption of the new law in May 1999, what the United

States would do if a foreign government receiving U.S. aid violated human rights, including freedom of association, he replied that all it could do in the case of a friendly government would be to continue to offer advice and encouragement but not exercise pressure. It is highly unlikely that advice and encouragement would be effective enough to dissuade an authoritarian government from its repressive course of action.[20]

Egyptian NGOs did not remain passive following the adoption of the new law on associations in May 1999. The draft law had been discussed in meetings between the minister of social affairs and several civil society organizations; these groups had criticized the provisions that defined banned "political activities" and the conditions for foreign financing of NGOs; eventually, all participants in these meetings had agreed on a final version of the draft law. However, the draft presented to and approved by the People's Assembly was different from what civil society groups had agreed to. Human rights organizations launched a campaign of criticism against the new law, and as a result the minister of social affairs promised that an executive bylaw would eliminate all causes of concern. The new bylaw was issued in November 1999 and indeed it addressed some of the criticisms. As a result, some organizations decided to seek registration with the Ministry of Social Affairs, reluctantly accepting the new law. Others considered ways of changing their legal status, or simply continued to fight this law.[21]

The government showed its displeasure with organizations that did not want to abide by the provisions of the new law. Both the Egyptian Human Rights Organization and the Ibn Khaldoun Center for Development were ordered by the governor of Cairo in January 2000 to cease publication of their news bulletins—ironically, the news bulletin of the latter is called "Civil Society." The order was transmitted to them by police officers. The Egyptian Human Rights Organization faced further problems: the prosecutor general reactivated the charge that the organization illegally received $25,000 to write a report on police action against Copts in the village of Kosh'h in Upper Egypt—during the investigation of the murder of one Copt there in 1998, police forces were reported to have rounded up most of the village Copt inhabitants.[22] There is no evidence that U.S. officials reacted to these developments.

U.S. diplomats have made, in the past, some gestures of support toward some beleaguered human rights organizations, visiting their headquarters or inviting their leaders to meetings in their homes or in restaurants; however, they stopped short of offering official assistance. Instead, they confined U.S. aid to associations engaged in development work, narrowly defined to include mostly economic and social dimensions of the development process, and have shied away from associations engaged in "political development." For these diplomats, who reflect U.S. policy, socioeconomic development in Egypt gets the top priority, with democratization coming far behind.[23] Obviously U.S. officials value the friendship of the Egyptian government more than the strength of civil society organizations.

Nevertheless, the NGO Service Center, which started operations in early 2000 with an annual budget close to $5.5 million although total U.S. economic assistance to Egypt is decreasing, is an indication that the U.S. government continues to support civil society in Egypt and that it is taking seriously the OECD policy directives that donor countries emphasize assistance for democratization and the building of civil society. The problem is that U.S. assistance to civil society in Egypt is very timid, for the time being at least.

USAID is not the only American donor assisting civil society organizations in Egypt, nor does such assistance come only from United States organizations. The Ford Foundation's extensive human rights program benefits many organizations in Egypt and other Middle Eastern countries, particularly in the occupied Palestinian territories and Sudan. Canadian, German, Dutch, and Scandinavian donors also offer assistance to human rights groups in Egypt and other Arab countries. The Egyptian civil society organizations that receive assistance from private U.S. foundations and other governments include, in addition to human rights groups, family planning associations such as the Egyptian National Committee for Population and Development, an umbrella organization; independent research centers such as the Ibn Khaldoun Center for Development Studies, Al-Ahram's Center for Political and Strategic Studies, and various university research centers; women's organizations; and even trade unions. The Friedrich Ebert Stiftung, a German foundation close to the Social Democratic Party, is particularly involved in helping trade unions. Thus private American donors as well as donors from other countries reach civil society organizations that cannot receive direct assistance from a USAID reluctant to offend or antagonize the Egyptian government.[24]

The U.S. and Islamist Associations

The civil society organizations that do not receive any kind of foreign assistance are probably the most influential. Professional associations and religious bodies such as the Al-Azhar spiritual leadership, led by a religious dignitary called the Grand Professor Chief of Al-Azhar Mosque,[25] Dar Al-Efta',[26] and the Coptic Church, do not benefit from the aid of Western governments or foundations. These institutions do receive support from Muslims and Copts, in Egypt and abroad. Coptic bodies receive donations from Copts who have emigrated to Western countries, and Muslim institutions get help from Egyptian Muslims living in Persian Gulf countries, and even from governments of these countries.

Organizations with religious affiliations were excluded from U.S. assistance despite the fact that USAID uses a very broad definition of civil society. Dr. Richard Brown, USAID director in Egypt, said that his agency defines civil society as including any organization independent of the government that is active either at the national or local level—a definition that should enable USAID to engage with a wide variety of organizations. In reality, most of the U.S. funding for civil society goes to the entities known as nongovernmental organizations (NGOs).[27] This excludes religious bodies, professional associations, and political parties. Egyptians, however, consider all these groups to be major constituents of the hoped-for civil society. Many of the professional associations, foremost among them those controlled by the Muslim Brotherhood, call for respect of human dignity as well as for freedom of association and of expression. The journalists syndicate, which was never totally controlled by the brotherhood, fought the government in 1995 over the question of freedom of the press.

The U.S. position on professional associations probably stems from American officials' belief that civil society is different from so-called political society and that organizations of the former do not concern themselves with politics. In their view, political parties are by definition not part of civil society. Nor are professional associations and trade unions, if they have ties to political parties or are themselves involved in politics—which is the case in all countries of the South as well as in a few post-industrial countries. However, in Egypt and some other Arab countries where the government severely restricts many civil rights, leaders and activists in professional associations and trade unions see political action as necessary to get the restrictions lifted, for the sake of their own operations and for all citizens' sake.

Politicization of civil society is also a product of restrictions on political activity per se. Political movements that, for one reason or another, cannot gain a legal presence in the formal political arena occasionally find an alternative forum in the relatively autonomous professional association or community organizations. It is not surprising that Nasserites, Marxists, and Muslim Brothers in the Sadat years found in professional associations an outlet that they could not find legally in political society, to continue borrowing the Gramscian term. Nor is it surprising that the Muslim Brotherhood, which still does not have a legal presence under the Mubarak government, should seek to make professional associations into its exclusive fora. Associations of engineers, medical doctors, scientists, and lawyers make up for the brotherhood's lack of a political party.

Perhaps for USAID the fault of the professional associations is not just their political involvement but their "bad" political involvement: the U.S. perceives them to side with an Islamist movement that does not oppose "terrorism" while being extremely hostile to U.S. efforts to promote a settlement of the Arab-Israeli dispute—in reality, these organizations only oppose a settlement because that does not do justice to Palestinian and Arab legitimate rights.

Many Egyptians, too, doubt the commitment to civil liberties of the Muslim Brotherhood and of the professional associations it controls. On the other hand, other political forces in the country—and the government itself—do not have a clean record on such matters, either. I believe that the Muslim Brotherhood and the associations they control should be judged on their actions rather than on what some people perceive their intentions to be. If the first criterion is accepted, one must conclude that they have contributed to the temporary flourishing of the incipient civil society in Egypt in the 1980s. In the 1990s, they were harshly repressed by the government, which attempted in several ways to preempt their electoral successes in professional associations, and in general elections. When such methods failed in the case of professional associations, the government resorted simply to postponing elections in those associations where Islamists were likely to be the major winners, notably the engineers', medical doctors', and lawyers' syndicates. No elections took place in any of these associations after February 1993 despite relentless efforts by their members to get government authorization to do so.

The U.S. government does not completely ignore all professionals and human rights activists. USAID financed trips to the United States for Egyptian journalists and human rights activists over the past two decades, giving them an opportunity to see how their American counterparts work. Furthermore, some U.S. congressmen, during the debate on the Freedom from Religious Persecution Act of October 10, 1998, claimed that Copts are persecuted in Egypt.[28] The overtly political character of these declarations, however, not only caused concern in the Clinton administration but also led many Egyptians, Muslims, and Copts alike to denounce them as flagrant interference in Egypt's internal politics.[29] The statements also demonstrated that the U.S. government is definitely not of one mind in its definition of civil society or in its choice of methods intended to promote that civil society abroad.

It is this suspicion of U.S. interference in Egypt's internal affairs that makes both Muslim and Coptic religious bodies reluctant to ask for U.S. aid. It is rare, in fact, for Muslim bodies to ask assistance of non-Muslim countries at a time when many Arabs and Muslims are rich and can provide well for them. Coptic churches, for their part, have become suspicious of other Christian churches and the countries in which they are located, particularly of Western Protestant churches that have been active in Egypt and have turned some Copts away from the faith into which they were born. Moreover, neither Islamic nor Coptic religious bodies in Egypt suffer from a shortage of funds, since Egyptians usually donate generously to religious institutions. In fact, the earliest voluntary associations in Egypt were founded by domestic religious bodies and made valuable contributions to education, health care, and charitable work in the country.

Assessing Civil Society Assistance in Egypt

In assessing civil society assistance in Egypt, it is crucial to consider the general context. And that context is clear: at the start of the new millennium, Egypt is a pure case of political deliberalization. The reversal of the liberalization process started with the adoption in 1992 of amendments to the penal code that stiffened penalties for terrorist acts, but terrorism was broadly defined to include also "incitement to the use of violence against the government." A year later, another law raised the quorum for elections in professional associations in the hope that this would prevent Islamists from winning majorities in their national councils. When it became clear that the new legislation would not prevent Islamists from mobilizing enough members to win huge electoral victories, the government opted to postpone elections in most professional associations. Moreover, it appointed councils to run the engineers' syndicate and the bar association, accusing their former leaders of financial irregularities.

The People's Assembly election of 1995 was marred by violence and rigging by officials, leading the courts to declare elections in nearly half the constituencies invalid. Voters returned only fourteen opposition deputies, the lowest number under the Mubarak presidency apart from the assembly elected in 1990, when most opposition parties boycotted the balloting. A year earlier, villagers had lost the right to elect their mayors and university professors the right to elect deans of faculties. In 1994, furthermore, the government attempted to curb the press, but this partly failed because of the journalists' vehement resistance to the law imposing the new restrictions. Finally, the already mentioned associations law that the People's Assembly adopted in May 1999 still leaves human rights organizations and independent research centers unhappy about some of its clauses.

Under these conditions, civil society has far to go to become an established element of state-society relations in Egypt—that much further now that the government has destroyed much of the limited progress it allowed during the 1980s. Civil society associations are under siege. Two of the largest and most active groups in the struggle for expanded civil and political liberties, the bar association and the engineers' syndicate, have been under direct government control for years, with no prospect of regaining their autonomy. A number of activists from several syndicates were arrested in December 1999, apparently while discussing preparations for new elections in the professional associations. Mostly Islamists, they are being tried in the winter of the year 2000 for "participation in a conspiracy to overthrow the government" and for belonging to an illegal organization—the Muslim Brotherhood.

The other rights and safeguards that make civil society possible are also under attack. Freedom of speech, though formally recognized by the constitution and protected by law, is limited in practice by the government monopoly on television and radio, and confined in the press to issues unlikely to arouse the ire of either the religious establishment or conservative Islamist circles. Nevertheless, the situation at present is far better than at any time since the revolution of July 1952: views critical of the government are expressed in the pages of several newspapers and even in a number of television programs.

Yet, the assassination of secularist writer Farag Fouda in June 1993, the attempted assassination of novelist and Nobel Prize winner Naguib Mahfouz in October 1994, and the divorce suit against Cairo University professor Nasr Hamed Abou Zeid in June 1993 were more than enough to convince liberal-minded intellectuals of the limits to freedom of speech.

Finally, among the legally recognized organizations of civil society, there is a clear imbalance between business associations, with their easy access to government and media and their growing influence, on the one hand, and muzzled professional associations and ineffectual trade unions on the other. Thus, while wealthy businessmen have their newspapers and organizations as well as easy access to all media, organizations of the so-called popular sectors are under siege. Western donors to the nascent civil society do not seem to be particularly upset about this kind of imbalance.

It would be easy to blame foreign donors for the setbacks of Egypt's emerging civil society, since the civil society organizations that suffered most are precisely those that got no help whatsoever from foreign donors. Professional associations, university Professors' Clubs, and Islamist organizations received no foreign assistance of any sort, with the exception of the journalists' syndicate, which got some travel grants for journalists. But most such associations, particularly the ones dominated by Islamists, would not have accepted Western assistance had it been offered anyway. They have a profound mistrust of Western governments and institutions, and they suspect imperialist designs behind offers of assistance.

It is also doubtful that Western donors would have welcomed an application for assistance from associations dominated by Islamists. The position of Western governments on democratization in Arab countries is ambiguous. They want democratization, but they want it to bring to power friendly governments. If democratization threatens to bring to power nationalist or Islamist parties such as the Islamic Salvation Front in Algeria or the Muslim Brotherhood in Egypt, Western governments would prefer the current authoritarian regimes, with which they generally get along well these days. With Hosni Mubarak, King Fahd of Saudi Arabia, Jordan's King Abdallah, Zein El-Abdin Ben Ali of Tunisia, and even Bashar Al-Assad of Syria, the West can make progress on the Arab-Israeli peace process and economic liberalization. Such might not be the case with Islamist governments in any of these countries. That does not rule out some Western government support for Islamist parties and factions, as with the U.S. government support for the various Islamist groups in Afghanistan during the Afghan civil war in the 1980s. An accommodation with more moderate Islamist groups is not at all impossible, but it would take a long time to become reality, and would be conditioned on the Islamists' dropping of their opposition to a regional peace settlement on Israeli terms, which Washington is trying to promote.

Despite these problems, foreign actors did have some positive influence on the evolution of an embryonic civil society in some Arab countries, including Egypt. Foreign economic assistance and some foreign investment, along with pressure to liberalize economic policy, fostered the growth of private entrepreneurship in Egypt (although the period when economic assistance was greatest, the 1980s and early 1990s, was also a time of stagnant or sluggish economic growth and increased unemployment and poverty, as documented by World Bank and IMF reports). The example of the working democracies and vibrant civil societies of the West fascinates minds and hearts of segments of the ruling elite in Arab nations, and those of the opposition leaders as well. Direct assistance, in the form of training, technical support, and financial grants, strengthened some organizations and enabled human rights groups in Egypt in particular to expand their activities and survive government restrictions. But foreign actors could never have reversed the trend toward a retreat of civil society in Egypt and other Arab countries like Jordan and Tunisia; even to suggest that they could have is absurd.

In fact, it would be unwise to ask Western donors, governmental and nongovernmental, to do more to help the embryonic civil society in Arab countries. It is doubtful the donors have the will to do more, so long as the rise of civil society is associated with a democratization process that could bring in governments less friendly to the West than those now in power. Furthermore, Arab countries do not believe that the West, and in particular the United States, is truly committed to democracy or to the legitimate interests of Arab countries. Washington's continued support of Israel, its disregard of the suffering of the Iraqi people, and its luke-warm response to Turkish incursions into Iraqi territory do not promote a positive image in the region. Large segments of the population in Arab countries, as well as most of the region's governments, are suspicious of any kind of external assistance provided to groups viewed as belonging to the opposition, which is the case for active civil society organizations in countries like Egypt, Jordan, and Tunisia. Nationalist and Islamist press campaigns against foreign sponsorship of social science research in Egypt is one of the latest manifestations of the profound mistrust of Western aid for any civil society organization.[30] Under these circumstances, increased support by Western donors would serve only to discredit civil society organizations in the eyes of ordinary Egyptians.

However, calling on Western actors, governmental and nongovernmental, to give up any interest in the emergence of a vibrant civil society in Arab countries would be unwise and even counterproductive. In my opinion, Arab peoples do need and deserve a vibrant civil society. The development of healthy civil societies would bring to power more responsible and accountable governments. Such governments might not readily accept all the United States' policies, particularly its unqualified support of Israel and attempts by Congress to dictate to Arab governments, as with the law on religious freedom. Nevertheless, the presence of responsible and accountable governments in Arab countries is in the West's best interest over the long term, helping shape a mutually beneficial relationship on solid grounds acceptable to all its parties. The emergence of such a civil society is a product of the historical process of social change in these countries and cannot be exported from other countries, as the experience of development of the civil society in the West itself has shown.

The situation thus requires Western peoples to realize this historical truth, while not giving up on the hope of witnessing such development in Arab countries. They should therefore remain engaged with the emergent civil society in these countries, but keep a low profile. Through constructive engagement, the West might succeed in persuading Arab regimes to remove legal and administrative hurdles that restrict the establishment and the functioning of civil society organizations. They should demonstrate all solidarity with the organizations of civil society, offering them publicity and standing beside them when their own government persecutes them. Limited amounts of technical assistance and training offered to them by their counterparts in the West would be most useful. Generous financial assistance, though occasionally necessary, is harmful in the long run, since it leads these organizations to depend on external funding, with no attempt to strike deep roots in their society that would provide them both funding and protection on a permanent basis. Finally, Western donor organizations should abandon efforts to impose their agenda on organizations in Arab countries or to sow discord by supporting some organizations while ignoring others that adopt the same goals. With low-profile constructive engagement on the part of Western peoples and donors, and some positive internal developments in the Arab world, a vibrant civil society in Arab countries might not be a wild dream after all.

Notes

1. John Keane, ed., *Civil Society and the State: New European Perspectives* (New York: Verso, 1988), pp. 13–21.

2. Mustapha Kamel Al-Sayyid, "The Concept of Civil Society and the Arab World," in Rex Brynen, Bahgat Korany, and Paul Noble, eds., *Political Liberalization and Democratization in the Arab World, Volume 1, Theoretical Perspectives* (Boulder: Lynne Rienner, 1995), pp. 131–47.

3. John Keane, "Despotism and Democracy, Origins and Development of the Distinction between Civil Society and the State, 1750–1850," and Norberto Bobbio, "Gramsci and the Concept of Civil Society," in Keane, ed., *Civil Society and the State*, pp. 35–99.

4. Jeno Szucs, "Three Historical Regions of Europe," in Keane, ed., *Civil Society and the State*, pp. 290–332.

5. Mustapha Kamel Al-Sayyid, "A Civil Society in Egypt?" in Augustus Richard Norton, ed., *Civil Society in the Middle East*, vol. 1 (New York: E. J. Brill, 1995), pp. 269–94.

6. Afaf Lutfi Al-Sayyid Marsot, *A Short History of Egypt* (New York: Cambridge University Press, 1985), chapters 3–5.

7. Ahmed Baha' El-Din, *Muhawarati ma'a al-Sadat* [My conversations with Sadat] (Cairo: Dar Al-Hilal, 1987), p. 64.

8. See different contributions in *Al-Munazzamah al-Misriyyah li houqouq al-insaan* [Egyptian Human Rights Organization] and *Hurriyat al-ra'y wa al-ëaquidah, quyoud wa eshkaliyyat* [Freedom of Opinion and Belief, Constraints and Problematics] (Cairo: EOHR, 1994).

9. John Waterbury, *Egypt Under Nasser and Sadat: The Political Economy of Two Regimes* (Princeton: Princeton University Press, 1983), pp. 207–31, 354–90.

10. For an example of the way elections are manipulated, see Sandrine Gamblin, ed., *Contour et Détours du Politique en Egypte, Les élections législatives de 1995* (Paris: L'Harmattan, 1997).

11. See data published on the Internet web site of USAID Egypt, www.Info.usaid.gov/eg/usegypt.htm, May 27, 2000.

12. OECD-Development Assistance Committee, *Development Cooperation, Efforts, and Policies of the Members of the Development Assistance Committee 1996* (Paris: OECD, 1997), pp. 32–33.

13. See the Internet web site of USAID Egypt, www.Info.usaid.gov/eg/usegypt.htm.

14. Ibid.

15. Brochure of the NGO Service Center (Cairo: The NGO Service Center, 1999).

16. Ibid.

17. Ibid.

18. It has become the Ministry of Youth in the new cabinet appointed in October 1999.

19. USAID official, interview by author, Cairo, February 1999.

20. The question was asked during a public lecture at the Center for Developing Countries Studies, Cairo University, May 4, 1999. I was the moderator of that session.

21. Leaders of human rights groups in Egypt, author interviews, November 1999.

22. "Balagh ela al-na'eb al-'am: 25000 thaman al-kheyana. Sefarah ajnabiyya toqaddem al-mablagh limisreyyin fi moqabel taqreer kadtheb 'an maza'em ittehad al-aqbaat" [Complaint to the Public Prosecutor, 25,000 price of treason. A foreign embassy offers the sum to Egyptians in return for an untrue report claiming persecution of Copts] *Al-Osbou* (Cairo), November 22, 1998, p. 1; and "Wa najahat hamlat al-Osbou'-e'adat al-sheeq al-mashbouh ela al-sefarah al-britaniyya" [The Osbou's campaign has succeeded. Suspect cheque is sent back to the British Embassy], *Al-Osbou'*, November 30, 1998, p. 1.

23. U.S. diplomat posted in Cairo, author interview, February 1999.

24. The Egyptian Human Rights Organization used to publish a list of donors who funded its activities. The 1993 annual report expressed thanks to international, Dutch, American, Swedish, Arab, and Egyptian donors. Of eight donors mentioned in this report, two were Americans, namely the MacArthur Foundation and the American Lawyers' Committee. See "Acknowledgment" in *Al-Munazzamah al-misriyyah li houqouq al-insaan-EHRO. Halat Huqouq al-Insaan fi*

Misr, al-taqreer al-sanawi li'am 1993 [The State of Human Rights in Egypt. The 1993 Annual Report].

25. In Arabic, "Al-Ustadth al-akbar, Shaykh al-jami' al-azhar."

26. The highest religious advisory body for Sunni Muslims.

27. Statement at public lecture moderated by the author, Center for Developing Countries Studies, Cairo University, May 4, 1999.

28. For information about the Freedom from Religious Persecution Act, see the Internet web site of American Atheists at www.atheist.org/flash.line/irfa2.htm.

29. This was expressed in several comments in Egyptian national and party newspapers throughout the fall of 1998 on the debates that preceded the passage of the bill.

30. "Al-ekhteraaq: Al-Ahram yujri estetl'a lihesaab jeha amrikiyyah 'an mawqef al-misreyyin men al-ra'ees Mubarak wa men qudraat quwwatehem al-musallaha" [The Penetration: Al-Ahram conducts a poll for an American organization on Egyptians' position towards President Mubarak the capabilities of their armed forces], *Al-Osbou'*, September 7, 1998, p. 3; and "Natlob tahqeeqat 'ajelah wa ehalat al-mutawarritin li al-muhakama-al-bahht al-mashbouh yaddor bi al-amn al-qawmi wa al-ahram laysa behaja ela 20000 dollar" [We demand immediate investigations: the suspect research damages national security and Al-Ahram does not need $20,000], *Al-Osbou'*, September 14, 1998, p. 1.

Part Two

Africa

3

Social Movements, Professionalization of Reform, and Democracy in Africa

Marina Ottaway

SINCE THE EARLY DAYS OF COLONIALISM, Africans, particularly in the cities, have organized a plethora of strong and resilient voluntary associations—in today's terminology, organizations of civil society—that have played important social, economic, and political roles.[1] Voluntary organizations have helped the millions of villagers who have migrated to African cities adapt to urban life and maintain strong ties back home, giving financial and moral support. Voluntary organizations have also tried to provide the services that incompetent governments do not: they have educated children and buried the dead, extended credit to microbusinesses with no access to the banks, and built, in the vacuum created by the collapse of the formal economy, parallel economies that are sometimes quite sophisticated.[2]

Africa's civil society organizations have also been significant forces in politics in many periods and in many guises. From the cultural societies and labor unions that blossomed into pro-independence political parties, to the sports clubs that supported such parties covertly, to the dense web of "civics" that contributed to apartheid's demise, organizations of civil society helped bring about all major political transitions in Africa. On their own, however, Africans rarely formed the kind of organizations donors consider essential to promote and strengthen democracy. Civil society as defined by the donors—that is, nongovernmental organizations (NGOs) involved in advocacy and civic education—is very weak in Africa and likely to remain so.

77

This chapter examines the differences between the civil society organizations promoted and funded by Western governmental and nongovernmental donor agencies and those that Africans form on their own initiative. It also explores whether organizations of the latter kind, which by definition reflect the social realities of African countries, are suitable for performing the functions that democratizing countries need civil society to perform. The discussion will help address the question of whether U.S. and other programs to assist civil society should look beyond the kind of organizations they now favor, working instead with ones better suited to conditions in Africa.

Civil Society and Politics in Africa

Political scientists in democratic countries have long been concerned with political pluralism—the participation of many different interest groups in the making of political decisions. Citizens should be able to attempt to influence government decisions directly rather than only indirectly through the election of officials, thus greatly broadening the scope of political participation. Discussions of pluralism assume that the organized groups that seek to influence decisions represent underlying social groups with well-defined interests. Social and economic pluralism is reflected in the pluralism of organizations, which in turn broadens political participation. For the United States and other established democracies, the assumption is largely correct—social, organizational, and political pluralism go hand in hand. The same does not always hold true for African countries today, particularly when the organizations seeking to influence decisions came into being mainly because donors were eager to finance them.

Without doubt, African societies are highly pluralistic. In all the continent's countries, numerous groups maintain their autonomy from the state and from—a point often forgotten—all rigid authority structures, whether traditional or modern, public or private. However, social, political, and organizational forms of pluralism are often quite distinct and do not necessarily support democracy. First, the social pluralism of African countries has a strong ethnic basis that, if politicized, leads more readily to conflict than to democracy. Second, many deeply rooted, active organizations of civil society have stayed out of politics and thus have not contributed directly to democracy. Third, the organizations of civil society that donors prefer often remain artificial creations with weak roots in the community; these free-floating entities promote an organizational form of pluralism without necessarily giving representation to genuine interest groups, thus without promoting political pluralism.

Pluralism and Conflict

In most African countries, social pluralism is based above all on region, ethnicity, and religion, while the rural-urban divide is somewhat important and social class and economic interests matter least. This is the result not of an African peculiarity but of economic realities. Whatever the cause, social cleavages based on ethnicity and religion tend to be much more rigid, and are potentially more explosive, than those based on economic interests.

Economic conditions in Africa do not readily support a definition of groups based on economic interests, and the strength of extended family relations and patron-client networks further decreases the importance of such groupings. The overwhelming majority of Africans are peasants, but landlessness, with the attendant chasm and conflict between peasants and landlords, is relatively rare; thus economic interests in rural areas often are not sharply differentiated. In urban areas, sky-high unemployment also flattens the class structure. The industrial working class is small, as is the business class, and a large segment of the urban population survives in the informal sector. The class structure, in other words, is relatively amorphous, and organizations articulating economic interests are weak—a situation that used to cause considerable analytical difficulties and ideological angst among Marxist scholars of Africa. The major exception is relatively industrialized South Africa, where both labor unions and business organizations are distinct, self-conscious socioeconomic groups with a very important political role.

In some countries, such as Kenya and the Ivory Coast, large farmers are a powerful interest group.[3] Peasants, on the other hand, never are. Their interests are usually poorly represented in politics, and when large peasant organizations exist, as in Ethiopia between 1975 and 1991, they are likely to become instruments of government control over the peasants rather than channels through which peasants express their demands.[4]

On the other hand, ethnicity and, increasingly, religion have been central to political life. All African countries are ethnically very diverse, because present states are new and the assimilation processes that forged a degree of homogeneity in the so-called nation-states have not taken place. (And even in seemingly homogeneous states, as is becoming clear, old ethnic identities can suddenly reacquire a saliency they appeared to have lost.) While all African governments have declared that they will work to overcome ethnic and religious divisions, most have not done so, instead playing the cards of ethnicity or religion in their bids to win support.

In the 1990s, the return to multiparty elections in most African countries, leading to the formation of ethnic political parties, has made the political role of ethnicity even more overt. The pluralism of ethnic parties reflects the underlying social pluralism, but it does not augur well for democracy because ethnic divisions tend to be rigid and to breed intolerance.

In all countries, there are groups whose definition of their interests goes against the essence of democracy—extremist groups with narrow agendas intolerant of other groups' right to pursue their own goals.[5] While such extremist groups are undemocratic and in some cases repugnant, in established democracies they are not seen as a real threat. In the cacophony of voices striving to influence policy, they are not widely heard and are even less heeded; a highly pluralistic political system can absorb and neutralize some undemocratic forces without serious consequences. But if inherently undemocratic interest groups dominate, as it is often the case when ethnicity becomes politicized, pluralism can easily lead to conflict.

The Disengaged Civil Society

Organizations based on ethnicity or religion are certainly not the only African groups with strong roots in society. As mentioned earlier, African countries have produced numerous voluntary associations of all types that have sought to help their members adapt to difficult environments. In the colonial period, those organizations became politicized and contributed to the development of the pro-independence parties and the success of their struggle. After independence, as economic conditions sharply deteriorated, voluntary organizations and even informal networks continued to protect their members from the failures and depredations of governments. Everywhere, small organizations developed to provide schooling for children who did not find a place in government schools, small loans to microbusinesses that banks ignored, water to neighborhoods that lacked pipes. Such organizations, however, were depoliticized: the single-party or military African regimes, more repressive than the colonial governments, did not allow them to take on any political role. Civil society resisted capture by the state, as Goran Hyden has pointed out, but did not itself try to capture the state.[6] It thus did not contribute directly to political pluralism or democracy.[7]

With the political openings of the 1990s, the political space has increased even in African countries that still fall far short of democracy. There is little sign so far, however, that the voluntary associations are taking advantage of the new climate to mobilize their members behind political agendas. This may be temporary, and voluntary organizations may again become politicized as they were under colonialism, becoming an important avenue for grassroots political participation. For the time being, it is not these groups but the pro-democracy NGOs organized with donor support that represent civil society in the political process.

Free-Floating on Donors' Funds

In seeking to develop civil society in African countries, donors have largely ignored existing voluntary associations and have turned instead to new kinds of organizations, particularly advocacy NGOs that attempt to influence government policy and civic education NGOs that see their role as educating citizens to become active participants in the politics of a democratic country. Both kinds of NGOs supposedly promote political pluralism, indeed a "healthy" political pluralism, since they are formed on the basis of interests and policy choices, not of ascribed, rigid identities such as ethnicity. Even women's organizations, which are based on the biologically ascribed gender identity, focus on policy reform rather than seeking power for women for the sake of power.

The problem with civil society assistance is that the political pluralism it promotes is not rooted in social pluralism but is often a free-floating political pluralism without a real social base.[8] The organizations it helps call into being and develop are the creations of donor funding rather than of social demands for representation and a role in policymaking. This is particularly true for organizations that engage in civic education.

Civic education NGOs in Africa arose with the return to multiparty elections that began in 1991. One example is the Foundation for Democratic Process (FODEP) in Zambia. In 1991, Zambia held multiparty elections for the first time since 1968. President Kenneth Kaunda, who had ruled since independence, had been increasingly discredited by seemingly endless economic stagnation. Unlike what would happen later in other countries such as Kenya, it was not donor pressure but a strong domestic opposition that forced Kaunda's hand. Western donors, however, strongly supported the elections. To ensure the credibility of the process, they provided international observers and also promoted domestic monitoring efforts. The elections were competitive and Kaunda was defeated.

Elated, donors put together a package of programs intended to consolidate democracy in Zambia by strengthening government institutions on one side and civil society on the other. Under the latter initiative, organizations formed to monitor the elections were encouraged to remake themselves as civic education NGOs. FODEP was the largest of these groups.

Poorly prepared to take on the new task, with weak leaders and no broad support, FODEP was a top-down organization, almost completely dependent on donors' financial and—yet more serious—managerial support. The U.S. Agency for International Development brought in an American consultant, Southern University, on a multiyear contract to help reorganize and build up FODEP. Nevertheless, the NGO remained notably weak and dependent, although it fielded a large number of monitors for the 1996 elections.[9] But even had it developed better leadership and a stronger sense of purpose, it would still have been free-floating, the product of a system of donor-supported political pluralism with virtually no social roots. If deprived of support from donors, FODEP would not simply retrench but would probably disappear. Its weak leadership and general lack of dynamism make it an extreme case among donor-supported NGOs. But it is not unique in owing its existence to the supply of cash that donors are eager to spend on civil society rather than to demand from a mobilized interest group in society.

A second case from Zambia illustrates the point.[10] Women for Change is a donor-supported NGO that seeks to educate women about their rights and help them organize to obtain respect for those rights in their private lives as well as in the public sphere. Much more activist and militant than FODEP, Women for Change organizes small groups of women in rural areas—partly consciousness-raising and partly mutual help—hoping that they will become self-sustaining and even spawn new groups. Like most donor-created and -supported civil society organizations in Africa, Women for Change is urban-based and headed by educated women. It is probably working harder than many to reach out to women in the countryside and build up some organization there. But even civic education NGOs can be much closer to the people they try to organize to defend their own interests. In Zambia, the Catholic Peace and Justice Commissions are probably more representative, or at least closer to those they seek to represent, than urban-based NGOs like FODEP or even Women for Change. The same goes for some other church-related NGOs in African countries, including Kenya and Zimbabwe. No matter how hard-working, determined, and sincere about helping village women its leaders are, Women for Change remains an organization created from the top down, and from the city out, to extend a helping hand to village women; it is not an organization *of* village women.

Representation and Trusteeship

Relations between most donor-supported civil society organizations and the constituency in whose name they speak can be characterized as trusteeship rather than as representation. Trustee organizations—unlike, for instance, labor unions and business associations—were not formed by a mobilized constituency that articulated its interests and created a vehicle to bring them to the attention of the government. Rather, they are organizations whose leaders have taken it upon themselves to define and represent the interests of people who do not speak for themselves.[11]

Trustee organizations exist even in democratic countries, and they contribute to pluralism and democracy to some extent. Groups disenfranchised by law or poverty have often been represented by others. Welfare legislation in most countries is a result of efforts of such "trustees"—for example, during the New Deal in the United States. Organizations representing the interests of children are always trustee organizations. At times, political systems have officially recognized a role for trustees; in South Africa from 1956 to 1970, for instance, blacks' interests were represented in parliament by a small number of whites elected for the purpose to specially reserved seats. In today's democratic South Africa, as throughout the continent, a disproportionate number of civil society NGOs supported by donors are trustee organizations.

Representation by trustees, however, works in a very different manner from representation by organizations in which those being represented play a part. A few white advocates in parliament could not substitute for the extension of political rights to the entire black population of South Africa. Donor-supported trustee organizations in Africa tend to resemble each other in their programs, leadership, and ideological outlook—and to be much closer to donors' preferences than to the needs and preferences of supposed constituents. The recent increase in the number of NGOs in Africa thus does not necessarily strengthen pluralism. And even with relatively representative NGOs, the question must be raised whether organizations that represent the interests of passive constituencies risk blunting more direct, though more problematic, forms of participation.[12]

Moreover, trustee organizations are much more vulnerable than representative NGOs to government depredations, particularly during a transition, when democracy is still threatened. Representative organizations, rooted in social groups, are more difficult for a government with no commitment to democracy to control and suppress. If the Zambian government closed down FODEP or Women for Change, the donors would complain, and if the suppression was part of a concerted attack on NGOs, they might even suspend assistance channeled directly through the government. Domestically, however, little would happen: Zambian crowds would not march in the street for FODEP as they did in 1991 for the Movement for Multiparty Democracy (MMD). Backed by many mobilized constituencies—in the labor unions, the churches, indeed most sectors of urban society—the MMD was not a free-floating organization, and went on to victory in the elections over the machine of a party that had been in power thirty years. The civil society organizations that donors created after 1991 do not have comparable clout and would have to change their character and manner of operation completely to acquire it.

Rethinking Civil Society Assistance

Civil society in African countries confronts a dilemma. The professional advocacy or civic education NGOs that donors favor are poorly rooted in the society, they are top-down rather than grassroots, they are trustee rather than representative organizations, they struggle with management problems, and they would not survive without outside support. Yet they are the organizations that seek to engage the state, influence its policies, and make it more accountable. The voluntary associations that Africans have formed themselves are grassroots organizations with a proven ability to organize and survive on their own, responsive to the demands of their members and thus more representative. But in recent years they have not attempted to represent the interests of their members in the political process and as yet have played no role in promoting democratization. They are more likely to disengage from the state than to seek to hold it responsible. Thus the organizations that contribute most to the democratic process are poorly rooted in society, while those with the strongest roots contribute little to the political process, although they have contributed in the past.

Are donors right to support Africa's professional NGOs despite those organizations' many shortcomings, or should they turn their attention to the more informal, broad-based organizations, steering them toward political activity and helping build them into social movement-type organizations? Are the professional NGOs at all suitable for fostering democratic transitions? Comparing the effectiveness of grassroots associations and social movements with the very limited impact of the professional, trustee organizations created with donor support, one is tempted to say that donors should redirect civil society assistance whenever possible to broader-based movements.

Such a conclusion is too sweeping, however. Probing deeper, let us turn to the experience of South Africa, which highlights the complicated relationship between social movements and professional NGOs, the effectiveness of each under different political conditions, and the distinct challenges each poses for donors. I will then attempt to draw some general conclusions about the problems civil society assistance faces in Africa.

The Rise and Fall of Civil Society: South Africa

South Africa offers the most recent and most dramatic example in Africa of spontaneously formed voluntary associations, organized into a broad social movement, forcing democratic change even in a well-organized, strong authoritarian system. Foreign donors, including the United States, worked with that broad movement. The movement's story is worth discussing in some detail because it raises issues crucial to the promotion of civil society: not only whether donors can work with social movements, but whether civil society organizations effective against an authoritarian regime can also be effective in building democracy, and whether social movement-type organizations are sustainable in the long run or require exceptional conditions to survive.

In the late 1950s the African National Congress (ANC), the first and the major movement fighting for the rights of disenfranchised South Africans, turned militant, seeking to build a broader following with mass actions such as the public burning of the passes the government required Africans living in the cities to carry. The ensuing repression convinced some ANC leaders of the necessity of transforming the movement into a tightly organized party with a military wing. Thus Umkhonto we Sizwe came into being. The change proved costly. A smaller, more formally and more tightly organized party was more vulnerable to repression than a broad, somewhat inchoate movement. The new ANC was practically destroyed by arrests among its leaders, including Nelson Mandela. The rest of the leadership was forced into exile.

The ANC strove for the next three decades to build up Umkhonto we Sizwe and liberate the country through military force, but the strategy was unsuccessful.[13] Separated from South Africa until the mid-1970s by a buffer of white-led countries, the ANC never succeeded in mounting military attacks that threatened the apartheid regime. The ANC as a professional politico-military organization was largely a failure.

Beginning in the early 1970s, however, internal opposition in South Africa revived, not because of steps the ANC had taken but because of the rapid growth of new organizations of civil society. The black labor

unions became active again and drew so much support that the government deemed it wiser to recognize them.[14] At the same time, the black
consciousness movement inspired by Steve Biko gave rise not to one large,
formal organization the government could infiltrate and destroy but to an
extremely broadly based and loosely organized network of small grassroots
organizations in the townships. Hundreds of student groups, church-related organizations, and, above all, township "civics" sprang up. Their
members were determined to make the country ungovernable by organizing boycotts of rent and electricity payments, paralyzing the schools,
and disrupting the operations of the township councils; and they succeeded. Government repression took a tremendous toll, with thousands
of people arrested or fleeing into exile, but the movement survived. Unlike the ANC with its hierarchical organization, the civil society hydra
had too many heads to be slain. Instead, it grew in strength. By the early
1980s, the civic organizations joined loosely under the umbrella of the
United Democratic Front (UDF). At the same time, the industry-based
labor unions came together in the Congress of South African Trade Unions
(COSATU). Later COSATU and the UDF formed the Mass Democratic
Movement (MDM) in an attempt to coordinate their efforts.[15]

During the 1980s, South Africa witnessed the triumph of civil society.
While it is impossible to precisely assign credit for the defeat of apartheid among South African civil society, international economic sanctions,
and the demise of communism—this last eliminating Pretoria's fear that
if the ANC came to power Moscow would be right behind it—there is no
doubt that pressure from organizations of civil society played the most
important role.

The segment of civil society that made the most significant contribution to the defeat of the National Party was largely organized not into
professional NGOs but along the lines of a social movement. Social movements are characterized by a "more or less spontaneous coming together
of people whose relationships are not defined by rules or procedures
but who merely share a common outlook on society"and a common goal.[16]
In the case of South Africa, while a core group emerged that sought to
channel popular discontent so as to exert maximum pressure on the government, to link the internal movement to the exiled ANC, and to mount
a major public relations campaign to put the antiapartheid struggle on
the international agenda, the muscle of the movement was people who
had simply had enough of apartheid and living conditions under it and

had spontaneously mobilized against the system. In the words of Jeremy Cronin, a member of the ANC National Executive Committee:

> After nearly total defeat, the [anti-apartheid] struggle finally reemerged in the mid-1970s, largely with the student riots of 1976. . . . To be honest, the ANC did not organize any of this. The students organized themselves around the issue of Afrikaans in the classroom. More than anything else, this shows that a movement's leadership is often several steps behind the grassroots movement. The ANC, however, was able to link this issue to the larger struggle by providing a framework to explain the larger significance of the local issue. This demonstrates that average people will mobilize—often without any centralized guidance—over issues that are of concern at the local level. The challenge then is to link these protests—grievances over daily life—with the larger political movement.[17]

The revival of the struggle inside South Africa forced the international community to focus on a battle it had chosen to ignore for many years. In 1986, the United States Congress adopted the Comprehensive Anti-Apartheid Act over the opposition of the Reagan administration. Soon after, the U.S. Agency for International Development (USAID) greatly increased the assistance it sent to South Africa, which had been very small, channeling all funds through organizations of civil society as required by the new law.

Assisting civil society in South Africa was a difficult trick for the United States as well as for international organizations and other countries. The Reagan administration remained suspicious of the ANC because of the party's historical link to the South African Communist Party and because of the aid it had received from the Soviet Union. Antiapartheid organizations, for their part, were deeply suspicious of the United States because of its past support of the apartheid regime. Moreover, the civic groups that comprised the movement, both for political and for administrative reasons, were not organizations through which aid could easily be channeled. Politically, some of the civic and student groups were out of control. They challenged the legitimacy of black township officials who were collaborating with the regime, and that was both understandable and acceptable. But the so-called necklacing of suspected collaborators—a gruesome form of execution in which a tire filled with gasoline was hung around the victim's neck and set on fire—was a different matter. While the civics were not advocating violence as such, they were committed to making South Africa ungovernable, a goal that inevitably entailed considerable violence at times.

Not all obstacles were political. The majority of the organizations in the movement would not have met USAID's administrative requirements. They were loosely organized, the leadership changed frequently and suddenly as individuals were arrested, and they had to operate clandestinely, without fixed offices. They were, in other words, an administrator's nightmare.

As a result, the organizations of civil society that USAID supported were not the hard core of the antiapartheid movement but NGOs that were professional in their orientation, better organized, and less militant in their activities. The largest component of the program in South Africa was support for "activities that are consistent with the objectives of the majority of South Africans for an end to the apartheid system," but such activities were very broadly defined, including "scholarships, assistance to promote the participation of disadvantaged South Africans in trade unions and private enterprise, alternative education and community development programs."[18]

In practice, the bulk of U.S. assistance—about 40 percent between 1987 and 1994—went to education, mostly for scholarships for South Africans to study in the United States.[19] While useful in itself, so long as students returned to South Africa after completing their training, the education of individuals does not necessarily build democratic social capital. Even less can it be considered a direct contribution to the building of civil society organizations capable of forcing a reluctant government to renounce separate development and recognize the political rights of the entire population.

Many other NGOs also received support under the U.S. program. They were organizations offering services to victims of repression rather than organizations that challenged apartheid or the government directly. The United States helped fund organizations that provided legal services for detainees, support for their families, and legal advice for people trapped in the myriad regulations that circumscribed the lives of black South Africans. The organizations chosen were considered politically neutral, or at least made their services available to anyone, irrespective of political affiliation. That is to say, they were not movement-type organizations, but more professionally oriented service-delivery or advocacy organizations.

The services they provided were important and much-needed. Education was crucial for a country in which the black population had systematically been undereducated in line with the apartheid policy of "Bantu education." Support for families of detainees helped decrease human misery a little. It is also possible, but difficult to confirm, that the knowledge that such support was available, or that political detainees could get legal counsel, encouraged participation in the antiapartheid movement. But it was not these more professional, service-oriented organizations of civil society that convinced the government that apartheid had failed and it was time to negotiate with the ANC. That was the movement's achievement, and violence was part of the process.

These observations are not meant as criticism of U.S. assistance in South Africa in the late 1980s. Such assistance was useful, and while it can be assumed that some was wasted, there is no indication that the program in South Africa suffered from unusual problems or a particularly high failure rate. Rather, the comments highlight two points. The first is that the organizations that donors, particularly the United States, can and do fund are not a representative cross-section of civil society. Assistance goes to NGOs even when it is social movements that are most effective.[20] The second is that the effectiveness of the more professional organizations and even their contributions to democracy, particularly in countries that are not yet democratic, may be heavily dependent on the existence of more radical and at times violent movements that donors cannot or are unwilling to support. The radical movements have the muscle to make the government feel threatened and thus to force it to consider change, although the more professional groups may be more adept at turning the cry for change into specific policy demands when the time actually comes to enact reforms. Promoting professional civil society organizations in nondemocratic countries where there is no strong social movement may be futile, although professional NGOs may be more effective in the final stages of a transition.

The Changing Role of Civil Society

The experience of South Africa suggests that civil society's role in broadening political participation and promoting democracy must be looked at dynamically. The contribution of civil society to democracy changes as a country experiences a political transition. First, some kinds of organizations are more effective in some periods than in others; second, civil society organizations need to relate to the government in different ways at different stages of the transitions; third, it is possible that the relationship of formal organizations of civil society and the interest groups they purportedly represent also varies over time. These issues will be explored below, looking at a number of African countries. The rapid evolution of the political situation in many of the countries in the last decade provides interesting evidence on all points.

Stages of Democratization and Civil Society

Social movement-type organizations survive much better than formal NGOs when governments are hostile to democracy and to all forms of organization they suspect of harboring political goals. Formal NGOs are vulnerable unless they abandon the demand for political participation and become purely service-delivery organizations. Under hostile conditions, the looser structure of a movement and the mass support it can generate are advantages, both in terms of the movement's survival and of the pressure it can bring to bear on a reluctant government. More professional NGOs, with their small memberships and often abstract goals such as "democracy," are less effective.

During a conference intended to help Nigerian and Zairean civil society organizations draw lessons from the success of the movement in South Africa, a Nigerian participant admitted that pro-democracy organizations in Nigeria "have called on people to rally around democracy as an ideal, but that this call has not yet successfully animated the Nigerian population." In contrast, the South African activists pointed out that in pursuing their ideal of a more democratic South Africa they had mobilized people around everyday issues such as stopping rent payments on government-owned houses or on electricity bills owed to the government-controlled company.

In a more liberal atmosphere, when repression and thus fear of outlawing are not a problem, social movements may be much less effective, if not downright dangerous. No government can satisfy all broad demands on issues affecting daily life, produce a house for every family, or put a good school within reach of every child; nevertheless, people must start paying rent and fees again, or services will collapse completely. Protest must cease and civil society must learn to be realistic, advocating policies that take into consideration not only what might be desirable but also what is possible given the government's financial and administrative limitations. Professional NGOs are better equipped to do those things than are social movements. But professional NGOs are poorly equipped to force closed, authoritarian political systems to open up.[21]

Some examples illustrate how these points play out in Africa. Contrast the relative effectiveness of women's NGOs in Uganda and such organizations' lack of effectiveness—indeed the threat of repression against them—in Zambia. On paper, women's rights advocacy associations in Zambia and Uganda are similar. They are urban-based trustee organizations led mainly by women from the urban educated elite, and they do not have a mass following. Ugandan groups, however, operate in a relatively favorable political context. Uganda is not a democracy, far from it: political parties are banned from participating in elections, although individual candidates compete for all posts, and the "movement" that governs the country, while theoretically welcoming everyone irrespective of political preferences, in reality bears a suspicious resemblance to a single party. But President Yoweri Museveni is genuinely interested in changing the country and improving the lives of citizens, so long as change does not threaten his power but only enhances his domestic and international image. Improvement in the status of women does not threaten him, and in fact may gain him support. Consequently women's organizations have successfully influenced government policy despite their lack of a large popular base. It is now accepted that women must hold at least a third of the top positions on all government committees; Uganda's family code has been reformed to strengthen the rights of women; and a land law parliament approved in the summer of 1998 gives every woman joint ownership of land she acquires with her husband, thus protecting her from the claims of the husband's family if he dies. In other words, women's NGOs in Uganda can point to some concrete achievements, the result not of an adversarial relationship with the government but of a cooperative one.

The situation in Zambia is very different. The government of Frederick Chiluba, elected in 1991 in the country's first multiparty contest in twenty years, rapidly slid again into authoritarianism. Not only does Chiluba appear determined to remain in power at all costs—so does Museveni—but he and his cabinet quickly lost their reforming zeal, power becoming not a means to an end but an end in itself. The situation has grown even worse since the 1996 elections, which the government won by an overwhelming majority after the leading opposition party refused to participate, protesting a controversial constitutional amendment that barred its presidential candidate from running.

In increasingly undemocratic Zambia, all NGOs are suspect in the government's eyes, including women's organizations. Purportedly championing the cause of women, the president's wife in May 1998 took the lead in castigating such groups for getting involved in politics or, worse, embezzling donors' funds, rather than actually helping poor women; she demonstrated what women's NGOs should do by handing out food in remote villages.[22] Under such circumstances, small, professional women's NGOs were ineffective. They could not cooperate with the government in promoting policy reform, and they remained unable to generate the mass support that might convince the government to reconsider its position.

The Evolution of Civil Society

Civil society's ability to bring about democratization in a country thus depends on the fit between the conditions in the country at a given time and the type of organizations that exist there. In countries where politics is still very closed, or in the early stages of a democratic transition when reversal is still likely, it appears that movements are more effective than professional NGOs, since they can more easily command mass support and make the government feel sufficiently threatened to accept change. But when democracy is more consolidated—which is not the case in most African countries—professional NGOs may be more effective.

This means that as countries democratize, or as they become more authoritarian, organizations of civil society must change as well. The process of conversion is not easy, and leads to waxing and waning of civil society's effectiveness. Around the world, civil society organizations in countries that have made noticeable progress toward democracy have faced at some point or are now facing a crisis of transformation.[23]

South African civil society was very successful under an authoritarian government but is still struggling to find a role in the young democracy. What makes the current difficulties of civil society organizations even more striking is that long before the 1994 elections many within the mass democratic movement were aware that civil society would have to redefine its role and strategies.

The "civics" and other township organizations that made civil society so powerful during the 1980s were mostly extremely close to the ANC, seeing that party as the rightful representative of black South Africans as well as of all those committed to a future not dominated by race. At the same time, the UDF was an autonomous organization, with its own leadership inside the country, while the ANC remained exiled until 1990. Furthermore, the township organizations remained independent of the UDF, which, as previously mentioned, was a loosely organized front rather than a tightly structured, hierarchical organization.

In 1990, Nelson Mandela was released from prison, the ANC was unbanned, and its leaders returned to South Africa to start the negotiations with the National Party that led to the April 1994 elections. The internal movement was thrown into disarray. In theory, it recognized that democracy required not only political parties but a politically active civil society, particularly in South Africa, where it was a foregone conclusion that the ANC would take its place as the dominant party with little competition for the black vote. In practice, UDF activists were ANC supporters, and for the politically ambitious, joining the ANC was a better career move than sticking with the movement. After agonizing a few months, the UDF, its leadership depleted, disbanded. Township organizations also began to atrophy.

It was not the end of civil society in South Africa. While the organizations of the mass movement declined, the professional NGOs prospered, bolstered by the lack of repression and by donor funding. A more developed, wealthier, and better educated country than others in Africa, South Africa saw a strong NGO sector emerge. The array of civil society organizations there looks more like that of established democracies than of other African states. Human rights, conflict resolution, women's rights, legal aid, gay and lesbian rights, educational reform, environmental concerns—every cause has an organization. Advocacy as well as service-delivery organizations thrive, and so do a variety of think tanks. By any standard, South Africa still has the vibrant civil society deemed necessary for a wealthy democracy.

But it is a different civil society from the one that led the way in ending apartheid. Today there are more trustee organizations and fewer groups with broad membership. The leadership is drawn more from the better-educated class and not necessarily from the people in whose name the organization speaks—and in South Africa, that also means there are more whites and Asians in the organizations than one would expect from their minority status in the population. Civil society in the late 1990s is still effective, but very different from ten years earlier. Some conservative critics argue that the ANC is trying to control all NGOs, preventing donor funding from reaching those of which they do not approve.[24]

Kenya's experience also illustrates the changing roles and effectiveness of civil society in different periods. Under the relatively benign if undemocratic government of Jomo Kenyatta in the 1960s and 1970s, Kenya developed both an NGO sector and a network of active community-based organizations. Securely in power, Kenyatta was willing to allow a degree of freedom in the country, and even welcomed it so long as his position was not challenged. Parliamentary elections were highly competitive, although competition was often between candidates from the same party; thus MPs were forced to develop ties to their constituents and to try to promote development in their district. The government, furthermore, promoted self-help development projects, the *harambee* system in the villages, encouraging people to raise money and volunteer labor for projects of common interest, very often schools or cattle dips. The mixture of active politics in the constituency and emphasis on mobilization for self-help contributed to the growth of community-based organizations. More formal NGOs also developed early, particularly on the initiative of the National Council of Churches of Kenya. The NGO sector in Kenya in this period stressed development rather than democracy. Nevertheless, the pluralism of organizations compared favorably with what most other African countries had at the time.[25]

With the death of Kenyatta in 1978, the situation changed. His successor, former vice president Daniel arap Moi, was less secure in his position and consequently more repressive, banning political parties where Kenyatta had been content to coopt the opposition. Moi's attempt to shift the ethnic balance of power away from the Kikuyu, who had dominated under Kenyatta, increased tension and also contributed to the more authoritarian climate. In the early 1990s, finally, Kenya too came under great pressure, domestically and above all from the international community, to accede to the new trend toward multiparty politics and democratic elections. Very reluctantly, the government agreed. Elections took place in 1992 amid violence and on a definitely unlevel playing field, and again in 1997 under somewhat improved but still marginal conditions.

Organizations of civil society did not play a major part in this attempt to force a political opening in Kenya. The battle was waged by political parties, which unfortunately for the future of democracy fought with each other almost as much as they did with Moi, allowing him to win the elections. It was also fought by international donors, who could put considerable pressure on Moi by suspending assistance or at least threatening to. Civil society organizations were less influential. To be sure, human rights and pro-democracy groups existed in Kenya. But the civil society that had proved strong and capable of organizing to promote development under a more benign government was not organized to bring pressure on an authoritarian government fighting for its political survival.[26]

Kenya teaches two lessons. First, it is not possible to talk about the strength or weakness of civil society in general but only in a specific context and in relation to a specific kind of activity. The village organizations that geared up villagers for self-help efforts could not prevent the Moi government from centralizing *harambee*, transforming it from self-help into forced contributions to a general fund the government controlled. Nor were they equipped to force the government to accept multiparty elections—possibly they were not even interested. The second lesson to be drawn from Kenya's experience is that the effectiveness of civil society organizations also depends on the government; organizations that perform well given some political space by a more tolerant government can prove ineffectual in a more authoritarian climate.

Changing Relations with Constituents

It is time to return to the issue, raised in the discussion of trustee organizations, of civil society organizations' relations with their constituencies. The term "constituency" is used here in a very broad sense to indicate the people an organization claims to represent, whether or not those people help decide who speaks for them and what is said in their name.

Organizations of civil society, movements and NGOs alike, often make extravagant claims of representing the people, the grassroots, and the public interest, in contrast to self-interested politicians in and out of government concerned only with power and, often, their personal enrichment. Their voice, civil society organizations claim, is thus the only truly democratic one.

In reality, the relationship between organizations of civil society and their constituents varies greatly. Voluntary, membership-based organizations with democratic internal structures can be said to represent their members because their members have voted for the goals of the organization by joining it and then by endorsing the leadership. But such democratic membership-based organizations are rare in Africa. The most common forms of representation are very different. Movements typically are backed by loosely organized constituencies that can be mobilized at least sporadically by the movement's leaders. In other words, at least occasionally there is a test of whether the movement has a following. Movements, however, invariably claim to speak for a much larger segment of the population than the one that has given them any active support. The ANC saw itself as the representative of all South Africans, and the Organization of African Unity routinely defined liberation movements in the remaining colonies as "the sole and legitimate representative" of the people. Similarly, in Poland before the transition, Solidarity was "civil society," in opposition to the state.[27] Finally, there are organizations, most often NGOs, that claim to represent silent constituencies. The most extreme—and unfortunately, not uncommon—case is that of the "briefcase" NGO comprised of little more than its leadership. But many established, even influential, NGOs act as advocates or trustees for virtual constituencies that are never consulted. Donor assistance makes it easier for such organizations to exist, since it frees their leaders from the necessity of soliciting funds from domestic supporters, though by doing so they might build up a real rather than a virtual following.

All the preceding forms of representation are important in democratization as it unfolds in a transitional country, even when they themselves are not democratic, and they also exist in established democracies. However, representation by organizations that neither have an explicit mandate nor are democratically controlled can hinder democracy.

Africa has endured many liberation movements whose leaders, not content with representing their people against a colonial power, insist that only they can continue interpreting the popular will after independence, thus turning the liberation movement into an authoritarian single party. This may become a lesser danger in the future because the days of liberation movements are probably over, barring a wave of secessionism. Much more likely is the possibility that trustee organizations, particularly those with donor backing, may crowd out organizations with more grassroots support, thus more representative of their constituencies, but less capable of playing the game of grantsmanship that supports successful NGOs in Africa.

One Size Does Not Fit All

If success is measured by the number of NGOs formed in the late 1990s, civil society assistance in Africa has been extraordinarily successful. Enthusiasm, however, is vastly premature since serious questions remain about the viability of these organizations and the degree to which they contribute to pluralism, except in a narrow sense, and to democracy. Donors continue to decry the weakness of any organization they support, assuming that it reflects a weakness of African civil society. Yet African societies have given rise both to voluntary associations that fulfill a great variety of needs and to strong social movements that have at times played a crucial political role. This suggests that donor-assisted organizations are failing to tap into a potential that other groups have exploited successfully.

The contrast between the difficulties donor-funded projects encounter and the seeming success of activities originating within the society is not exclusive to democracy assistance but is a well-known problem of development assistance. African countries—and many countries elsewhere—are dotted with boreholes that silted up because nobody took responsibility for them. They abound in rusted skeletons of tractors nobody maintained. But they are also dotted with clean wells that have given water since before anyone can remember, and their roads are clogged with ancient vehicles that carry startling loads of people and merchandise in apparent defiance of the laws of mechanics. Civil society assistance is running into many similar paradoxes.

Development assistance experts have painfully learned the lesson of sustainability: projects nobody except the donors care about will eventually fail. Sustainability depends on "ownership" of a project by those meant to benefit from it. People will do their best to keep alive something that is important to them.

The problem of ownership holds for civil society organizations created with the assistance of donors. Many NGOs are likely to go the way of the silted borehole and the rusty tractor because nobody will take responsibility for them. It is difficult to conceive of money being raised in a village to support the full-time staff of a civic education NGO, with its secretaries, computers, and four-wheel-drive vehicles. But much money has been raised, and volunteer work contributed, to support schools, cattle dips, and even political movements. Sustainability depends on what people want, and forms of organization on what they can afford. Many of the organizations of civil society that donors have created are neither what people want nor what they can afford.

This is not to suggest that Africans do not want a say in what their governments do—that they are indifferent to the issue of democracy in a broad sense. But what they want, and what they are ready to do, are not necessarily in line with the donors' vision of the active civil society.

Assistance programs for civil society assume they can help create NGOs that are simultaneously representative, willing to pursue democratic goals as defined by the donors and through the kind of activities defined by the donors, and effective in exerting pressure on the government. In reality, most civil society organizations in African countries are not likely to possess all those attributes simultaneously.

As the contrasting experiences of Nigerian and South African organizations indicate, organizations that truly represent mobilized constituencies will probably have more immediate, concrete goals than an abstract ideal of democracy, and those goals will probably be several steps removed from what democracy advocates have in mind—consider the leap from a boycott of rent payments to a democratic government in South Africa.

Organizations that reflect the donors' view of democracy both in their immediate goals and in the means they use to pursue them—the NGOs created with donor funding—are likely to be trustee organizations. Such trustee organizations may play a useful role, particularly when dealing with a government open to reform, but they are not necessarily representative and are likely to remain dependent on donors. Their sustainability is very much in doubt.

Finally, in countries where the government's commitment to democracy is weak or nonexistent, broad-based social movements—despite all their shortcomings, including lack of internal democracy and unrealistic, populist promises—may be the only channels through which citizens may have an impact on the government.

The major challenge facing agencies seeking to assist civil society is understanding better what an effective, mobilized civil society means in a certain country, at a certain time. Organizational structures, forms of representation, relations between leadership and constituencies—all can vary a great deal, and there is no formula that makes civil society effective everywhere at all times. Even in the same country different circumstances require different organizations of civil society. The South African civics that helped defeat apartheid are not the organizations that can strengthen democracy today, and conversely, professional trustee NGOs would not have gotten good results in the 1980s.

As pointed out earlier, donors operate under political and administrative constraints that make it difficult or impossible for them to support representative organizations or social movements whose goals are not clearly democratic, even when they play an important role in the process of change. That limits the effectiveness of civil society assistance. The more serious problem, particularly in countries with large civil society assistance projects, is that donor-assisted NGOs of limited effectiveness may weaken potentially more effective organizations by depriving them of leadership, as enterprising individuals move to the greener pastures foreign assistance creates.

While a vibrant civil society is undoubtedly an important factor in any democratic transformation, vibrancy comes in many forms, and the professional, donor-supported NGO is only one of them—one that does not fit all situations, and one that can even weaken rather than strengthen civil society.

Notes

1. The literature on civil society in Africa is rich; only a few studies can be mentioned here. See Donald Rothchild and Naomi Chazan, eds., *The Precarious Balance: State and Society in Africa* (Boulder: Westview Press, 1988); John Harbeson,

Donald Rothchild, and Naomi Chazan, *Civil Society and the State in Africa* (Boulder: Lynne Rienner, 1994); Atul Kohli, Joel Migdal, and Vivienne Shue, eds., *State Power and Social Forces: Domination and Transformation in the Third World* (London: Cambridge University Press, 1994); and Michael Bratton, "Beyond the State: Civil Society and Associational Life in Africa," *World Politics*, vol. 41, no. 3 (1989), pp. 408–30.

2. See, for example, Kenneth Little, *West African Urbanization: A Study of Voluntary Associations and Social Change* (Cambridge: Cambridge University Press, 1967); Akin Mabogunje, *Urbanization in Nigeria* (New York: Africana Publishers, 1968); Howard Wolpe, *Urban Politics in Nigeria: A Study of Port Harcourt* (Berkeley: University of California Press, 1974); Immanuel Wallerstein, "Voluntary Associations," in James Coleman and Carl Rosberg, eds., *Political Parties and National Integration in Tropical Africa* (Berkeley: University of California Press, 1966); Thomas Lionel Hodgkin, "The New Associations," in *Nationalism in Colonial Africa* (London: Muller, 1956); F.M.N. Heath, "The Growth of the African Councils on the Copperbelt of Northern Rhodesia," *Journal of African Administration*, vol. 5, no. 3 (July 1953), pp. 123–33.

3. See Jennifer Widner, "The Rise of Civic Associations Among Farmers in Cote d'Ivoire," in Harbeson, Rothchild, and Chazan, *Civil Society*, pp. 191–214; Joel Barkan, "Resurrecting Modernization Theory and the Emergence of Civil Society in Kenya and Nigeria," in David Apter and Carl Rosberg, eds., *Political Development and the New Realism in Sub-Saharan Africa* (Charlottesville: University Press of Virginia, 1994), pp. 87–116. In most countries, even large farmers have been a weak voice, or their organizations have been co-opted by the government; see Kimberly Ludwig, "Democratization and Economic Interest Groups in Zambia," Special Study No. 6, Delivered to USAID/Zambia by Michigan State University in Terms of Cooperative Agreement No. 623-0226-A-00-3024-00, September 25, 1997, pp. 19–27.

4. Marina and David Ottaway, *Afro-Communism* (New York: Africana, 1986), pp. 139–144.

5. Giovanni Sartori argues that pluralism presupposes tolerance, indeed that the concept of pluralism "covers the trajectory from intolerance to toleration, from toleration to respect of dissent, and, via that respect, to believing in the world of diversity." See Giovanni Sartori, "Understanding Pluralism," *Journal of Democracy*, vol. 8, no. 4 (October 1997), pp. 58–69.

6. Goran Hyden, *Beyond Ujamaa in Tanzania: Underdevelopment and an Uncaptured Peasantry* (Berkeley: University of California Press, 1980); see also Michael Bratton, "Peasant-State Relations in Postcolonial Africa: Patterns of Engagement and Disengagement," in Kohli, Migdal, and Shue, eds., *State Power and Social Forces*, pp. 231–54; Naomi Chazan, "Africa's Democratic Challenge," *World Policy Journal*, vol. IX, no. 2 (Spring 1992), pp. 279–307; and Naomi Chazan,

"Engaging the State: Associational Life in Sub-Saharan Africa," in Kohli, Migdal, and Shue, eds., *State Power and Social Forces.*

7. Chazan, in "Africa's Democratic Challenge," and Claude Ake, "Rethinking African Democracy," *Journal of Democracy,* vol. 2, no. 1 (1991), point out that proliferation of civil society organizations may weaken rather than strengthen civil society vis-à-vis the state by encouraging people to withdraw into their separate spheres.

8. Leadership of political movements, particularly movements on the Left, has often been provided by individuals who did not personally belong to the social stratum whose interests they represented. Karl Mannheim, *Ideology and Utopia,* trans. Louis Wirth and Edward Shils (New York: Harcourt, Brace & Co., 1985), pp. 155–58, refers to them as "socially unattached" or free-floating intellectuals. However, the intellectuals Mannheim discussed became part of movements with a real social base. Donor-promoted NGOs usually do not develop such a social base, leaving them poorly connected to the society, or "free-floating."

9. See Zambia Democratic Governance Project, "Mid-term Review," delivered to USAID/Zambia by Michigan State University in Partial Fulfillment of Cooperative Agreement No. 623-0226-A-00-3024-00, July 18, 1995, pp. 48 ff.; and "Civic Education" in "Zambia Democratic Governance Project: Final Evaluation," report prepared for USAID by Dale Pfeiffer, Neo Simutanyi, and John Holm, March 14, 1997.

10. This discussion, like the one on FODEP in the three preceding paragraphs, is partly based on interviews carried out by the author during two trips to Zambia in May 1997 and May-June 1998.

11. The concept of trusteeship has often been used in relation to organizations seeking to defend the interests of the poor in the United States. Such trustee, or advocacy, organizations define problems and formulate strategies quite differently from the poor themselves. On the controversy surrounding this issue, see Frances Fox Piven, "Whom Does the Advocate Planner Serve?" in Richard A. Cloward and Frances Fox Piven, eds., *The Politics of Turmoil: Essays on Poverty, Race and the Urban Crisis* (New York: Pantheon Books, 1972), especially pp. 47–48.

12. See also Piven, "Whom Does the Advocate Planner Serve?"

13. See Howard Barrell, *MK: The ANC's Armed Struggle* (New York: Penguin Books, 1990).

14. On the revival of black labor unions, see Steven Friedman, *Building Tomorrow Today* (Johannesburg: Ravan Press, 1987); Johann Maree, *The Independent Trade Unions* (Johannesburg: Ravan Press, 1987); and Eddie Webster, "The Rise of Social Movement Unionism: The Two Faces of the Black Trade Union Movement in South Africa," in Philip Frankel, Naom Pines, and Mark Swilling,

eds., *State, Resistance and Change in South Africa* (Johannesburg: Southern Book Publishers, 1988), pp. 174–98.

15. See William Cobbett and Robin Cohen, eds., *Popular Struggles in South Africa* (London: Review of African Political Economy, 1988); Jeremy Seekings, "Political Mobilization in the Black Townships in the Transvaal," in Frankel, Pines, and Swilling, *State, Resistance, and Change*, pp. 197–228; Mizana Matowana, Shirley Walters, and Zelda Groener, *The Struggle for Democracy* (Cape Town: Center for Adult and Continuing Education, University of the Western Cape, 1989); and Marina Ottaway, *South Africa: The Struggle for a New Order* (Washington, D.C.: The Brookings Institution, 1993), pp. 55 ff.

16. See the entry on "Social Movements" on the Internet web site of Encyclopedia Britannica Online at www.eb.com, October 1999.

17. International Human Rights Law Group, "Nigeria-South Africa Consultative Meeting, Johannesburg, South Africa, September 27–29, 1996," conference proceedings, p. 5.

18. Cited in Douglas Tilton, *USAID in South Africa* (Washington, D.C.: Africa Policy Information Center, 1996), p. 27.

19. Ibid., p. 30.

20. On the role of social movements, as opposed to NGOs, in political transitions, see Michael Bratton, "Civil Society and Political Transitions in Africa," in Harbeson, Rothchild, and Chazan, *Civil Society*, especially pp. 60 ff.

21. For a very interesting elaboration of the role of NGOs in democratization and their relation to social movements, see Stephen N. Ndegwa, *The Two Faces of Civil Society: NGOs and Politics in Africa* (West Hartford: Kumarian Press, 1996), especially pp. 1–13, 109–18.

22. See "Shang'ombo Women Touch Vera" and "Opinion," *Times of Zambia*, May 19, 1998; "NGOs Speak Out," *Times of Zambia*, May 20, 1998; "NGOs Gang Up Against Vera," *The Post*, May 20, 1998; "Women's Lobby Hits at Detractors," *The Post*, May 21, 1998. The *Times of Zambia* is a government newspaper, and *The Post* is the country's only independent daily.

23. See, for example, Kynn Kamenitsa, "The Process of Political Marginalization: East German Social Movements After the Wall," *Comparative Politics*, vol. 30, no. 3 (April 1998), pp. 313–33; Brian Loveman, "NGOs and the Transition to Democracy in Chile," *Grassroots Development*, vol. 15, no. 2 (1991), pp. 77–97; Elizabeth Jelin, "The Politics of Memory: The Human Rights Movement and the Construction of Democracy in Argentina," *Latin American Perspectives*, vol. 21, no. 2 (1994), pp. 38–58; Kenneth Roberts, "Economic Crisis and the Demise of the Legal Left in Peru," *Comparative Politics*, vol. 29, no. 1 (1996), pp. 69–92; William Dan Perdue, *Paradox of Change: The Rise and Fall of Solidarity in the New Poland* (Westport, Conn.: Praeger, 1995); and Tomek Grabowski, "The Party that Never Was: The Rise and Fall of the Solidarity Citizens' Committees in

Poland," *East European Politics and Society,* vol. 10, no. 2 (Spring 1996), pp. 214–54.

24. See R. W. Johnson, "Destroying South Africa's Democracy: USAID, the Ford Foundation, and Civil Society," *The National Interest* (Fall 1998), pp. 19–28.

25. C. J. Gertzel, Maure Goldschmidt, and Don Rothchild, *Government and Politics in Kenya* (Nairobi: East African Publishing House, 1972), pp. 167 ff.; Barbara Thomas, *Politics, Participation, and Poverty: Development Through Self-help in Kenya* (Boulder: Westview Press, 1985).

26. Jennifer Widner, *The Rise of a Party-State in Kenya* (Berkeley: University of California Press, 1992), especially chapters 5 and 6; Michael Bratton, "Civil Society and Political Transitions in Africa," in Harbeson, Rothchild, and Chazan, *Civil Society,* p. 52; Ndegwa, *Two Faces of Civil Society,* pp. 109 ff.; Frank Holmquist and Michael Ford, "Kenya: State and Civil Society the First Year after the Elections," *Africa Today* (Fourth Quarter 1994), pp. 5–25.

27. See Elizabeth C. Dunn, "'A Product for Everybody is a Product for Nobody': Niche Marketing and Political Individualism in Polish Civil Society," *Anthropology Today,* vol. 14, no. 4 (August 1998), pp. 22–23.

4

Voicing the Voiceless: Foreign Political Aid to Civil Society in South Africa

Christopher Landsberg

SINCE THE 1960S, South Africa has undergone what can be described as four waves of democratization. The first wave (1960–89) was the struggle against apartheid and the white-minority regime upholding it. The antiapartheid protest movements inside and outside South Africa, together with the banned liberation movements, particularly the African National Congress (ANC), worked to weaken the apartheid state and nudge, even compel, the government into negotiations on a transfer of power. This wave was at its highest in the mid- to late 1980s. Domestic and international structural and contingency pressures converged powerfully to snap open the apartheid edifice. The combination of internal and external pressures and inducements—that is, balancing carrots and sticks—had compelled the apartheid state to enter into negotiations with its liberation adversaries.

The second wave (1990–94) was the transition—what Michael Bratton and I have labeled South Africa's "triple transition."[1] The country underwent: 1) a political transition from apartheid to democracy; 2) an economic transition from a closed economy dominated by the white minority to an open, globalized economy; and 3) a military transition from quasi-civil war to peace.

Between the first universal franchise elections in April 1994 and the second one in 1999, South Africa experienced the third wave, namely that of consolidation. During this phase, the young post-apartheid state was preoccupied with efforts to anchor its fragile, infant democracy by focusing essentially on the politics of nation-building and reconciliation.

In the aftermath of the 1999 second democratic polls and the inauguration of Thabo Mvuyelwa Mbeki as president, South Africa entered the fourth wave of democratization. There are already signs that this phase is likely to be dominated by the politics of delivery and strengthening of the state machinery to more effectively tackle South Africa's heavy burden of socioeconomic challenges.

While the political dimensions of South Africa's four waves of democratization are much-chronicled and celebrated, the role of civil society—and international donors' support for it—has received scant attention. This chapter is a modest attempt to fill that void.

1960–90: Loosening Apartheid's Grip

Only now is it becoming public knowledge that what ultimately dragged the apartheid regime to the negotiating table was not the military wings of the African National Congress (ANC) and others; rather, it was the intensified political revolt spearheaded by civilian organizations that mobilized a large portion of the population of the black townships, coupled with substantial international pressure.

Analysts do not always appreciate that, between 1960 and 1990, civilian organizations in South Africa engaged in the struggle against the apartheid state fell into two distinct sectors.[2] The better known of the two can be called *political society*, and it included formal extraparliamentary political organizations like the ANC, the Pan-Africanist Congress, the South African Communist Party, the Black Consciousness Movement (BCM), the Azanian People's Organization (AZAPO), the United Democratic Movement, the New Unity Movement, and the Unity Movements of South Africa.

The other sector, more properly termed *civil society*, included community-based organizations formed in the 1970s such as the Port Elizabeth Black Civics Organization, the Soweto Civics Organization, Civic Associations of Southern Transvaal, and the Black Community Programs, as well as groups established later, like the South African National Civics Organization, the Action Committee to Stop Evictions, United Municipalities of South Africa, the Urban Councils Association of South Africa, and the Urban Foundation. The trade unions and trade union associations were also part of civil society; among the country's most important in this period were the United Workers' Union of South Africa, the Congress of South African Trade Unions (COSATU), the National Council of Trade Unions, and the National Union of Mine Workers. Of course, given the nature of resistance against apartheid, civil society was highly politicized.

During the 1960s and 1970s, both political society groups and civil society groups received extremely beneficial support from progressive international donors such as the Nordic countries, the Netherlands, the Soviet bloc, the United Nations, and the Commonwealth; in Africa, Nigeria, Libya, Tanzania, and Zambia provided support for political and civil organizations, as did the Organization of African Unity's liberation committee.[3] In the 1980s, Swaziland, Botswana, Lesotho, and Zimbabwe added their support for the battle against what was commonly called the "authoritarian racist regime." Conservative countries like the United States, Britain, Germany, and France were conspicuous in not providing support until quite late. Financial, diplomatic, material (travel costs, pamphlets, and other overhead expenses of campaigning), and physical (office space and sanctuary) support from foreign donors were vital to the victories that both civil and political society won in South Africa. On the downside, however, during the apartheid years civil and political society became highly dependent on donors' backing—a virtual "cargo cult" developed. (The question that today hovers over the future of civil society organizations, in particular nongovernmental organizations [NGOs], like an albatross is whether these South African entities will survive a total disengagement of donors from the country. Evidence points in the direction of a demobilization, if not collapse, of a majority of NGOs in the event of donors' totally withdrawing from the republic.)

The progressive donors mentioned above supported both civil society organizations (CSOs) and political society organizations (PSOs), understanding that the two were inextricably intertwined. Civil society, the organized realm operating outside the formal political arena but within the public sphere, typically concerned itself with bread-and-butter issues affecting the population of the townships, such as education or house rents. Political society, comprising a plethora of political groups on both the left and the right, had avowedly political objectives, as its name implies: the movements that made it up sought either to weaken the state and end the apartheid system or to rally support for the apartheid state. Progressive donors seemed to appreciate that political and civil society interacted closely and fed off each other in the struggle against apartheid and the white minority regime, meshing into what was known as "the extra-parliamentary opposition." By and large, political society was the dominant element, pulling civil society into its realm and politicizing it. During the 1980s in particular, community-based organizations mobilized as part of the political project.

During the antiapartheid struggle, the close relationship between civil society and political society was strategic. CSO tactics included refusal to cooperate with the authorities so as to create a crisis of legitimacy and confidence for the state. To mobilize for their *uhuru*—freedom—civil society groups and political society groups created no-go areas in the townships, fought councilors and mayors appointed by the apartheid government, refused to pay rent and electricity bills, and boycotted white-run central business districts. In short, they set out to create means and courses of action that would give a voice to the voiceless and show the power of the hitherto powerless. They incorporated both practical and consciousness-raising elements, such as campaigns for lower school fees and basic services and participation in rallies against apartheid. Civil society provided the local, community-based context, while political society provided the political context and direction. Together, they made for a powerful extraparliamentary opposition to the apartheid state.

Interdependence was the key to the movement's success. Working alone in the 1960s, political organizations opposing apartheid had had almost no impact. The revival of South African civil society in the 1970s was crucial, but it would have accomplished little had the organizations of political society not been there to bring civic organizations together.

The most instructive illustrations of the importance of combining political and civic action are offered by two movements, the Azanian People's Organization (AZAPO), a black consciousness group founded in 1978, and the United Democratic Front (UDF), established in 1983.[4] While the raison d'être of both AZAPO and the UDF was overtly political, the two also emphasized civic issues such as education, training, and strengthening local participation in decision-making through community forums; thus they became known as the Mass Democratic Movement.[5] The UDF benefited much more from international aid than did AZAPO, with foreign funds enabling the UDF to strengthen its organizational structures, open offices, and pay for rallies, workshops, training, and the like.

AZAPO was established in May 1978 to fill the vacuum left by the banning of numerous black consciousness groups the previous October. The organization's broad aims were: to create political awareness among black workers and to mobilize them by means of the philosophy of black consciousness; to fight for an educational system that fulfilled the demands of the "Azanians" (black South Africans); to propagate and interpret religion as a liberation philosophy relevant to the black struggle; to expose the injustices of the apartheid system and the exploitation of blacks; and to build unity among the oppressed in order to distribute wealth and power among all the peoples of Africa. AZAPO became the major exponent of black consciousness in the 1980s and was consequently opposed to the organizations supporting the ANC's Freedom Charter—the so-called charterist organizations.[6]

Despite its opposition to charterism, AZAPO saw itself as a bridge-builder between black organizations. The group received strong support from black academics and other intellectuals and eventually became more dependent on their backing than that of the masses. Because of its success, AZAPO was one of seventeen extraparliamentary organizations the South African government effectively restricted in February 1988. In 1990, after the de Klerk government unbanned opposition groups and started instituting reforms, AZAPO appealed to socialist groups to create a "socialist agenda" for liberation and transformation. Negotiations on the transition, AZAPO insisted, "must take place between resistance organizations and not the ruling class." AZAPO would only participate in the transition if the process included the election of a constituent assembly, the resolution of the land issue, the social liberation of blacks, and the restructuring of the economy.

The organization's rigid stance on participation in negotiations triggered deep divisions within AZAPO. Hard-liners regarded the organization's position as too close to that of the ANC, while conservatives argued for pragmatism in the matter. Unable to bridge the divisions in its ranks, AZAPO fell back on its second-best alternative: the need to create a "liberation solidarity front." The organization's youth wing also pushed for the creation of a "youth patriotic front." In the end, the divisions greatly weakened AZAPO, leaving it isolated from the mainstream and thus unable to influence South Africa's transition from apartheid to democracy.

The United Democratic Front (UDF) was formed in May 1983 in the Transvaal, Cape Province, and Natal in response to a call by antiapartheid activist Dr. Allan Boesak for all opposition movements to boycott the elections for the tricameral parliament created by the 1983 constitution. These elections would have enfranchised whites, "coloureds," and Asians at the expense of "Africans."[7] As Boesak said, "The politics of refusal should unite us."

During the 1980s the UDF established itself as one of the chief political organizations in the country; at one point more than six hundred township, student, and church groups were affiliated with it. The front declared its main objective to be the creation of a single, nonracial, unfragmented South Africa, and it welcomed support and participation from all races. Unlike AZAPO with its black consciousness ethos, the UDF supported the ANC's Freedom Charter. Its opposition to apartheid was manifested in two ways: boycotts of all elections not based on universal suffrage, and establishment of local structures that played a vital role in the political education and mobilization of the masses. The UDF saw itself as an umbrella organization that would gradually merge into the ANC.

AZAPO and the UDF were overtly political organizations that also resorted to civic action in pursuit of political change. Other organizations formed in this period emphasized the civic more openly than the political aspect, but in pursuit of the same interrelated goals: to challenge the subjugated, oppressed, third-class status of black South Africans; to fill the vacuum left by a security-obsessed state that sought to repress opposition and preserve its power but failed to deliver even basic services to the majority of the population; and to weaken and finally topple the apartheid state. There was never any doubt that the latter was the ultimate goal of all organizations. Civic organizations in the townships, for example, organized around residents' grievances over the lack of government services, but their ultimate goal was the overthrow of the apartheid regime. And student grievances over "Bantu education," the second-rate schooling offered to Africans, not only led to the formation of student organizations in the townships but culminated in the 1980s with the founding of the National Education Crisis Committee (NECC), a frankly political group which received significant amounts of foreign political aid.[8]

The unprecedented series of militant student actions in black schools had given rise to another crisis in education for blacks, since schools were frequently closed and educational activities virtually came to a halt. The

Soweto Parents' Crisis Committee convened a national education crisis conference in March 1986, at which participants agreed to launch a nationwide organization, the NECC. This decision was supported by the UDF and COSATU. By 1987, NECC had representatives across the country. It called on all students to celebrate May Day as Workers' Day; vowed to expose, isolate, and oppose Inkatha, the Zulu party backed by the South African government; declared June 16 a national youth day; encouraged all progressive teacher, parent, and student bodies to implement "people's education," clearing time on the school calendar for the study of alternative material provided by student councils, parent committees, and support organizations; urged that all banned organizations, including the ANC, be unbanned and all political prisoners released; and called on communities and democratic organizations to mount regional and national campaigns to support all rent, consumer, and other boycotts. Thus the education of blacks was transformed, with guidance from the crisis committee, into another arena for mobilization against apartheid.

Attempting to separate the civic from the political in the extraparliamentary opposition in South Africa in the 1970s and 1980s is almost impossible, and it misses the point. Much of the strength of the antiapartheid movement inhered in the overlap of the political and the civic. The black townships had both student organizations, which could be considered part of civil society, and youth leagues, which were overtly political; all cooperated closely, and membership was cross-cutting or dual. Civic and community groups included seemingly apolitical ones such as burial societies, *stokvels* (revolving credit associations), and spiritual movements, as well as more political residents' associations, development associations, education-support groups, and the like. Workers and labor organizations, for their part, organized not only around issues relating to basic working conditions but around civic and community problems. Progressive professional and occupational associations—many of which benefited substantially from foreign aid—did not just protect the interests of their members but opposed apartheid and were sympathetic to the civic and political organizations with a broader focus. Examples include the National Medical and Dental Association, Lawyers for Human Rights, the South African Black Social Workers Union, and the Black Management Forum. Progressive extraparliamentary political movements formed alliances with trade unions, independent church groups, businesses, taxi-driver associations, and student movements.

The mix of political society organizations and civil society organizations that characterized what came to be known as the mass democratic movement was not accidental but the result of a deliberate strategy by the UDF, COSATU, and fifteen other protest organizations that the regime restricted in February 1988. The designation Mass Democratic Movement (MDM) gained currency among protesters as opposition leaders and members of various groups pulled together more and more. It was a movement rather than an organization—a temporary, broad resistance front against apartheid at a time when more formal movements like the UDF and COSATU were constantly battling state repression.

The Pillars of Struggle[9]

The mass democratic movement, together with the banned ANC, envisaged an antiapartheid struggle based on "five central pillars."[10] The first pillar was building a strong civil society that could fill the vacuum in governance created by apartheid.

The second pillar was mass mobilization, to foster a climate of change and transformation. The idea was to create vehicles through which people could participate in influencing the policies, strategy, and tactics of political opposition forces in South Africa. Broad participation was crucial because political repression risked isolating the leaders of the mass democratic movement and removing them from the realities on the ground. Thus it was the deliberate tactics of the democratic movement to create a strong civil society that could not easily be repressed, but would resist and ultimately weaken the draconian state.

The third pillar of the antiapartheid struggle was establishing a strong underground movement. This movement organized on the basis of clearly defined rules, seeking to turn the townships into liberated zones. At the high point of the struggle during the 1980s, the apartheid state was unable to exert control over the townships, which became bases from which the democratic movement organized and where it held meetings. Many of the campaigns organized in this period revolved around boycotts and labor strikes, and workers would simply stay in the townships during stay-away actions.

The fourth pillar was the "armed struggle" waged by the banned liberation movements including the ANC, the Pan-Africanist Congress, and the South African Communist Party since the early 1960s. The armed struggle was invoked as an option by the exiled liberation movements after other, peaceful efforts to engage the state ended. In reality, the armed struggle never acquired major importance. It was difficult to wage in South Africa and the apartheid state kept it from acquiring popular support at home. At times the armed struggle even drove a wedge between the political class and civil society movements, which saw their resistance as the key to liberation and resented the political movements insistence on armed struggle. While the armed struggle helped create a security crisis in South Africa, it remained too ineffectual to topple the apartheid state.

The fifth pillar was building international support and solidarity for the antiapartheid cause. The chief objective here was to turn South Africa into the world's number one polecat and ostracize it internationally. Civil society and political society movements in South Africa campaigned to delegitimize the apartheid state and put forward the liberation movements as the "sole and authentic representatives of the people of South Africa." The support the international donor community provided to the white state's opponents at home and abroad were critical reinforcing elements of the antiapartheid crusade. South Africa came to feel the effects of political and diplomatic isolation, of economic sanctions, and of military and sociocultural seclusion. This fifth pillar proved critical in the late 1980s in moving the apartheid state toward the negotiating table, as South Africa felt the effects of international trade sanctions and extreme political isolation.

Leaders of the mass democratic movement understood the importance of making connections between the five pillars and South Africans' daily lives. By the 1980s, the mass mobilization campaigns involved constant boycotts and labor strikes, and the black townships became "no-go areas" for the government. It was in these mass campaigns, which sought to link the day-to-day struggle for survival of the common people—the struggle to pay rent and electricity bills, to get children schooled, to find transport to get to work—with the struggle against the apartheid regime that civil society and political society almost became one. Local issues were related to larger concerns involving the legitimacy of the state. The strategy of the movement was to build self-confidence around a series of small victories and to develop militancy in areas where militancy would not be expected.

No issue was too trivial to become part of the political struggle. The struggle for the washing lines in the Western Cape, for example, took on political dimensions far beyond the confines of the community. Residents of the area known as the Cape Flats lacked sufficient space to hang their laundry out to dry. Local civic leaders politicized this very ordinary grievance, complaining to and organizing a march on the Cape Town city council to demand additional clotheslines. In innumerable cases like this, the mass democratic movement seized on local issues to open up political space and build constituencies.

Both AZAPO and the UDF continued to embody the strategy of building a political movement on the daily struggles of poor and racially oppressed communities. While AZAPO gained widespread support within South Africa, particularly among intellectuals, it was the UDF that came to epitomize in the eyes of the outside world the grassroots struggle of black South Africans against apartheid. As a result, the UDF attracted large amounts of what today would be called civil society assistance, long before donors tried it elsewhere. Organizations affiliated with the front received the bulk of the attention and help, with donors buying into the popular UDF slogan that "the politics of refusal needed a united front." By the late 1980s, more than six hundred organizations nationwide affiliated with the front—including some three hundred youth movements, eighty civic organizations, and fifty student and educational bodies—had benefited from foreign assistance. Above all, the UDF could boast of impressive grassroots support. Protesting the white-ruled state's attempt to institute the tricameral parliament, the UDF mounted the successful "one million signatures campaign." Foreign assistance was key in helping the front stage such campaigns.

Foreign Political Aid for Civil Society

The fight against apartheid had attracted some form of international support since the 1960s because the system established by the South African regime conflicted with the post-World War II democratic wave of morality of human rights and decolonization. Apartheid was indeed a counter-wave to the Huntingtonian second wave of democracy. That repellent system both violated all UN principles and was completely out of step with the changes and decolonization that were sweeping the African continent. In seeking to influence developments in South Africa, donors supported political and civic organizations alike. Their goal was avowedly political: donors sought to break down the apartheid edifice and to replace it with a democratic form of government—indeed, progressive donors provided democracy assistance to South Africa long before they started doing so in other African countries or indeed elsewhere in the world. The moral repugnance of apartheid overrode the donors' normal reluctance to interfere in the domestic politics of another country. Donors even engaged in "struggle bookkeeping," asking few questions of the NGOs that received the funds about how the money was managed and spent.

International organizations used diplomatic and cultural sanctions that isolated South Africa to convey their condemnation of government policy. UN efforts began with a 1961 General Assembly resolution that called the racial discrimination in the country "reprehensible and repugnant to human dignity."[11] In 1963, the Security Council called on all UN members to end the sale of arms, ammunition, and military vehicles to the white-ruled republic. In 1976, the General Assembly imposed a comprehensive arms embargo against South Africa. The country's isolation also increased with its expulsion from the International Olympic Committee in 1970.

In addition to condemning and seeking to isolate the perpetrators of apartheid, the international community supported organizations fighting the system. Assistance for what is now known as civil society played an important role, along with aid for political organizations. Donors, in fact, did not make a clear distinction between political assistance and civil society assistance until the transition of the 1990s. Before then, their main concern was supporting the opponents of apartheid, and they did not bother much about which organizations were political and which were not. For donors like the United States, which had serious reservations about the ANC, the overlap between organizations of political society and of civil society during the 1980s made it possible to support the antiapartheid effort without directly assisting a political movement they considered too radical and too close to Moscow.

Sweden was in the vanguard of political aid efforts, supporting the exiled liberation movements and civil society organizations in South Africa. Under the banner of humanitarian assistance, some $400 million in aid flowed to the ANC, labor unions, and progressive NGOs from the 1960s to 1994.

During this time, the UN operated an active trust fund for South Africa supported by several governments, notably of the Nordic states.

The fund served as a vehicle for collecting and distributing substantial humanitarian, legal, and educational assistance to victims of apartheid and organizations representing them. Foreign governments showed solidarity with political prisoners by contributing to the International Defense and Aid Fund for Southern Africa (founded by the late Canon Collins and the British Anti-Apartheid Movement in 1966) and other civil society forces.

The European Commission (EC), along with the U.S. Agency for International Development (USAID), was a latecomer, providing support for development activities in South Africa in 1985.[12] The Special Program for Victims of Apartheid was established in September 1985 by the development ministers of the countries of what was then the European Community and later became the European Union (EU), on the initiative of the European Parliament. Through the Special Program, the EU supported a range of NGOs involved in educational, legal, and humanitarian efforts. After President F. W. de Klerk announced the political reforms of 1990, the program channeled assistance to NGO projects intended to ease the transition. Between 1986 and 1994, the EU committed 450 million ECU, about R200 million, to the Special Program, making it one of the EU's largest aid programs in any country.

Britain began providing aid to civil society organizations only in 1979. Prior to that time, Britain was more interested in maintaining its family ties with its former colony. Until the 1994 elections, all British support was channeled through NGOs and community groups. The aid program gradually expanded, with the British government disbursing an estimated R50 million in 1990. The government of the Federal Republic of Germany, like that of Britain, had controversial ties with the apartheid regime that kept it from supporting South Africa's NGO sector until the 1970s. At that time, it switched its support away from the government and toward civil society.

Foreign Assistance, 1990–94: Leveling the Playing Field

Soon after South Africa's triple transition began in 1989 with the ouster of the hawkish President P. W. Botha and the ascent of the more dovish de Klerk, donors had to alter their tactics and strategies.[13] When Nelson Mandela was released from prison in 1990, signaling the final phase of the dismantling of apartheid, the political organizations, in particular the ANC, turned into a government-in-waiting. Relations between political society and civil society, notably what we can here call elite civil society, viz. NGOs, changed. The dealings between the two strata at times even became tense as NGOs that formed part of the mass democratic movements started fearing domination by the unbanned ANC.

Donors could no longer work closely with both political and civic organizations in the name of resistance against apartheid, but faced a new decision on how to channel assistance during the transition phase. What emerged as the dominant theme were attempts to level the playing field in South African politics. While most progressive donors continued to support organs of both civil society, in particular NGOs, and political society, they began to emphasize that these actors needed to play a role in the nascent triple transition. Many donors developed programs that focused on preventing violence, readying political parties for elections, and educating voters. Foreign donors also stressed broadening public participation in the transition; in other words, they wanted to see a participatory approach that would directly involve community groups, NGOs, and the grassroots in the political transition. Promotion of human rights became popular among both progressive and conservative donors. Donors often gave funds to elite pockets of NGOs in the belief that they would reach out to real civil society.

Aid flowed in new directions. Some donors began to develop foci for real CSOs, not only the elite types, as they promoted small entrepreneurs in black communities, for example, or helped the inhabitants of the informal (squatter) settlements, women's associations, professional associations, and charitable NGOs. As 1993 drew to a close, however, almost all donors began to shun civil society and diverted the bulk of their aid to preparation for the election. At the same time, many of the ANC's progressive friends abroad hinted that they would end their formal ties with the liberation movement after the first democratic elections. Instead, they would concentrate on cultivating ties with the new state and would stress relations and cooperative partners between what they saw as CSOs—which by then became a euphemism for elite NGOs—and the new government.

After 1994: Donors Scale Down

When in 1994 apartheid finally ended and democracy began—the apartheid state replaced with a democratically elected ANC-dominated government of national unity—political society as South Africans had known it changed. The symbiotic relation between political and civic organizations all fighting the apartheid state together abruptly ended. Instead, the ANC took over the reins of state power, forming the new, legitimate government. Civic organizations and other NGOs were left to redefine their roles in the new state and vis-à-vis the new government. Foreign assistance reflected the new situation, albeit with major flaws. After 1994, all international donors, as they normalized ties with South Africa, began to commit large sums of money to the new government. While they did not abandon completely their traditional nongovernmental friends, their support waned as they split their budgets between alleged civil society (that is, the NGOs) and the state. The question arose: could donors tilt toward the state without alienating and abandoning CSOs?

That many CSOs emerged from the transition to democracy both weaker and more diverse than they had been before 1994 compounded donors' dilemma. Civil society, including very many NGOs, also appeared to be highly demobilized. The glue that had held civil society together—opposition to apartheid—had come unstuck as the white-minority government began to capitulate to domestic and international pressure. One of the first casualties of civil society demobilization was the depth of the CSOs—that is, the extent to which citizens at the grassroots level participate in and are represented by voluntary organizations. Loss of depth cut into the CSOs' actual and potential role as guarantors of government accountability and transmitters of democratic culture in South Africa.

CSOs were caught off guard by donors' decision to tilt toward the young, fragile post-apartheid state. In short, an ailing civil society started to feel the effects of declining support just as democracy arrived in South Africa. Donors typically conveyed two contradictory messages. On the one hand, they were adamant that CSOs should now help sustain transformation and consolidate sustainable democratic governance. The idea of "strategic partnerships" between government and NGOs, notably in service delivery, was high on donors' aid radar screens. On the other hand, donors were emphatic about the need to strengthen civil society's capacity to "counterbalance" and "oversee" government. They expected CSOs to offer "constructed alternatives" to government and play a "watchdog" function. In a similar vein, donors stressed the need to build up CSOs' ability to provide policy information to the public and analyze public policy issues.

Few donors, however, were prepared to put their money where their mouth was. They underestimated the gaps in civil society's organizational and management capacities and fundraising know-how. They had not fully realized that many CSOs lacked financial and technical sustainability, or how dependent on foreign assistance South African civil society remained. The many people leaving to take up posts in the Mandela government, triggering leadership crises at many organizations, exacerbated CSOs' other problems. Thus the much-touted strategic partnership between government and CSOs came to little. To add insult to injury, many of the overseas donors began to talk about winding down their activities and considering exit strategies. As they saw it, the arrival of democracy was equal to the end of the transition.

Enter elite society! In the wake of the disempowerment of many genuine CSOs connected to the heart of grassroots communities, a new type of society emerged that paraded as civil society: grand NGOs, with the notable exceptions of course. Its sudden embrace by donors of this noble civil society was indeed conspicuous. What is more, there was a striking similarity, even overlap and duplication, among donors' themes and programs.[14] The new civil society was entrusted to play a key role in anchoring the republic's infant democracy. The EU's European Program for Reconstruction and Development declared a commitment to "good governance and democratization."[15] The Canadians focused on a program for "strengthening civil society" through the promotion of "good governance," while Denmark's civil society program in South Africa was marked by assistance for "democratization and the prevention of violence." Ireland provided assistance for "human rights" and "democratization" as Sweden proclaimed support for "democracy and human rights." And USAID financed a program that supported "democratic consolidation." The Netherlands championed support for "democratization and governance," while Switzerland sought to promote "democracy and good governance" through assistance to organs of civil society. Germany also provided support to civil society, mainly through the foundations of the German political parties—the Friedrich Ebert Stiftung, the Konrad Adenauer Stiftung, the Hans Seidel Stiftung, and others.

USAID has tended to give priority to efforts that would "improve the quality of governance." That has involved working with the government and civil society to make the new democratic institutions viable and secure and ensuring the success of the transition to full majority rule in the 1999 elections. The USAID mission in South Africa has supported efforts to develop the electoral system, strengthen the culture of human rights, create a more equitable justice system, and integrate NGOs into the delivery of services. USAID said in 1995 that some of its aid was aimed at "supporting civil society as a balance to, and check on, government." Institutions it assisted included the Institute for Democracy in South Africa (IDASA) and the Institute of Race Relations. The ANC-led government at times showed a remarkable sensitivity about and resentment of USAID's support to organizations that made it their business to monitor government performance, provide information to the public, and help protect human rights.

The EU in 1995 decided that its assistance for the reconstruction of South African society would be implemented partly through the central government, partly through provincial and local governments, and partly through NGOs, as with previous EU programs. The budget was split, with almost exactly one-third going to each of those three stakeholders.

The British government also opted to provide funds to national government, subnational tiers of government, and NGOs. A key objective of British Official Development Assistance was to strengthen local NGOs and the Independent Development Trust, an outfit geared toward promoting partnerships between the government and organs of civil society. As much as a third of British assistance went to civil society organizations.

The Netherlands was one of only two donors—Sweden being the other—to split its aid equally between government and civil society. It intended support for civil society to deepen the democratization and reconciliation processes in South Africa. The Hague targeted safety and security as an area that needed its backing. Sweden's assistance of NGOs involved in police development, capacity-building, and implementation has been notable. Since 1995, Stockholm has provided SEK 8 million ($1.2 million) to the Truth and Reconciliation Commission, the statutory institution established to investigate, reveal, and pardon "gross violations of human rights" committed in South Africa during the apartheid years. The Center for Conflict Resolution at the University of Cape Town, the Center for Policy Studies, the South African Institute for International Affairs, and the Institute for Security Studies all benefited from Swedish support. Sweden has also helped finance the South African National NGO Coalition, the Independent Mediation Services of South Africa, and the Legal Forum on Education.

Norway has supported numerous projects and institutions promoting democracy and human rights. The Norwegians have assisted IDASA, the African Gender Institute, the University of the Western Cape, and the Truth and Reconciliation Commission, Denmark has also assisted the commission, especially its trauma center in Cape Town and its research division.

Switzerland has provided assistance to NGOs on condition that "the quality and relevance of the work done by the respective organizations justifies it." The Swiss believe that "NGOs not only play a vital role in creating a strong civil society in South Africa; they also play an important role in advising, and helping to implement, the government's development programs." Switzerland has assisted the Legal Resources Center, Lawyers for Human Rights, the Black Sash, IDASA, the Independent Mediation Services of South Africa, the Institute for Strategic Studies, and South African Institute of International Affairs.

Canada has channeled aid to the Center for Education Policy Development, IDASA, the National Cooperatives Association, Kagiso Trust (a development agency that was also part of the internal resistance movement in the past), and the Mining and Energy Policy Center. From 1994 to 1996, Ottawa sponsored a Civil Society Capacity Development Program. In addition, Canada committed Canadian $3.2 million to partnership projects involving South African and Canadian NGOs. In each case, a Canadian NGO worked with one or more key South African partners, sharing knowledge about how to plan and implement programs—the idea being that the South African NGOs could then contribute more to their country's democratic development and reconstruction.

Another important category of funders of CSOs and PSOs has been foundations and related agencies that are not bilateral donors.[16] Those long involved in South Africa included the U.S.-based Ford Foundation; the U.K.-based Westminster Foundation; the Friedrich Ebert, Konrad Adenauer, and Hans Seidel stiftungen from Germany; and the European Union Foundation. Recently, a new breed of foundation—for example, the Open Society Foundation financed by George Soros—has been set up in the country.

After 1994, multilateral donors like the United Nations Development Program and the World Bank joined in the fray, supporting organizations of South African civil society.

A gap seems to have emerged between the stated intentions and goals of donors and the realities CSOs face on the ground. While many donors sought to assist in the consolidation of democracy by providing aid to a combination of delivery and watchdog NGOs, many chosen NGOs typically faced technical and organizational stresses and strains that made it difficult for them to perform their functions. Some struggling ones simply fell by the wayside. Many, though not all, of the beneficiaries were also of the elite type, which claimed to have connection with grassroots communities but in reality did not. They often attracted large sums of donor support simply based on claims that they fulfilled a grassroots, or watchdog, or delivery function. Very few donors had in place the monitoring and evaluation mechanisms to determine the validity and claims of such stated assumptions. Just as puzzling was how many past recipients seemed to lose their attractiveness while others grew in prestige in donors' eyes. In short, there was something very sexy about the donor-NGO game in South Africa.

Donors were also ambivalent in how they handled NGOs independent of the state. On the one hand, they stressed the importance of such organizations for building a vibrant democracy. On the other, they handled such outfits awkwardly because of their ability to upset the state through their watchdog and critical roles. Thus, it became fashionable for donors to openly cooperate with independent CSOs if the new government would be happy about them.

Then there is the sustainability debate. Many donors are truly trying to build up the institutional capacity of CSOs in order to make them more sustainable. Sustainability has a further aim, to make CSOs less dependent on both donors and the state. But many of the ideas on sustainability remain just that: ideas. It is again the nobility that sticks out as only a few NGOs are targeted and strengthened, all in the name of sustainable civil society. In the meantime, (real) civil society in South Africa continues to live in a rather difficult present en route to an uncertain future.

USAID: A Case Study

Let us home in on a specific case of foreign political aid: that dispensed by USAID from 1986 to 1999. This case highlights the intricacies and dilemmas of foreign political aid to South Africa. It also reveals the complicated interplay between foreign aid and the political relationship between donor country and recipient country.

The United States began to support South African civil society organizations only in the mid-1980s, a full twenty years after the Nordic countries and other donors decided to do so. Before that, when the Cold War was still in full swing, Washington collaborated closely with the white government in Pretoria. Its policy proceeded from its preoccupation with containing Moscow's thrusts into regional vacuums and trouble spots and from its view of the South African regime as a bastion against communism.[17] The antiapartheid crusade in the United States, meanwhile, was confined mainly to members of the civil rights movement, academics, and church activists.

By the mid-1980s, a shift in U.S. policy toward South Africa started. A mobilized domestic lobby challenged the executive branch and State Department monopoly on foreign policy, imposing its views. Apartheid became a rallying point for civil rights movements, particularly in the African-American community. Public opinion, organized in interest groups and lobbies, pushed Congress forcefully to adopt a policy that ran in the opposite direction from President Ronald Reagan's. In 1986, the United States' relationship with South Africa changed dramatically. Faced with a broad-based and effective domestic lobby, Reagan had little option but to accept a new policy toward South Africa. In September 1986, Congress passed, over the administration's objections, the Comprehensive Anti-Apartheid Act, which imposed sanctions against South Africa and directed USAID to "strengthen the leadership and institutions of the disadvantaged community so they can better respond to the legitimate needs of their constituencies."

Responding to the congressional mandate, USAID established the Community Outreach and Leadership Development Project (COLD). COLD's goal was "to promote political and social change in South Africa that leads to an end of apartheid and to a political system based on the consent of the governed." COLD sought to develop the leadership and capacity of community development organizations in the disadvantaged segments of South African society so as to make them more responsive to the people they claimed to serve. Organizations receiving assistance had to "evidence community support" and "demonstrate genuine commitment to promoting black South African leadership and experience."

In practice, however, it was difficult for USAID—and other donors—to ensure that organizations applying for grants were genuinely community-based and committed to promoting black South African leadership and expertise. Because USAID and many other donor agencies were under pressure from their governments to speedily pledge and disburse funds, a lot of less-than-democratic NGOs disconnected from the society around them slipped onto the funding rolls. Some organizations that claimed to be community-based were unable to define the scope of their activities and their community affiliations. Furthermore, many organizations promoting black leadership remained white-led—understandable considering that education and opportunities were skewed in favor of white South Africans, but diminishing their representativeness.

From its inception, COLD singled out five priority areas. The first was "Women's Self-defined Needs," a very awkward expression that is actually used in the COLD documents. Cooperation with women was part of a broader strategy for urban or community development.

Rural-based community development was the second priority under COLD, and many organizations were funded that worked primarily in rural areas. Here, too, irony prevailed: the bulk of South African NGOs established for, and professing to do, rural outreach were based in cities. But rural areas under the political repression of the time were extremely complex, not easily understood by outsiders. Further decreasing the effectiveness of these organizations, South Africans in general lacked the expertise to execute rural projects.[18]

USAID saw the third priority area, shelter, as relating to all disadvantaged South Africans, in both urban and rural areas. The agency supported programs that sought to help communities defend themselves against the forced removals of population by the apartheid state.

Another priority was developing skills among youth, particularly skills useful in the non-formal sector of the economy. In reality, a sizable chunk of the budget of COLD's education program went for formal education, and above all for tertiary education, and USAID typically neglected areas such as skills training for and job creation in the non-formal sector.

The final priority was information and communications. USAID assisted the print media and helped other organizations develop tools, such as newsletters, to disseminate information.

During the 1990–94 period, USAID also pursued a policy aimed at leveling the playing field and building capacity for the post-apartheid period. By and large USAID was preparing the post-1994 era. USAID still decided against cooperating with the state or political society actors. But while there was a clear focus to what USAID did—that is, building leadership capacity—it was not clear how it was decided to support which actors. Assistance seemed piecemeal in practice. What, for example, were the demonstration effects showing that genuine leadership capacity was being built? This is not to argue that proof was difficult to gather. The scholarships programs are proof of success. It is simply to argue that not enough is done to gather proof and to learn some lessons from successes and failures.

With regard to NGOs too, USAID shifted its focus to supporting and strengthening the leadership and institutional capacity. A significant number of grants were awarded to South African NGOs through COLD, which sought to promote leadership development, organizational development, and general capacity-building; the goal was to empower black communities to pursue their development priorities and promote democratic practices.

COLD also funded political party training and party-strengthening activities intended to level the political playing field, but it did not support political parties directly in the form of direct assistance. Instead, programs and activities were aimed at spreading information about elections and democracy to majority parties. The idea was also to enable the then recently unbanned parties to actively participate in the 1994 elections.

As far as election support is concerned, the COLD project assisted three principal activities in this sub-sector: 1) voter education, broad civic education, and democracy training through South African NGOs and American technical support organizations; 2) election monitoring; and 3) technical assistance and support for the Independent Electoral Commission.

Furthermore, COLD supported activities in conflict resolution and mediation. Working through a small number of specialized NGOs, it funded an array of programs and activities including labor mediation, training of specialists in community conflict resolution, support for conflict resolution specialists and conflict intervention specialists, and special programs for communities seriously troubled by violence and conflict.

Another category of support went for advice centers, paralegal assistance, street law, and human rights. COLD-supported activities in this subsector were intended to strengthen a system of alternative legal services. COLD targeted support for defense of human rights and direct challenges to human rights abuses. Funding also went to activities to increase awareness and knowledge of legal rights and remedies in highly marginalized populations.

An interesting shift that emerged in the post-1994 environment resembled a dichotomy. USAID decided to support NGOs both close to and independent of the state, yet it appeared obsessed with getting government's consent to and encouragement for that. The outcome was an overall trend of tension between USAID, the government, and CSOs.

After 1994, support to civil society was given under the auspices of USAID's Strategic Objective 1 (SO1) Democracy and Governance Program. This program sought to strengthen civil society, elections, parliament, and human rights and to reduce and mitigate violence. Strategic concerns motivated NGOs' integration into the government's service-delivery operations and their assigned key role in areas such as electoral systems development, the strengthening of political parties, the building of a human rights culture, and construction of a more equitable justice system.

But what was striking about USAID's program in South Africa after the 1994 elections was the continuing influence of partnerships with CSOs that had been established during the antiapartheid struggle. By and large, USAID continued to support the organizations it had supported back then. However, the environment had changed radically, demanding new approaches to assisting CSOs, such as pluralism. What South Africa needed was support to CSOs that would continue to contribute to the consolidation of democracy as policy advocates, service deliverers, and public watchdogs. It seemed not to have dawned on USAID that CSOs themselves were grappling with their old relationships; they sought to carve out new roles in the post-apartheid age. Instead, USAID seemed obsessed with getting political recognition and staying in government's good books, while convincing its CSO partners that it is ultimately on their side. This approach, not surprisingly, was viewed by many as a rather ungainly one, and it seemed that USAID was always on the defensive doing fire-fighting and trying to restore a damaged image, if not credibility.

So what can USAID do differently? For starters, there should be a clear distinction between supporting government versus supporting

CSOs, as opposed to the safe option of supporting strategic partnerships between CSOs and government. Furthermore, there is no real justification for a support strategy to CSOs that must first get government's prior behind-the-scenes rubber stamp. Such a move is bound to result in a lot of politicking. Government should have as little as possible say on who in civil society gets to be supported. But there is a rub here: what is urgently needed is an even-handed attitude toward CSOs. There is urgent need to move away from the position of supporting CSOs that are either very close to or vehemently oppose the ANC-dominated government. Apart from CSOs on the left and right, there are important players who engage in critical solidarity and are ardent supporters of democracy. Above all else, donors should go back to the drawing board and rediscover the authentic civil society of the grassroots, the truly voiceless, who have become neglected in the process, and help them to develop a loud voice to force themselves back onto the political and socioeconomic agenda.

As for the idea of setting up trust funds and endowments as ways of making CSOs more sustainable, there is again need to move away from supporting a chosen few, "safe" CSOs. The challenge remains how to reach as diverse a spread of NGOs with fast-dwindling resources.

Conclusion

While donor support to civil and political society has long been a feature of South African politics, it is clear that the nature of foreign political aid changed substantially in the 1990s. It was very simple for donors to support civil society and political society against apartheid; one could easily distinguish between the good guys, or antiapartheid nonstate actors, and the bad guys of the apartheid regime. After 1994 there were no bad guys anymore; both the reconstituted state and civil society now belonged to the good side. Foreign political aid supporting efforts to circumvent the white state was replaced with an aid regime that backed the new democratic, black-led state. While CSOs were the sole beneficiaries of foreign political aid before 1994, after democracy's arrival they were forced to share the spoils with the new state. This new reality triggered its own set of intricacies and dichotomies. CSOs were expected to do much more with a great deal less support from donors. It also increased competition among CSOs for the largest slices of the small aid cake. An even more important fallout caused by this new balance of forces is that, while many NGOs claimed to have close ties with communities and grassroots constituencies, many were becoming disconnected from those constituencies and repackaged themselves as blue-blooded types in order to meet with donors' approval. A new type of CSO has emerged in the post-apartheid age, and it is elitist and oligarchic in character. The new NGOs are run by a small circle of leaders who spend more time making themselves attractive and hustling to attract ever-dwindling resources to ensure their survival than doing all-important grassroots work. Thus, while many speak of voicing the voiceless, they are in fact voicing the already voiced. In the months and years to come, this pattern is likely to become more common as donors begin to scale down their activities in South Africa and prepare to shut up shop. In short, the cargo cult of dependence on external donor aid has not prepared CSOs for life on their own. Nor did overseas donors prepare CSOs for such an eventuality by, for example, taking the issue of sustainability seriously enough. Today's attempts at building sustainability are too little, too late. Donors' withdrawal will be devastating for South African CSOs. While in most other African countries bilateral government-to-government aid forms the bulk of overseas assistance packages, in South Africa, foreign political aid to CSOs has long been an inordinately large part of aid packages.

The major objective of foreign political aid to South Africa was overtly political and strategic: it sought to assist in the overthrow of the apartheid regime and to replace that regime with a democracy. Support to civil and political society in South Africa was a means to that end. Foreign political aid went to both civil and political society because donors were almost forced to concede that society in South Africa was heavily politicized by the repressive machinery of apartheid. CSOs would not have been as effective in achieving the transition if not for the support from the international donor community. It is, therefore, conceivable that without continued support CSOs will be less successful in helping consolidate South Africa's young democracy.

To be sure, it was easy for donors to give foreign political aid to civil society and political society organs in the past as both were vibrant and alert to opportunities. Even at the height of apartheid repression, donors were able to disburse aid to organizations speedily and secretively. In the post-apartheid age, it is far more difficult for donors to give; but this should be more reason for them to appreciate that it is imperative they give to CSOs. The question is: which civil society do they prefer to embrace?

Without South Africa's CSOs, the young democracy would be even more fragile than it is now. For decades, CSOs in South Africa busied themselves with, and struggled for, procedural democracy, and that stood them in good stead with the foreign donor fraternity, made up almost entirely of liberal democracies. What is needed now is for CSOs to shift focus to the more substantive aspects of democracy, such as helping secure the participation of grassroots communities. This is, therefore, a call for donors to rethink the need for continued involvement in South Africa, while seriously considering ways of helping secure the sustainability of CSOs. It is also a call for the nonstate aristocrats to become less civil and more part of society.

Notes

1. Michael Bratton and Chris Landsberg, "From Promise to Delivery: Official Development Assistance to South Africa, 1994–98," Research Report no. 68, Foreign Policy Series, funded by the Ford Foundation and the MacArthur Foundation (Johannesburg: Centre for Policy Studies, March 1999), p. 3. The original version of this paper has been published by the Centre on International Cooperation (New York: Lynne Rienner Publishers, 2000).

2. The terms "political society" and "civil society" and their usage are borrowed from Peter M. Lewis, "Civil Society, Political Society and Democratic Failure in Nigeria," in International Human Rights Law Group, "Using Community-based Mobilisation Strategies to Effect Change in Nigeria," Compilation of papers, Accra, Ghana, May 6–8, 1998.

3. For an elaborate outline of foreign assistance to the liberation movements and struggle, see Scott Thomas, *The Diplomacy of Liberation: The Foreign Policy of the ANC since 1960* (London: Tauris Academic Studies, 1996).

4. Ibid.

5. Some information on the mass democratic movement and the AZAPO is taken from Hennie Kotze and Anneke Greling, *Political Organisations in South Africa: A–Z*, updated edition (Capetown: Tafelberg, 1994).

6. While black consciousness promoted the idea that black South Africans could only be emancipated by themselves, not the white man, charterist organizations subscribe to the ideal that "South Africa belongs to all who live in it, black and white," as proclaimed by the Freedom Charter. Charterists were therefore more nonracial in their beliefs.

7. Tom Lodge, Bill Nasson, et al., *All, Here, and Now: Black Politics in South Africa in the 1980s,* Ford Foundation Series "South Africa: Time Running Out" (Cape Town: David Philip, 1991), pp. 47 ff.

8. On the NECC, see Kotze and Greyling, *Political Organisations in South Africa.*

9. For a discussion of the pillars of struggle, see the presentations of Cheryl Carolus, Jeremy Cronin, Azhar Cachalia, and Titus Mafolo in International Human Rights Law Group, "Nigeria-South Africa Consultative Meeting," Workshop proceedings, Johannesburg, September 27–29, 1996 (Washington, D.C.: International Human Rights Law Group, 1996).

10. See "Phases of Mass Mobilisation in South Africa," in International Human Rights Law Group, "Report of the Nigeria–South Africa Consultative Meeting."

11. On the UN and South Africa, see Chris Landsberg, *Exporting Peace? The UN and South Africa,* vol. 7, no. 2, International Relations Series (Johannesburg: Centre for Policy Studies, October 1994).

12. On international development assistance for South Africa, especially from the EU, see Chris Landsberg, "An Overview of International Development Co-operation with South Africa" (paper commissioned by the German Development Association, Pretoria, June 1997), p. 16; see also "Agreed Minutes, Annual Consultations on Development Co-operation between South Africa and the EU on the European Programme for Reconstruction and Development" (Pretoria: International Development Co-operation, Department of Finance, March 25–26, 1998).

13. Chris Landsberg, "Directing from the Stalls? The International Community and South Africa's Negotiating Forum," in Steven Friedman and Doreen Atkinson, eds., *The Small Miracle: South Africa's Negotiated Settlement* (Johannesburg: Ravan Press, 1994), p. 281.

14. For an overview of this, consult the compendiums of annual consultations between the South African government and overseas donors that have taken place since 1994. These compendiums are kept by the chief directorate, International Development Co-operation in the Department of Finance, Pretoria.

15. The following quotations are taken from "International Development Co-operation: Compendium of Agreements between South Africa and Certain Countries Regarding Development Assistance" (Pretoria: Department of Finance, August 1, 1995).

16. Julie Hearn, "Foreign Aid, Democratisation and Civil Society in Africa: A Study of South Africa, Ghana and Uganda," Discussion Paper no. 368 (Sussex: Institute for Development Studies, 1999), p. 22.

17. Chris Landsberg and Cedric de Coning, "From 'Tar Baby' to Transition: Four Decades of US Foreign Policy towards South Africa," vol. 8, no. 6, *International Relations Series* (Johannesburg: Centre for Policy Studies, March 1995), p. 7.

18. USAID-South Africa, *Concept Paper* (Pretoria: USAID-South Africa Mission, March 1993).

Part Three

Asia

5

Democracy as Development: A Case for Civil Society Assistance in Asia

Stephen J. Golub

VIEWS ABOUT THE LINKS BETWEEN civil society assistance and democracy promotion in Asia substantially depend on where one works. In Washington, where supporters of civil society aid justify the cost of such work by declaring that it builds democracy and the rule of law, evaluation of aid efforts frequently hinges on a given Asian nation's overall progress in those regards. Taking a more realistic view, Asian nongovernmental organizations (NGOs) that receive U.S. aid look for progress in specific policies, practices, or groups of people. Rather than declaring, "We are building democracy" or "We strengthen civil society," they talk about work to strengthen laws against rape or to improve farmers' livelihoods. Their staffs may cooperate with the state to the extent possible but also challenge government or vested interests at great personal risk, sometimes even dying for doing so. Relatively lucrative donor-supported salaries motivate some NGO personnel, but many serve at great sacrifice and regularly venture into fetid slums or isolated rural areas, enduring discomfort that both government officials and comfortably perched Western critics of civil society assistance shun. Many Asian NGOs pursue a participatory development approach that helps address the greatest needs of people in the societies in question: sometimes physical security, often socioeconomic progress, even a blend of the two. Their work frequently takes place at a nexus of democracy and development.

This chapter argues in favor of Asian NGOs' more realistic perspective on civil society assistance, and for increased U.S. support to such organizations. The discussion focuses on the United States Agency for International Development (USAID) because it specifically supports civil society work under the rubric of democracy and governance (DG, in USAID parlance) and because it is the largest U.S.-based donor active in Asia. Driven by congressional and internal pressures to demonstrate dramatic change, USAID often sets overly ambitious goals. The agency funds much good work in civil society. But its bureaucratic requirements are burdensome, and the agency's drive for results becomes a pursuit of the perfect that can block achievement of the good.

This chapter looks favorably on assistance for democratic practices such as civic education and advocacy. Those often work best, however, when framed around issues that appeal to the legitimate self-interest of Asian citizens who otherwise participate little in governance and benefit little from development. Except for the dramatic toppling of dictators or ensuing transitional elections, issue-oriented work advances participation more than clarion calls to a larger conception of democracy.

The analysis here thus distinguishes between assistance for "Big D" and "small d" democracy. Assistance geared toward formal systems of governance—"democracy with a Big D"—attempts to make elections, judiciaries, legislatures, political parties, and other core democratic institutions and practices operate responsibly, accountably, and effectively. Its goal is success on the national level, in overall progress on democracy and the rule of law. It is process-oriented and largely outcome-neutral. The results of an election, a parliamentary vote, or judicial deliberations do not matter, so long as the process unfolds appropriately. "Big D" democracy assistance supports advocacy by NGOs. But it is largely indifferent to whether NGOs win policy battles, except insofar as victories are indicators of greater capacity in policy advocacy.

In contrast, assistance intended to foster "democracy with a small d" aims in part at socioeconomic progress for disadvantaged people, and in any event at impact on specific policies, practices, and populations. It differs from much mainstream development work (in health or livelihood enhancement, for example) in that the means it employs—community mobilization, legal assistance, media, advocacy, civic education—are important threads in the fabrics of many sturdy democracies. That is, it does not teach farmers how to maximize crop yields or mothers how to safeguard their children from childhood diseases. But it can help farmers get their land rights enforced or help women protect their own health and that of their children by combating domestic violence. And sometimes "small d" efforts build on mainstream development work: women who are first organized around family planning needs, for example, are better able to learn about their rights.

Civic participation, while a goal of both types of democracy assistance, is not outcome-neutral in "small d" democracy. Often it blends with socioeconomic progress. Democracy in this sense is very much a matter of both the process and the products of equitable development.

The two kinds of democracy promotion can overlap. NGOs that seek to get women into legislatures may have in mind specific substantive policies, not just elections. Groups that battle corruption may define themselves in terms of that problem's "Big D" implications, or they may have an environmental, gender, or agrarian focus as they tackle graft. "Small d" democracy advocacy can yield change at the national level, for instance in government policies and appointments. And "Big D" democracy assistance can operate at a community level to get people to press for good governance. The former uses democratic means to advance such development goals as good health for women, higher rural incomes, and better urban housing, while valuing affected people's participation in achieving those goals. The latter supports NGOs engaged in development out of a conviction that civil society is a crucial component of a vibrant democracy.

Despite the large overlap, it is important to distinguish between the two types of democracy promotion. Doing so builds appreciation of "small d" democracy assistance in Asia. The best ways of achieving progress in both development and democratization—again, as indicated by effects on specific policies, practices, and populations, not national transformation—often involve appealing to people's pressing concerns in their daily lives. Battered women, subsistence farmers, street vendors, and urban squatters usually respond far better to appeals to their legitimate self-interest than to their democratic spirit. They may well care about important concepts like democracy, and may be moved to action in times of dramatic national transition. But once the smoke has cleared and their personal needs reassert themselves, they are much more likely to act when they see the large concepts as linked to their specific circumstances. In development parlance, they act on "felt need."

Greater attention to "small d" democracy can also increase aid providers' understanding of how it both buttresses and builds on mainstream development work in the fields of health, population, livelihood, and the environment. Connections between democracy work and development work already exist to a certain degree. The challenge is to explore further possibilities and establish strategies for fortifying useful links.

Perpetuating the inflated notion of "Big D" democracy assistance is misleading and even counterproductive. It raises unrealistic expectations in the many cases in which USAID, other funding agencies, intermediary organizations, and indigenous groups really seek "small d" progress. Again, the two are not mutually exclusive and "Big D" work can be legitimate and important. There is much to be said for intellectual honesty, however, particularly where it lends itself to institutional effectiveness. Democracy assistance *does* have national impact on laws, policies, and high-level appointments—for example, in the area of the environment. But usually it makes a country's processes and institutions more democratic only in the most gradual, issue-specific ways—and that is enough of an accomplishment to strive for.

This chapter does not attempt to summarize Asian civil societies in their enormous variety or to come to any sweeping conclusions about foreign aid's effects on half of humanity. Instead, it scrutinizes individual programs to get at the true value of civil society aid when understood close up. Donors' decisions should of course factor in underlying societal needs, forces, and phenomena, but that is only part of the programming puzzle—and sometimes not the most important part. Donors do not fund needs, forces, and phenomena; they fund institutions, individuals, and opportunities.

Thus this chapter spotlights U.S.-based organizations' aid to specific programs in specific places at specific historical moments. First, it examines cases in which civil society support has achieved worthwhile results. It then considers a stream of DG assistance emblematic of the "Big D" approach that has proved problematic in Asia: aid to central government institutions. The discussion focuses on USAID but also considers work supported by other American groups: the Ford Foundation, which uses its private endowment to operate completely independently of the U.S. government; the Asia Foundation, which receives funding from USAID projects and through a line item in the State Department budget, as well as from donors outside the U.S. government; and the International Human Rights Law Group, which receives support both from USAID and from other donors. It does not examine civil society aid by non-U.S. actors, such as European bilateral donors, although the conclusions reached are intended to be broadly generalizable.

The conclusion emerges that USAID can best respond to opportunities and constraints by refining how it goes about its business. Experience teaches that generally it should support "small d" over "Big D" initiatives; indigenous NGOs over government institutions; and flexible, evolving projects instead of rigidly predesigned ones. Above all, it should link democracy with development and with people's difficult daily lives. To accomplish all this, it must rethink some of its strategies, streamline its bureaucratic operations, and get closer to the people in not-yet-fully-democratic countries that it says it wants to benefit.

Going With NGOs

Incubators of Innovation, Sources of Replication

One reason for donors to channel support to nongovernmental organizations is that NGOs are incubators of innovation and reform. They often have flexibility, creativity, dedication, and independence that government institutions lack. In the field of legislative strengthening, support for the Center for Legislative Development, a Philippine NGO, has resulted in congressional capacity-building that both is more effective and allows for more civil society input into the reform process than a purely governmental approach. The center has served as a resource for related efforts elsewhere in Asia.

Asia Foundation and Ford Foundation funding for the Philippine Center for Investigative Journalism has supported innovative reporting on a plethora of issues. Often that reporting is of better quality than the usual products of the country's sensationalistic press, and it has more effect on society. For example, a Supreme Court justice resigned the day after the center documented unethical behavior on his part. Other reports, together with NGO advocacy, helped block in 1992 the appointment as the country's top environmental official of a member of Congress with ties to the illegal logging industry. To some extent the center has been a model for similar initiatives in Thailand and Nepal. Not everyone has appreciated the center's stories, however; some of the center's writers have been harassed and have even received death threats.

Neither the Center for Legislative Development nor the Philippine Center for Investigative Journalism would claim that Philippine democracy overall is stronger because of its work. What they can take credit for is limited but significant "small d" reform in government processes and decisions, as well as contributions to important development goals (most notably gender legislation for the Center for Legislative Development and environmental policies and practices for the Center for Investigative Journalism).

In Bangladesh, assistance from the Asia Foundation, the Ford Foundation, and the Norwegian Agency for Development Cooperation played a pivotal role in the evolution of the Madaripur Legal Aid Association, an NGO named for the rural district where it mainly operates, serving a population of more than one million. The association's broader significance stems from its development of a mediation scheme (selectively backed by litigation) that has served as a model for other NGOs across the country and for a nationwide legal aid NGO led by Madaripur's executive director. USAID has supported much of this replication.

Madaripur and other NGOs in Bangladesh function in a harsh social context. Well over half of Bangladeshis are illiterate, more than a third are "very poor" by World Bank standards, and the country ranks near the bottom on the United Nations Development Program index of human development indicators. Lack of resources both in the government and among citizens, together with the inefficiency, corruption, expense, unfair treatment of women, and incomprehensibility (for most Bangladeshis) of judicial operations, has made the courts a last resort for redress. And though traditional dispute resolution is free, efficient, and easily understandable, it too is plagued by corruption and, even worse, by gender bias, as well as legal ignorance. While the NGOs' mediation efforts ameliorate rather than cure these deep-rooted problems, they offer impoverished Bangladeshis, particularly women, a measure of choice they would not otherwise have.

Bangladesh NGOs do not claim to be contributing to such "Big D" goals as overall rule of law or to fully functioning democracy. On the other hand, even though Madaripur's approach to its clients' problems is rather straightforward and law-oriented, the potential mainstream development benefits should not be discounted. To the extent that the organization addresses violence against women, for example, it advances socioeconomic goals that a 1995 World Bank study indicates such abuse undermines.[1]

Building on Mainstream Development Efforts

The discussion thus far has sketched ways in which mainstream socioeconomic development fields can benefit from efforts that are squarely democracy-oriented. The reverse is also true: many democracy efforts build on mainstream work in health, livelihoods, education, and other fields. For example, a 1995 Asia Foundation-commissioned study of a pilot effort to integrate family planning and legal services in Bangladesh shows that the two can be mutually beneficial.[2] The activities of NGOs dealing with reproductive health and related services provided a means by which their outreach workers could educate and assist people in legal issues.

In a related vein, the Asia Foundation has financed mediation and other legal services provided by Banchte Shekha, a women's movement that has made significant inroads against the gender biases and power imbalances faced by rural women in Bangladesh's Jessore district. The movement's legal successes, however, build on a foundation of years of programs relating to literacy, organizing, livelihood, and health for its members. And that in turn rests on the courage of Banchte Shekha's founder and staff, who have endured harassment and threats from legal, political, and religious quarters.

Banchte Shekha's experience, both its good and bad aspects, resonates in India. The Ford Foundation grantee Hengasara Hakkina Sangha, based in Bangalore, conducts paralegal training for *sanghas* (very basic community-based organizations comprised of women), and for small development-oriented NGOs that organize them around such concerns as family planning or access to credit. *Sangha* members report that the combination of organization and knowledge of their rights has helped them combat domestic violence in their communities and, more sporadically, to negotiate higher pay for their agricultural labor. Yet it would have been impossible for them to discuss rights if they had not previously been organized around less controversial topics (which themselves can meet resistance in communities dominated by conservative attitudes about gender).

Similarly, the Ahmedabad-based Center for Social Justice builds much of its legal work on mainstream efforts carried out by its parent development organization or other bodies. Much of the work is geared toward benefiting women and *dalits* (a term preferred to the pejorative "untouchables"). The center has won notable court victories in such matters as obtaining potable drinking water and restraining police misconduct. It also pays a price; a mob attacked a field office for challenging religious orthodoxy and seeking to improve *dalits'* status.

Nepal offers yet another variation on these themes. Only with the nation's transition to democracy in the early 1990s did NGOs burgeon. Some would call it a donor-funded explosion—many of the NGOs that sprang up were purely Kathmandu-based, were motivated more by donor dollars than by altruism, and were organized with donors' democracy rhetoric rather than long-term development in mind. In recent years, more indigenous NGOs have established a presence beyond the Kathmandu Valley. But geographical barriers and past squandering of development aid contribute to poor physical infrastructure, which hampers Kathmandu NGOs' contact with outlying areas. Traditional economic relations and political patronage continue to hold sway. Finally, perhaps because of the nature of the democracy movement in Nepal, many NGOs have strong political affiliations.

Partly in response to these circumstances, USAID/Nepal's democracy-oriented support has in recent years moved away from Kathmandu NGOs (as well as central and local government bodies) and focused on the Empowerment of Women Program, based in rural regions. That effort seeks to blend literacy, economic participation, and legal rights and representation for women. It works with a combination of Western and indigenous NGOs with offices in Kathmandu and outlying districts. The NGOs in turn build on their existing relationships with community-based organizations and groups of women. Some of these groups (of men as well as women), organized by intermediaries with donor support, predate democratic Nepal.

The program is still too new to have compiled much of a track record. But preliminary USAID-supported field research indicates that women's collective actions have had some effect, notably in the matter of village alcohol production, sale, and consumption and public drunkenness by men. Establishing controls over alcohol may not seem like a democracy objective. But considering how alcohol both diverts scarce family resources and exacerbates domestic violence, women's concern is understandable. At the same time, praise for the program must be tempered by criticism of the way the agency runs it, a potential restraining approach that will be discussed below.

Policy Reform and Implementation

NGOs affect policy reform, legal implementation (that is to say, actually getting worthwhile laws enforced), and capacity-building among the people with whom they work. With support from the Ford Foundation, the Asia Foundation, and other donors, numerous Philippine legal services NGOs in the 1990s helped bring about significant positive change in all three categories. Such NGOs call themselves "alternative law groups" (ALGs) and carry out what they call "development legal aid," working with disadvantaged populations on development issues, inspired by a philosophy and ethic distinct from those of most of the lawyers who dominate the country's bar. ALGs operate on both the national and the grassroots level, undertaking work in women's rights, the environment, agrarian reform, small business deregulation, and a host of other matters.

In line with a general trend in civil society in the Philippines, recent years have seen increased cooperation between ALGs and local and national government. As part of coalitions of NGOs and associations of groups representing the disadvantaged, ALG lawyers have made crucial contributions to most of the progressive social legislation and attendant regulatory reform in the country over the past decade, regarding rape, agrarian reform, natural resources, urban housing, and several other issues. Those civil society coalitions have also helped formulate scores of implementing rules and regulations, as well as provincial ordinances. Their accomplishments are no mean feat, especially since elite interests still dominate the national legislature and politics in the Philippines.

One sees more clearly the value of the work of these lawyers and their allies through a developmental, "small d" lens. Various donors have supported ALGs under various rubrics: democracy, governance, rule of law, civil society, reproductive health, and natural resources, to name a few. The common thread is that the ALGs work with development-oriented socioeconomic development NGOs on problems that can be framed in terms of both development and democracy. And though Philippine democracy on a national scale may have taken a step backward from the somewhat technocratic 1992–98 administration of President Fidel Ramos to the more traditional politics and patronage of his successor, Joseph Estrada, NGOs remain a vibrant force for progress in some regards (agrarian reform and local governance, for instance) and a means of weathering the storm in others (for example, the environment).

Against All Odds

In some cases, whatever else might or might not be accomplished, the argument for civil society assistance is that it supports groups that are making the best of a bad situation. Cambodia is such a case. The nightmarish Khmer Rouge regime (1975–79) intentionally wiped out all religious, professional, media, cultural, and community associations that existed in even rudimentary forms, along with many of the organizations' members. Subsequent repressive governments have only grudgingly permitted such groups to emerge, often with foreign assistance. Today, the environment in which voluntary organizations operate ranges from barely tolerant to hostile, under the gaze of a government that killed more than a hundred of its enemies in mounting a 1997 coup.

USAID-funded (through the Asia Foundation) Cambodian NGOs help keep a democratic flame burning in the midst of the repression. They provide information to international human rights monitors based abroad and in the Phnom Penh office of the United Nations Center for Human Rights. They helped publicize the dumping on Cambodian shores of toxic chemicals from Taiwan. (That publicity got two NGO activists jailed.) And when the government discouraged the formation of an international tribunal to try former Khmer Rouge leaders, NGOs collected tens of thousands of signatures on petitions demanding a trial before such a panel. Particularly in light of the country's history and current government, collecting names for or even signing such a document was an act of singular courage, the kind usually lost in broad-brush Washington discussions of civil society. The same courage could be ascribed to such NGO activists as the late Neelan Tiruchelvam, director of Sri Lanka's International Centre for Ethnic Studies, whom terrorists assassinated in 1999 for daring to press for what seems the impossible dream of ethnic reconciliation in his country.

Two International Human Rights Law Group projects in Cambodia further demonstrate the merits of civil society assistance even where civil society is decimated. The group's Human Rights Task Force provided advice and other aid that got human rights groups up and running. It helped teach the groups' staff how to document, strategize, systematize, publicize, and otherwise conduct their work. And its USAID-assisted Defenders Project introduced the notion of criminal defense to a legal system accustomed to throwing the accused in jail and almost literally throwing away the key.

Ironically, Indonesia has received noteworthy U.S. civil society support. For many of the years that the U.S. government supported the Suharto regime politically and diplomatically, USAID focused its assistance on organizations working in legal aid, environmental defense, even human rights advocacy. The contributions of these Indonesian organizations to date go far beyond those of their Cambodian counterparts that merely kept the flame burning, though they may not reach the level of replication seen among Bangladeshi legal services NGOs or the policy impact that Philippine groups have delivered. But that such NGOs are in place and have amassed valuable experience over the years, in part because of USAID assistance, may enable them to play a leading role in the post-Suharto era.

The results of aid to civil society go beyond specific NGOs' successes on specific issues. In countries like Pakistan, Sri Lanka, the Philippines, and Thailand, NGO leaders have entered government service without forfeiting their commitment to public service. Equally important, people whom U.S.-supported NGOs have helped organize and train are beginning to enter the lower levels of local government in the Philippines, India, and elsewhere in Asia. The impact on government, then, proceeds not just from external advocacy but from participation on the inside.

Sustainable Impact, Realistic Expectations

Why fund a civil society organization if there is no assurance that it is sustainable—that it can survive once its grant ends? While there is no guarantee that an NGO will continue its operations after any given donor's funding runs out, enough do to make support for a promising group a worthwhile bet. In addition, donors may hold NGOs to too high a standard if they demand sustainability from groups whose Western equivalents depend on outside funds. Even in the United States and Europe, many nongovernmental groups are not truly self-supporting. For example, a recent paper on U.S. public interest law groups concluded it is unreasonable to expect them to achieve such financial independence.[3] Furthermore, donors themselves are in a far better position than NGOs to creatively plan to ensure the continued existence of worthy grantees.

But perhaps donors should view sustainability in a different light. The most important consideration may be whether the *impact* of NGOs is sustainable, not whether the particular organizations themselves are. Policy changes that flow from the work of such groups may become permanent. The material conditions of individuals and communities that NGOs assist may change for the better and stay that way. And NGO leaders may go on to serve in government. Looked at in terms of impact, sustainability is not a matter of whether an organization has a permanent funding source but of whether outside support helps it do quality work.

Trouble at the Center

Civil society's track record appears even stronger compared with that of another approach to strengthening Asian democracy: assistance for central government institutions such as parliaments and judiciaries. That "Big D" experience ranges from ambiguous to counterproductive.

Nearly two decades spent trying to strengthen the administration of Asian courts provide perhaps the starkest illustration of the flaws of democracy aid to central governments. The Asia Foundation, for example, undertook a wide range of international and country-specific initiatives in that field throughout the 1980s. Its efforts were well intended; a key objective, for instance, was to reduce the delays common in Asian courts. Nevertheless, the attempts generally failed. Under new leadership with far more experience in development work, the foundation focused less on central governments in the 1990s.

The problems plaguing many Asian legal systems run much deeper than the solutions that foreign-funded projects offer. Delays in the court system, other administrative problems, and a lack of judicial transparency and accountability derive more from corruption, patronage, personalism, and indifference than from narrow technical deficiencies such as judicial personnel's lack of training. A landmark study of Indian civil courts discounts familiar diagnoses like insufficient resources, complex legislation, and litigiousness and highlights factors that include countervailing interests and incentives.[4] Nor can training or other technical fixes always overcome such problems, rooted as they are in a society's politics, economics, and culture. Partial solutions, to the extent they exist, may lie in grappling with interests and incentives, and may include incorporating civil society forces into the fray.

After my 1987–90 stint with the Asia Foundation in the Philippines, the country that was the centerpiece of the foundation's judicial programming in Asia, I concluded that the decade of intensive engagement with the judiciary there had achieved very little. A foundation staff member elsewhere in Southeast Asia considered analogous work in that country "a black hole." Similar foundation efforts in South Asia met similar fates.

Nor has failure to reform judiciaries been confined to foundation-sponsored programs. A recent USAID-funded International Human Rights Law Group effort, the Cambodian Court Training Project, left a number of insiders and outside observers convinced that the attempt had failed.[5] The reasons, again, included pervasive corruption, patronage, and political control in the courts. (A relative showcase of a court, for example, turned out to be what many agreed was one of the country's most corrupt.) *Weighing in on the Scales of Justice*, a broad USAID review of selected rule-of-law programs (including those in the Philippines and Sri Lanka), concluded that a strategy oriented toward civil society was usually preferable to a "[government-focused] paradigm featuring a 'technical fix' or engineering approach to institutional change."[6]

In addition, a rule-of-law project can create the illusion that a government cares about improving a legal system, when the reverse is the case. And as was perhaps true in Cambodia, it can make democracy assistance a cover or a scapegoat for the failure of the United States and the international community to exercise the political, economic, and diplomatic pressure that might more immediately curb a regime's lawlessness. More broadly, a development organization's focus on the technical details of the administration of justice may downplay social justice and the political economy of reform, stunting the perspectives of both its staff and its programming partners in foreign governments.

For the Asia Foundation and the International Human Rights Law Group, any unproductive work in central government institutions is outweighed by the contributions they have made through civil society assistance. But their experiences are cautionary.

Room for Improvement

There is a case for civil society assistance intended to foster democracy, particularly when oriented toward development and "small d" democracy. But considerable room for improvement exists, both in the manner in which USAID provides such support and in what is supported. This section offers suggestions regarding the nexus of the "how" and "what" of the agency's civil society support. In the process, it addresses some considerations that reach beyond USAID. The main point about USAID is that while some of its civil society support goes for good projects that yield good results, these come about despite rather than because of the way the agency works.

At a Distance

How *does* USAID operate? All too often, it operates at a great remove from the local organizations it indirectly supports and the people it attempts to benefit. Literal physical separation is one manifestation of this distance. Many USAID staff get out of the office all too rarely, and out of capital cities even less frequently. In many cases they never meet with subgrantees they fund through intermediaries. During consulting assignments stretching over eight years in the Philippines, I repeatedly found myself explaining the work of legal services NGOs to those USAID personnel who were managing the funding for them. Such separation means an even greater distance from, and virtually no contact with, the people the NGOs work with and supposedly serve.

Lack of contact often translates into lack of perspective—or rather, a perspective at odds with the realities on the ground. Projects that make sense inside the walls of a USAID mission may make much less sense in their real-world setting. What recipients of USAID support say about their work may well sound different (sometimes worse, but sometimes much better) if one observes their work first-hand or interviews its beneficiaries. How things look from any national capital often conflicts with the view from the rest of the country. "Big D" impact seems more possible when contemplated in the capital; "small d" results seem more marginal. Lack of contact seriously affects USAID personnel's perspective in all these regards.

The World Through Intermediaries' Eyes

USAID's limited contact with the organizations it supports and the difficulties with which those organizations grapple daily is especially harmful in developing societies. The agency's eyes and ears in a foreign country tend to be the Western grantees and contractors it funds and the Western consultants it imports for advice.[7] Perhaps there is no great harm in that in other fields in which USAID works. But democracy programming, particularly in the area of civil society, requires a clearer sense of what one is doing. It is one thing to have a general understanding of the need for effective NGO advocacy, for example. When deciding which specific efforts and local organizations to fund, however, one must know the institutions, organizations, and personalities in play.

Unfortunately, the way USAID operates blocks agency personnel from gaining that knowledge, with especially negative repercussions for civil society assistance. The agency relies heavily on consultants, often brought in from outside the country in question, for advice at all stages of its project cycle. Such outsiders can provide useful input in matters that USAID personnel have neither the time nor training to investigate. Consultants may also offer knowledge gleaned from development efforts in other countries. In my experience, however, USAID is overly dependent on consultants for advice on matters that its in-country personnel do or should know better than any visitor. That dependence sets up a vicious cycle in which the handling of consultants consumes the time and energy of overstretched agency staff.

Trapped in the Project Cycle

The project design stage of USAID initiatives locks a mission into a rigid approach to a complicated situation. The fact that projects have to be "designed" means that they lack the flexibility to respond to the obstacles to and opportunities for effective advocacy. The upshot can be expensive projects with poor results. Civil society support is particularly prone to this problem.

A current "coalition project" in the Philippines serves as illustration. USAID channels funds to Western or large Philippine NGOs for them to forge coalitions of local civil society groups. Each coalition focuses on a specific sector or issue: fishing communities, labor, administration of justice, urban housing.

The project began with the fundamental misconception that USAID funding was necessary for the forging of coalitions. The truth is that the Philippines abounds in coalitions of NGOs and people's organizations, including ones working on many of the same issues as coalitions brought together by American dollars. An even more serious design-driven error is the project imperative of formalizing the kinds of links that in many instances are best left informal and allowed to flourish or wither on their own. The proof lies in the troubled histories of the coalitions. As the saying goes, money changes everything. Intense infighting over too-abundant cash all but destroyed certain coalitions. Some good results have come out of the project, but not nearly so many and not nearly as quickly as if the money had been awarded in a more flexible manner.

The Empowerment of Women Program in Nepal is another case in point, although it may be yielding some benefits. It too has taken a "one size fits all" approach, requiring intermediary organizations to partner each other and indigenous organizations in a predetermined manner. A more efficient and effective approach would have set general parameters for the program and then provided funds to different organizations to work in the ways they deemed best.

In theory and on occasion in real life, USAID creates projects that incorporate great flexibility, mainly through grants, whether direct or through intermediaries, to local NGOs. The Indonesia mission's funding of NGOs even under the Suharto regime may be a good example. This "foundation-style" approach, taken to its logical and praiseworthy extreme, basically says to local partners, "Tell us what you want to do and we'll fund it, if it makes sense in view of your capacities, our broad objectives, and other programming opportunities." It is particularly effective where it supports those local groups' core office, salary, and related costs, thereby giving them the flexibility they need to address evolving needs and challenges. In such cases the design process melts away or at least becomes much simpler.

Much more typically, however, the subtext of the discussion is "This is what USAID wants to do. Now we need to find partners to do it." The result is a process that builds in rigidity and excludes more effective—and sometimes more cost-effective—means of reaching the desired goals. Yet an additional drawback of the USAID project cycle is the substantial delay its many requirements often engender.

Nothing But Results

"We don't focus much on specific activities or accomplishments any more. We just track results." This comment from a USAID official involved in civil society programming in a major Asian nation sums up a disturbing trend in the agency's "Managing for Results" (MFR) system. The new system was introduced at USAID in the mid-1990s as part of the Clinton administration's larger "Reinventing Government" initiative and in response to congressional pressure. It was intended to be an advance over the old system of assessing projects which mechanically involved applying narrowly conceived measures of what USAID funding achieved (for example, the number of people trained in a particular project). Senior officials believed the new system would help agency personnel focus on real results—for example, how much the people learned during the training or how much they later applied it. They also saw it as a way of measuring annual progress of various projects and field missions, and for adjusting budgets accordingly.

Managing for Results, however, tends to substitute one set of mechanical, rigid attitudes and procedures for another, preventing the agency from getting the kind of results it says it is seeking. The system does not do away with mechanical indicators; in fact, it has created a new impetus to generate numbers, at the expense of the quality and ultimate impact of the agency's projects. The Empowerment of Women Program in Nepal is a case in point. It may well sacrifice ultimate impact by trying, at least partly in response to MFR pressure, to reach as many women as possible—an ironic, partial return to the days of simply counting heads. However praiseworthy the project, in certain respects it is a mile wide and an inch deep. Even worse than the fixation on quantitative results, MFR often leads the agency to choose short-term over long-term results. One reason USAID/Nepal has sought quantity over quality is that the system forces it to justify the project's very existence on a yearly basis.

MFR sends USAID field missions scurrying to document misleading results that can blow up in their faces. Before the 1997 coup in Cambodia, for example, the Phnom Penh mission considered conducting annual surveys in which it would pay Cambodian leaders of government and civil society to assess the country's democratic and human rights progress. The mission would have taken credit for favorable survey results. Even had the coup not taken place, the problems with the idea were manifold. But in the coup's aftermath, any honest survey would have shown democracy's position much weakened, the important achievements of the mission (in bolstering progressive NGOs) swamped by negative developments for which USAID, through MFR, was inadvertently assuming responsibility.

The Face of USAID

This chapter has suggested that USAID is not sufficiently in touch with the actors and factors that shape civil society's development. One partial exception to the rule of inadequate inquiry into local organizations' work is the individuals and units in the agency generally known as the "bean counters." As used here, the term applies to some, though certainly not all, internal auditors and members of the Inspector General's office. Though they occasionally bring needed discipline to indigenous NGOs' accounting practices, all too often they display excessive interference with the operations of the agency's partners, whether contractors, grantees, or subgrantees. The interference affects civil society assistance particularly, in at least three ways.

First, of all the agency's partners, indigenous NGO subgrantees struggle most with USAID's rigid accounting and reporting requirements. The paperwork is substantially the same for a $50,000 grant to an NGO as for a $5 million project. Meeting the requirements consumes tremendous amounts of time—and in effect, money. In one extremely minor but emblematic episode several years ago, agency auditors disallowed a

Philippine NGO's purchase of a rice cooker (common in offices in the Philippines) for staff meals. The person-hours that the NGO, the agency, and the intermediary grantee put into negotiating and corresponding on the matter exceeded the appliance's value by a factor of ten or twenty. Extrapolated over countless costlier instances, this rigid approach both impinges on partner organizations' operations and costs the agency far more than it saves.

Second, internal battles at the agency over ways of counting beans hurt civil society grantees more than other partners. For the bulk of 1998, for example, the Inspector General tussled with other agency units over whether and how tightly results should be linked to funds spent in a specific fiscal year. One wonders whether the Inspector General's office should even be concerned with this issue when its central mandate is to scrutinize misuse of funds, and whether its concern reflects proper understanding of the long-term nature of development assistance. In any case, a dispute of this sort particularly threatens support for civil society organizations, whose results often take years to materialize.

Finally, but most fundamentally, excessive attention to financial reporting combines with inattention to substantive work to reveal to indigenous partners the worst face of USAID. The many dedicated people at the agency, given time and opportunity, could build productive partnerships with local groups. These groups' contact with USAID, however, is often confined to the auditor or accountant who views their operations with suspicion. A Bangladesh organization, for example, was put in the position of having to certify that its USAID-funded computers were not being used for projects the agency had not funded. In the words of one of the organization's leaders, such requirements "seem designed to catch us doing something wrong."

Some Possible Solutions

Maximum Engagement with Limited Control

Perhaps this chapter's most basic suggestion is that USAID field personnel become better acquainted with what they fund, while exercising less control over grantees' operations. Such engagement could help them put MFR data in context and greatly enhance their decisions about funding. In fact, USAID should consider adopting two across-the-board indicators for its civil society programs, to at least assess whether it is sufficiently reaching out beyond the confines of its field missions: 1) the amount of time its personnel devote to outside meetings and observation of grantees' activities, and 2) the time they devote to such meetings and observation in places other than the capital city.

On the other hand, once agency personnel reach funding decisions, they should refrain from interfering with grantees unless clear abuses occur. In theory, minimal interference is an aspect of USAID grants, as opposed to the much tighter control of contracts. In practice, some missions too often seek to substitute their relatively uninformed judgments for grantees' judgments. They are much likelier to constructively influence grantees and subgrantees by engaging with them in a well-informed but nondirective manner.

The Importance of Simplification

A bureaucratic snarl of procedures enmeshes agency operations, and the effect on civil society assistance is particularly severe. One place to start untangling is the project cycle. Flatly stated, the agency should drop the cycle. (All other funding organizations mentioned thus far, as well as the National Democratic Institute, the International Republican Institute, and the National Endowment for Democracy, survive without this cumbersome vehicle.) USAID missions could prepare annual reports of what they plan to do and have done, subject to approval from headquarters. But these can and should allow for plenty of flexibility in the funding. Would dropping the cycle engender congressional wrath? Working on the grand scale of the federal budget, Congress rarely focuses on a few million dollars spent to build up NGOs in a given country. Nor should it.

Another emphasis of administrative reform should be the ways in which USAID procures goods and services. A third could be an accounting system that attributes intermediary organizations' personnel expenses to programs, and therefore counts them as part of the real meat of development aid, but treats such personnel costs at USAID as part of the allegedly fatty excess of overhead.

Reducing Pressure from Congress

This chapter mainly has portrayed USAID's operating methods as an independent variable, a product of its institutional culture. Other forces, however, are at work, not least of which is Congress. Foreign aid's harshest critics in the House and Senate help create the conditions that undermine aid's effectiveness. USAID strives to avoid criticism from Congress (as well as from its own Inspector General, other executive agencies, and the press). It piles up protective procedures, and bureaucracy's triumph over common sense grows ever more dizzying. A balance needs to be struck. But particularly when it comes to civil society assistance, which demands considerable flexibility, one thing the agency's congressional critics could do that would most improve its work would be just to let it go about that work.

Political Society and Civil Society

While this chapter does not offer the Philippines as a model of democratic development, the influence of NGOs there on the making and implementation of policy is noteworthy. It raises questions about the relationship between political society (that is, political parties and attendant forces organized around electoral victory and political power) and civil society, and about democracy assistance strategies based on those relations.

One important factor in the Philippines (and to a lesser extent in India and other countries) has been the government's openness to input from civil society. To a degree, that openness stems from the appointment of NGO leaders to key posts; it also springs from the contacts those leaders had or cultivated in key agencies and Congress. In view of these connections, and since the NGOs' impact and the country's overall democratic progress have flowed in part from the relatively effective 1992–98 administration of President Fidel Ramos, should democracy assistance seek to link civil society and political society? Does the effectiveness of civil society interaction with democratic development hinge on such links? And does the partial return to more traditional politics under the current president, Joseph Estrada, mean that political society should take precedence over civil society as a focus of assistance in the country?

One could argue that if the current central problem with democratic development in the Philippines is the nature of politics there, a foreign assistance focus on the country's political parties is in order. But the Philippines, along with many other Asian nations, differ from Eastern European countries that possess both reformist and regressive (and even repressive) parties, so that assistance can be directed mainly at the former. Nor would increasing the Philippine parties' capacities across the board change their nature, largely patronage-driven and elite-controlled, impervious to foreign training or advice. A realistically modest and far more nuanced and effective approach would be to fund civil society forces that work with relatively progressive political and government personnel while pressuring or working around more traditional or corrupt officials. To varying degrees that nevertheless merit greater emphasis, USAID and other donors are taking this approach in the Philippines and elsewhere in Asia.

Beyond Advocacy and NGOs?

As is perhaps the case in other regions, advocacy-oriented NGOs have been a central focus in Asia of USAID's DG assistance for civil society development. Notable exceptions to this rule exist: work with a Muslim federation in Indonesia, with community-based women's groups in Nepal, with coalitions of NGOs and people's organizations in the Philippines. But even the last two examples feature advocacy, though they do not focus exclusively on NGO support. Should there be much more to the overall Asia civil society program, then, than advocacy and NGOs, or NGOs alone?

The above examples demonstrate that USAID support has reached organizations other than NGOs, from religious networks to the most basic community groups. What is more, funding an indigenous NGO does not mean that support is strictly confined to that NGO. Across Asia, USAID funds have benefited community-based groups, unions, and religious institutes that partner with NGOs.

Practical considerations also weigh in favor of continuing to channel significant support to and through indigenous NGOs. They may be far more capable of handling administrative, accounting, and reporting duties than community-based organizations. Is the central focus on advocacy advisable, however? Even given that indigenous NGOs often are the logical recipients of USAID support, might it be preferable to pro-mote civic education and inculcate democratic values, perhaps by work-ing with unconventional aid recipients such as social clubs and seeking to affect the attitudes of their members? Certainly the agency has sup-ported civic education efforts, particularly in connection with elections.

A few factors must be borne in mind. For one, development experi-ence indicates that people learn best when education focuses on specific issues of immediate interest to them. Groups of farmers concerned about land rights or women plagued by domestic violence may be more atten-tive and willing to act than social club members whose purpose is a good time. Second, even to the extent that it makes sense to reach out to new groups, the best vehicle for doing so may be NGOs with develop-ment training experience and a dedication to their work.

Finally, and perhaps unconventionally, long-term inculcation of demo-cratic values may prove most effective if it can be woven into commer-cial media, as the Asia Foundation and its local partners have started to do in Thailand. Commercial movies, music, television, and, particularly, radio may reach far larger populations in Asia far more effectively than public education campaigns. Whether and how commercial media could incorporate appropriate messages is an evolving art. Advocacy-oriented NGOs might be interested in exploring the terrain, and might craft the best strategies for discovery.

Conclusion: Banking on Civil Society

Civil societies, NGOs, and NGOs' donor partners are not going to be the saviors of "Big D" democracy in Asia. Whether it thrives, survives, fades, or crashes in a given country hinges only in part (at most) on civil soci-ety, and to an even smaller degree on democracy aid. By scaling back our expectations, to focus more on "small d" democracy and its nexus with development, we can scale up that aid's actual impact. That more realistic perspective also includes a realistic view of Asian NGO person-nel. Some are truly heroic; some are just in it for the money; some sacri-fice more lucrative careers in the private sector; and most occupy the same middle ground as many of us. They want to do good and have impact. But quite understandably and legitimately, they also care about job security and feeding their families.

With this realistic view of democracy assistance and civil society in mind, perhaps USAID and other donors can best see themselves as intellectual venture capitalists. By banking on civil society, they invest in the home-grown ideas of individuals and organizations most likely to blend dedication, innovation, and flexibility. Just as a private sector venture capitalist would not pour funds into enterprises that lack those qualities, donors should be cautious about large state institutions bound by large bureaucracies and powerful vested interests. Similarly, just as venture capital does not come with so many strings that it strangles the recipient, donors might be well advised to value grantee flexibility over rigidly designed projects. Banking on civil society comes with risks and inevitable failures. But so do all forms of foreign investment and even the most effective strategies for development.

Notes

1. Lori L. Heist with Jacqueline Pitanguy and Adrienne Germain, "Violence Against Women: The Hidden Health Burden," World Bank Discussion Paper no. 255 (Washington, D.C.: World Bank, 1994).

2. Karen L. Casper and Sultana Kamal, "Evaluation Report: Community Legal Services Conducted by Family Planning NGOs," report prepared for The Asia Foundation, Dhaka, March 1995.

3. Helen Hershkoff and David Hollander, "Rights into Action: Public Interest Litigation in the United States," in Mary McClymont and Stephen Golub, eds., *Many Roads to Justice: The Law Related Work of Ford Foundation Grantees Around the World* (New York: Ford Foundation, 2000), p. 118.

4. Robert S. Moog, *Whose Interests Are Supreme? Organizational Politics in the Civil Courts in India* (Ann Arbor: Association of Asian Studies, 1997).

5. The author evaluated CCTP in 1997.

6. Harry Blair and Gary Hansen, *Weighing in on the Scales of Justice: Strategic Approaches for Donor-Supported Rule of Law Programs*, USAID Development Program Operations and Assessment Report no. 7 (Washington, D.C.: USAID Center for Development Information and Evaluation, February 1994), p. 51.

7. Two of the main funding mechanisms USAID employs are grants, which are given to NGOs, and contracts, which the agency awards to for-profit consulting firms. The former ostensibly leaves the agency with less control of the project, the latter with more. A third mechanism, cooperative agreements, falls between these two poles in terms of USAID control.

6

New Visions and Strong Actions: Civil Society in the Philippines

Mary Racelis

IRONICALLY, CIVIL SOCIETY IN THE PHILIPPINES owes much of its flowering in the late twentieth century to the dictatorship of Ferdinand Marcos (1972–86). The fifteen years of arbitrary governance, crony protection, profligate living, and gross human rights violations, capped by economic collapse, heightened organized resistance to the repressive regime. In four momentous days in February 1986, Filipinos cried, "Enough!"

More than a million demonstrators spanning the entire range of civil society and disaffected business and military groups took to the streets in peaceful protests on EDSA (Epifanio de los Santos Avenue), adamant that Marcos, his family, and his cronies had to go. They camped out, sustained by food and drink donated by people from the neighborhood. They chanted their protests, sang, and prayed in the face of approaching tanks. They put flowers in the muzzles of guns, urged the tank corps to join them, and on the fourth day overthrew the regime when Marcos and his minions fled to Hawaii.[1] Across the nation, Filipinos celebrated People Power. EDSA united many countervailing forces in society—nongovernmental organizations, or NGOs, people's organizations, or POs (the Philippine equivalent of community-based organizations), religious groups, labor unions, professional associations, academics, media, business, a sprinkling of the Left, and ordinary citizens. For civil society, it was the culmination of a long struggle against an abusive, morally bankrupt leadership and the beginning of an era in which, it was believed, new leaders would champion human rights, freedom of thought and speech, and diversity, and would usher in good governance founded on bureaucratic efficiency, accountability, transparency, and popular participation. Economic growth with equity seemed a real alternative at last in a country where, by 1995, over half the population (54 percent) was living below the poverty line.[2]

Today, NGOs and the POs working as their partners are at the forefront of innovation and social change in the Philippines. Government and business recognize, sometimes grudgingly, the partners' power to mobilize the nation's poor and their remarkable ability to pressure government into reforming specific anti-poor policies and practices, especially at local levels. NGOs are in the forefront of reform efforts, but until they rouse large numbers of the poor themselves to demand nationwide reform and sustain those efforts, their work is far from done.

Indeed, their vitality has earned the country the reputation of "NGO paradise" or "NGO superpower."[3] Speaking at the U.S. Agency for International Development's (USAID) Partners Annual Conference in Roxas City in October 1999, Mission Director Patricia K. Buckles declared the Philippine NGO community one of the world's most vibrant and sophisticated. Before an audience of NGO leaders from Asian countries, she observed that "the amazingly rich and diverse experience of civil society organization in the Philippines now benefits not only Filipinos, but also people beyond the country's boundaries."

This chapter begins with an overview of civil society in the Philippines, paying attention to the roles NGOs and POs have played in promoting democracy. Because civil society's interaction with the state has depended on how the state was structured at the time, the account focuses on significant periods in that evolution. It traces the historical roots to Filipino welfare activities and protest in various forms during the Spanish and American colonial regimes and into the post-independence period. Next featured are civil society's coming of age in the crucible of Marcos's martial law regime and its increasing capacity and influence under the next three presidents—Corazon Aquino, Fidel Ramos, and the incumbent, Joseph Ejercito Estrada. Discussions of donor assistance to NGOs and more generally civil society and of its implications for development and democracy in the Philippines round out the chapter.

NGOs as Promoters of Democracy and Development

The years since EDSA have witnessed an explosion of civil society groups in the Philippines. From 27,100 NGOs registered as nonstock, nonprofit with the Philippines Securities and Exchange Commission in 1986, the number almost doubled to 50,800 by March 1992. That figure has increased to anywhere from 60,000 to over 95,000 NGOs today. However, only an estimated 5,000–7,000 of these are grassroots NGOs whose organizers focus on empowering poor and excluded people and who live and work with them to overcome poverty and powerlessness in rural, urban, and indigenous communities. The other registered NGOs center their activities around more middle-class interests, as in professional associations, church-related groups, welfare associations, student alliances, professional organizations, labor unions, academic institutions, and the like.

Formally registered POs number in the thousands, augmented by 35,000 registered cooperatives and a large but uncertain number of unregistered community groups.[4] Although the total figure for POs in the Philippines is difficult to estimate, one can confirm that their numbers are growing. The local as well as national influence of NGOs, and increasingly POs, is all the more remarkable when one considers their aim of transforming a society now estimated at over 75 million Filipinos. A 1998 nationwide survey revealed that no more than 15.9 percent of families listed themselves as affiliated with POs or NGOs, while another 12.9 percent cited membership in cooperatives. While these figures may appear small, in actual numbers NGOs and POs reached 2,384,943 families out of the 14,370,711 total for the entire country. Cooperatives covered 852,385 families.[5] This is no mean feat.

The exponential increase in the number of NGOs after the fall of Marcos stemmed from several factors. The determination of President Aquino to expand democratic space for civil society helped immeasurably, but significant too were the large sums of money earmarked for NGOs that foreign donors poured into the country.[6] These grants recognized the NGO roles in resisting the dictatorship, reestablishing a democratic society through grassroots organizing and advocacy efforts, and delivering services to poor people more honestly and efficiently than government had done. The expansion of democracy and the prospects of a better future for the country thus freed young people from having to go underground, which under the Marcos dictatorship had been the only viable option open to many. The Aquino era saw them now begin moving into government, private sector, or NGO work.

The five thousand empowerment or development NGOs typically organize poor people into people's organizations able to take conscious control of their lives and develop their communities through active participation in decisions affecting their lives. Such decisions are not limited to local matters, although these naturally dominate community concerns. As people come to understand the links between their situation and events in the national as well as international arenas, they begin systematically to engage government and business at those levels as well.

Empowerment or development NGOs embody dedication and a determination to bring justice, peace, and equity to poor people through organization and advocacy. Accordingly, NGOs constitute intermediary support organizations with salaried professional organizers and development workers, while POs represent voluntary membership associations. POs owe their existence in large measure to thousands of NGOs nationwide that have worked side by side with them. For nearly four decades NGO activists have helped poor and once-powerless communities recognize and demand their rights to assets, technology, credit, information, basic services, and improved livelihood skills. As POs master these challenges with enhanced competence and confidence, partner NGOs turn their attention to the more complex problems affecting the POs.

In recent years, both NGOs and POs have begun turning to other NGO groupings for their help in more specialized activities, like micro-finance enterprises, architecture for low-income families, educational scholarships, health care, farming technology, gender sensitization, vocational training, and instituting peace processes in warring areas. Other civil society groups find themselves being asked to respond to PO and NGO needs, including the media, research institutes, counseling groups, professional associations, and training departments of private business and universities.

By organizing thousands of POs, Philippine NGOs have promoted democracy where it counts most—in people's everyday lives as they are affected by community, national, and even global developments. The NGOs have enabled people largely excluded from the benefits of society to claim a meaningful share of the assets and resources. Because poor people soon learn that complex and long-term solutions require action beyond the boundaries of their community, NGOs have facilitated PO linkages with networks and federations around their primary concerns as well as in coalitions and alliances embracing different kinds of stakeholders. This enables POs and NGOs to engage directly with government and to a lesser extent the private sector as they promote their interests through advocacy, demand, negotiation, and (usually) peaceful protest.

Political scientists who question Philippine democracy because political power remains concentrated in relatively few hands nonetheless affirm that NGOs make the Philippines more democratic:

> It is true that NGOs have not succeeded in electing any sizable body of officials to provide genuine representation for ordinary Filipinos. . . . Notwithstanding, NGOs have increased the capacity of middle- and lower-class Filipinos to act autonomously; consequently, the state is less completely captive of elite interests than previously. Furthermore, NGOs are shaping the national political agenda through their participation in the public policy debate. As advocates [for poor groups] they bring pressure to bear on both decision makers and the agencies that implement government policy.[7]

Leaders of NGOs and POs have begun to win elections for local office or to accept government appointments and have used their new power to incorporate people-centered values into the political arena. Sobered by earlier failures in which they backed promising candidates from established parties who either lost the election or reneged on their promises after winning, some NGOs and POs have joined activist-academics and other civil society groups to form their own nontraditional political parties with explicitly pro-poor platforms. Others focus on the interests of society's basic sectors (peasant farmers, women, workers in the informal sector of the economy, members of cooperatives, urban poor, and so on). Still others have promoted progressive agendas that span a wide range of basic sector interests.

In 1998 several such progressive parties along with the basic sector parties took advantage of the new party-list system to enter candidates in the election for the House of Representatives. Although only a few made it to Congress, owing to confusion over the new voting procedures for which a lethargic Commission on Elections was partly to blame, the race became an important milestone in the drive to challenge and dislodge traditional patronage politics. Already, NGOs and their PO and progressive party allies are developing strategies for reforming the political system in the next election.

Historical Evolution of Civil Society

Civil Society in the Making: The Colonized Philippines, 1565–1946

Against a backdrop of centuries of native resistance to external threats, the dynamic Philippine civil society of today traces its organizational roots to nineteenth-century Spanish colonial welfare associations and Roman Catholic parish organizations.[8] These proto-NGOs, like their more sophisticated counterparts of the present day, envisioned an empowering of the marginalized; alongside quasi-religious peasant protests organized by secret anti-church organizations like the Masons, they helped Filipinos hone their resistance to authoritarianism.[9] Those educated in Spain brought back news of cooperatives and labor unions. They applied the liberal principles of the French and American revolutions in the planning of the Philippine Revolution of 1896–99. With the ceding of the Philippines to the United States in 1899 as spoils of the Spanish-American War, and with it the end of the short-lived Philippine Republic, Filipino revolutionaries felt cheated out of their hard-won claim to independence. Many refused to be "pacified" and fought until as late as 1907. The new American colonizers countered with carrot and stick tactics, using both military action and the introduction of American institutions and welfare organizations to bring Filipinos into the American fold.

The first NGOs appeared early on, many of them local versions of American or international associations, like the Philippine National Red Cross and, in the 1930s, women's suffrage groups. Private nonprofit organizations in the form of religious and academic institutions were recognized as foundations in the Philippine Corporation Law of 1906. Farmers organized the first Farmers Cooperative Marketing Association in 1926, and by 1939 the country had 160 with 5,000 farmer-members. Government-supported rural credit cooperatives could claim 105,000 members in 570 groups by 1939. Socialist peasant movements made significant inroads by the 1920s, and some transformed themselves two decades later, during the Japanese occupation, into the People's Army to Fight the Japanese, or *Hukbong Bayan Laban sa mga Hapon*. In addition to the Huks, thousands of Filipinos went underground in a massive guerrilla resistance movement against the Japanese.

Colonization under three foreign occupiers taught Filipinos many lessons. Resentment at oppressive treatment reinforced nationalist perspectives and encouraged them to organize against the authorities either in open conflict or employing devious tactics intended to undermine the enemy from below or within. At the same time, they readily adopted institutional arrangements that reinforced their own values, such as church-affiliated welfare groups run by women, or that gave them access to power or some kind of security, such as labor unions and religious brotherhoods for men. The separation of church and state and the expansion of public primary education and literacy in English in the early twentieth century fostered more secular concerns. These centered around basic education, vocational training, business capabilities, and administrative skills to staff the colonial bureaucracy.

Laying the Groundwork: Civil Society from the New Republic to Martial Law, 1946–72

Ravaged by World War II and the Japanese occupation, the newly independent Philippines struggled to get government functioning again. Welfare agencies at first focused on relief and reconstruction but, soon realizing the need for longer-term strategies, they began shifting from relief to welfare, then to rural development activities. The beginnings of NGO networking came with the creation in 1949 of the Council of Welfare Foundations of the Philippines. That umbrella organization catered to the needs of disadvantaged groups like children, destitute mothers, and disabled and older people and brought together the country's major welfare and civic organizations, such the Girl Scouts and Boy Scouts, Catholic Women's Clubs, and the Philippine National Red Cross. Soon after came family, corporate, and scientific foundations, encouraged by government tax exemptions.

The increasingly serious threat that peasant movements in the countryside posed to the government sparked the community development approach to rural poverty. The Philippine Rural Reconstruction Movement (PRRM), founded in 1952 by Y. C. James Yen after Chinese and Taiwanese models, furnished the model. Its slogan of "release not relief" and its mobilization of village communities for improved livelihood, health, education, and governance were adapted on a nationwide scale by a new government entity, the Presidential Assistant on Community Development (PACD). This group promoted the fourfold approach to rural improvement as the government's alternative to communism and was strongly supported by American foreign assistance.

To counteract the atheistic elements of communism while fostering social justice, and already espousing the orientation to this world reflected in the pronouncements of the Second Vatican Council two decades later, Jesuit priests as early as 1947 had organized the Institute of Social Order. This institute spawned the Federation of Free Workers and the Federation of Free Farmers, which established branches in many parts of the country. By the early 1960s, most Catholic parishes had formed credit unions and cooperatives in response to the call for social action. The Catholic Church formed its National Secretariat for Social Action (NASSA) in 1967 to serve as a clearinghouse and coordinating body for Catholic social involvement. Protestant Filipino ministers and lay leaders incorporated the World Council of Churches' strong concern for social justice into their activities.

As it became apparent that community development and economic self-help projects left untouched the structural roots of injustice and poverty and in themselves could not transform the lives of the rural poor, NASSA explicitly recognized this in 1969 by adding "Justice and Peace" to its name, with active support from the more progressive bishops. By that time, many priests, nuns, and lay church workers had embraced the progressive Catholic perspectives first popularized in Latin America—Paolo Freire's pedagogy of the oppressed and Gustavo Gutierrez' theology of liberation. Others went further by espousing more leftist Christian democratic ideas as the rationale for their work. In Mindanao, church-related activism expanded rapidly, with the assistance of the Jesuit and Maryknoll religious orders, which administered many of the island's parishes.

Basic Christian Communities, a major program of the Catholic Church that combined community organizing and action with religious precepts and spirituality, sprang up in parish after parish, serving as the training ground for thousands of men and women lay leaders. The Federation of Free Farmers, which grew in membership and efficacy, trained many of the peasant and NGO workers who are still recognized today as outstanding leaders. Church-supported producer cooperatives, rural community organizing, and radio stations and other media efforts to popularize social justice and social development issues also date back to the dynamic 1960s.

The last years of that decade saw the beginning of community organizing around broad-based power relations. Young Filipino trainees learned strategies and tactics from associates of Saul Alinsky, the American sociologist–community organizer who successfully mobilized poor people in neighborhoods around the Chicago stockyards to demand better living conditions and opportunities. Alinsky's *Rules for Radicals* became part of Filipino organizers' regular vocabulary, and his ten steps in organizing for power underlie demand-oriented people mobilization even today.

By the early 1970s, the Zone One Tondo Organization (ZOTO) in Manila, comprised of sixty neighborhood associations in the largest slum and squatter colony of Southeast Asia, was achieving significant victories through conflict-confrontation tactics vis-à-vis the government. In a series of cleverly planned actions, ordinary poor people learned to negotiate as equals with powerful figures. They forced recalcitrant officials, corporate managers, and conservative church leaders to concede to their demands, initially centering around simple issues like installing more public water taps in their area, supporting a community health center built and staffed by ZOTO, preventing the construction of warehouses on land already occupied by large numbers of poor families, and taking over the distribution of typhoon relief goods to ensure their reaching the neediest.

Underlying all negotiations with the government was the tenure issue. Community organizers mobilized Foreshore residents through ZOTO actions aimed at resisting relocation and demanding on-site upgrading, while those located on the sites of planned major roads insisted on nearby resettlement.

Over the next decade, most of these demands were met, with ZOTO instrumental in training its leaders and members in basic issue or empowerment organizing. Filipino organizers affiliated with the Philippine Ecumenical Council on Community Organization (PECCO) developed over time a distinctive Filipino-style community organizing that blended local culture, values, and social organization with the conceptual framework and methodologies of Alinsky, Paolo Freire, Gustavo Gutierrez, and Karl Marx. All this took place not in classrooms but right in the neighborhood, in the belief that learning occurred and attitudes of powerlessness changed through iterative action and reflection.

By the mid-1970s, issue-based organizing, despite and perhaps because of Marcos's martial law regime, had firmly entrenched itself in the Tondo Foreshore and had spread to several cities, towns, and villages in Luzon, Visayas, and Mindanao. PECCO's nonpolitical stance in terms of ideology stood in sharp contrast to the Marxist-Maoist ideology underpinning organizing under the auspices of the Communist Party's National Front under way at the same time.

Alarmed at the increasingly radical student and worker movements and encouraged by progressive religious and business leaders, the private sector too turned to social reform. The Philippine Business for Social Progress Foundation (PBSP), organized in 1971 and today the country's largest NGO, persuaded member corporations to pledge a modest percentage of their gross earnings to development programs that strengthened poor people's skills and capacities. Local corporate funds for the first time systematically extended credit for small-scale entrepreneurs and cooperatives, and trained the enterprising poor in organizational management and community development.

Like PRRM in its earlier stages, PBSP aimed at expanding people's capacities to gain access to and utilize resources more efficiently. In promoting more socially responsible business, it favored a model of development featuring cross-class collaboration and harmony rather than conflict-confrontation, and stopped short of challenging traditional power structures that reinforced poor people's dependent postures. At the same time, PBSP played a crucial role in conscientizing private sector groups to engage in upgrading the situation of the Filipino poor on a productivity-enhancing and social justice basis rather than through welfare approaches. These linkages between corporations and communities negotiated by PBSP certainly played an important role in sustaining later coalitions formed between NGOs and POs for the purpose of ousting President Marcos.

By the early 1970s, more and more student activists, urban workers, and peasant groups were taking to the streets in strong protest against continuing poverty in the countryside and urban slums, abusive landowners and armed private warlords, graft and corruption, electoral fraud, and political violence. Massive protest demonstrations were daily occurrences, their magnitude and intensity causing those critical years to be dubbed the First Quarter Storm.

In summary, from independence to the eve of the imposition of martial law, civil society groups grew increasingly disillusioned as they contemplated lagging development and continuing poverty, corruption, violence, greedy elites, and a deteriorating society. Gone was the hope that Filipinos in power, after nearly four hundred years of colonization, would relegate widespread poverty to a thing of the past. Elite power consolidated in business and political spheres now excluded millions of citizens from the benefits of a decent life in a free nation. The Philippine communist movement had been revitalized by Mao Zedong's successes in China, while the Muslim separatist movement in Mindanao was gaining ground. Freewheeling debate and confrontations with government reached fever pitch in 1972. In September, President Marcos declared martial law.

Confronting the Dictatorship: Civil Society under Marcos and Martial Law, 1972–86

The paralysis that greeted the proclamation of Marcos's New Society proved short-lived. Activists went underground in droves to join the armed struggle of the National Democratic Front (NDF). Others joined the radical Social Democrats, who supported a parliamentary struggle to promote Marxist-Maoist ideas mixed with Catholic social teachings. Still others opted for legal community organizing and social development, often under the aegis of progressive Catholic groups or Catholic college and university organizations concerned about social justice. The Catholic Bishops Conference and the Association of Major Religious Superiors championed human rights and set up institutions featuring grassroots action, which they saw as an aspect of the social obligations of all Catholics.

Courageous NGOs' wide-ranging legal organizing and insistence on human rights forced the expansion of the narrow political space allowed under Marcos's "constitutional authoritarianism." The president, ever conscious of his image, sought to maintain a façade of democracy. He hesitated to attack the church head-on, lest he goad it into open opposition. Besides, some conservative bishops seemed sympathetic to him, resisting the progressive stance of their brethren committed to social justice and activism while upholding the constitutional principle of separation of church and state. The National Council of Churches, encompassing the 5 percent of the population that was Protestant, proved similarly divided and prone to NDF infiltration of its social-development ranks.

As repression and corruption in the Marcos regime increased, citizens groups, including many middle-class business and civil society stalwarts, directed their energies to trying to make the 1978 elections work. Refusing to condone the sham electoral exercises Marcos had set up, they launched widespread educational campaigns. Ordinary citizens learned techniques for getting out the vote and monitoring the balloting. Government attempts to integrate the independent cooperative movement into a publicly organized institution were rebuffed, leading to the formation of an independent National Association of Training Centers of Cooperatives. But the power of the repressive Marcos machinery proved too great to reform the political system. With no viable opposition party in sight, the Marcos forces won again. Although martial law was ostensibly lifted in 1981, the ongoing denial of human rights spurred continuous organizing and protest. The ability of federations, alliances, and coalitions to sustain resistance enhanced horizontal and vertical solidarity as well as unsettling the regime. Solidarity gave people the courage to oppose large-scale government projects, such as the Chico River Dam, scheduled to flood upland tribal communities. The dramatic efforts of Cordillera indigenous women to fight off project engineers and loggers elicited widespread admiration and support from international environmental groups and advocates for indigenous people. The collective efforts of anti-dam coalitions and the pressures they placed on prospective international donors to withdraw support worked. The dam was never built.

International partnerships gained further impetus from United Nations conferences that reinforced the validity of NGO and civil society efforts in environmental protection, community-based resource management, people's participation, peasant organizations, and women's and children's rights among others. Singling out the progressive statements of the 1972 UN Conference on the Human Environment in Stockholm, Filipino environmental groups defended their community-level activities as essential for development. Community organizers working with peasants and urban poor men and women cited the affirmation of people's participation as crucial to development, seen in the documents of FAO, UNESCO, UNICEF, and the United Nations Development Program. Women's organizations found similar protection for their organizing activities with poor women. They could, after all, remind the authorities of the Philippine government's commitment to implementing such programs of action made at several UN women's conferences from 1975 to 1995. How then could this be "a Communist plot"? UNICEF's Child Survival and Development Revolution, launched in 1982, enabled enterprising Filipinos to seize every opportunity to mobilize around "safe" issues like children, all the while building up their capacity to confront and undermine a repressive regime. This firm base for aboveboard organizing was thus laid and reinforced under the repressive but credibility-seeking atmosphere of the Marcos era. Community organizers who struggled to remain in the realm of legal organizing developed all kinds of clever but often dangerous ways to throw the political and military hounds off their scent.

Meanwhile, in mountain hideouts and urban slums, the National Democrats were busy conducting clandestine teach-ins advocating Marxist-Maoist visions of society and the logic of armed struggle being undertaken by its military arm, the New People's Army (NPA). Although many articulate local leaders received this kind of training, they often faced difficulties sustaining community action once the public protest demonstrations they were taught to organize were over. The National Democrats frequently undermined their own strong appeal because of internal dissension over ideology and strategy and by carrying out often ruthless military-type actions, sometimes against their own members charged as traitors.

The 1983 assassination of opposition leader Benigno "Ninoy" Aquino, believed to have been engineered by Marcos and some of his military cronies, was the catalyst that united civil society groups in opposition to the regime. After Aquino's widow, Corazon, was clearly cheated of her victory in "snap" elections called by an overconfident Marcos, mass action bringing together virtually all citizen groups got under way. Civil disobedience in the form of a massive boycott of goods produced and enterprises owned by Marcos cronies, along with nonviolent demonstrations, became everyday events.[10]

In such a volatile situation, negotiating across interest and class lines to maintain a united front against the regime sorely tested civil society groups. Nonetheless, they stuck together in common cause. When in

February 1986 Cardinal Jaime Sin called on all Filipinos to defend military leaders who had turned against Marcos, over a million people responded by taking to the streets. People Power had begun its push. Only the National Democrats took a diverging path. Their decision to boycott the elections and minimize their involvement in EDSA was a tactical mistake that would haunt the Left for many years to come.

Civil society activists thus melded a heritage of resistance to arbitrary authority and a commitment to freedom and democracy with the dangerous, heady experience of organizing oppressed people under martial law. In due course, they linked up with aroused middle- and upper-class citizens to overthrow the regime and forge a strong civil society. The solidarity among Filipinos of all classes and political persuasions (except for the extreme Left) has kept three administrations keenly aware of their responsibility for protecting the country's hard-won democracy—and of their accountability to citizens in the matter.

Seizing the Democratic Space: Civil Society in the Aquino Administration, 1986–92

Popular President Corazon Aquino saw restoration of democracy to the Filipino people as her administration's first mandate. Despite six military coups d'état attempted during her administration, Aquino's commitment to human rights and the rule of law prevailed and gained her the avid support of the NGO community. Many NGO leaders joined her government. Political openness and the prevalence of liberal ideas during the Aquino administration gave the lie to Marcos's claim that "constitutional authoritarianism" was rooted in Philippine culture. In international human rights forums, Filipinos now disagreed vociferously with the contention of Singapore's Lee Kwan Yu and Malaysia's Mohamad Mahathir that human rights and democracy were Western concepts incompatible with "Asian values." Nearly fifteen years of dictatorship had convinced the people of the Philippines that "enlightened authoritarianism" was a despotism in disguise rather than a solution for Eastern countries' problems.

Although early admiration for Aquino faded within the NGO sector in the wake of her administration's ambivalence on agrarian reform, vulnerability to political destabilization, and lackluster efforts at economic recovery, her role in reestablishing a free and open society earned her a place in history as a true champion of democracy. Her insistence on stepping down after the six-year term limit mandated by the 1986 Freedom Constitution promulgated during her incumbency offered the ultimate proof of her democratic commitment.

That 1986 constitution also strengthened the democratic agenda and supported state-civil society interaction. The participation of many civil society members in the writing of the constitution resulted in mandated consultative processes that institutionalized the active participation of NGOs, POs, and, more broadly, civil society in governance and policy-making. The more prominent Articles read as follows:

(Art. II, Sec. 23) The State shall encourage non-governmental, community-based, or sectoral organizations that promote the welfare of the nation.

(Id., Art. XIII, Sec. 15) The State shall respect the role of independent people's organizations to enable the people to pursue and protect, within the democratic framework, their legitimate and collective interests and aspirations through peaceful and lawful means.

(Id., Art. XIII, Sec. 16) The right of the people and their organizations to effective and reasonable participation at all levels of social, political and economic decision-making shall not be abridged. The State shall, by law, facilitate the establishment of adequate consultation mechanisms.[11]

The Local Government Code of 1991 likewise placed a high value on NGOs' and POs' participation in governance, affirming their roles as active partners in the pursuit of local autonomy (Sec. 34), legitimizing joint ventures with government for basic services delivery, capability-building and livelihood projects, and other development activities in local communities (Sec. 35) for which the local government unit could provide financial and other assistance (Sec. 36). Mandated too were seats for NGOs and POs on local development councils and special bodies to monitor and improve government implementation.[12]

Similarly, the crafting and passage of the Comprehensive Agrarian Reform Law, the Urban Development and Housing Act, and the Women in Development and Nation Building Law owed much to the research and lobbying of NGOs and their partner POs. Many government departments with community outreach arms, such as Environment and Natural Resources, Agrarian Reform, and Health, established NGO liaison desks to foster interaction between government and NGOs and establish a registry of qualified partners. Those contact points served as mechanisms for joint planning and implementation, advocacy, and protest.

Meanwhile, leftist political groups underwent a different kind of transformation, set off not only by the state's unaccustomed openness and the legalization of the Communist Party but by international developments featuring the unraveling of the Soviet Union, cautious steps by China and Vietnam toward a market economy, and, more generally, the end of the Cold War. The National Democratic Front's split into several factions weakened it. The New People's Army, the military wing of the party, declined as members looked to the Aquino administration for new kinds of justice and meaningful socioeconomic development. With the government now actively seeking to redress the wrongs suffered by victims of martial law, the Catholic Church hierarchy also changed its position, retreating from its highly visible role as human rights champion to the more traditional one of spiritual guide.

As the Aquino administration ended, the achievements of NGOs centered around four breakthroughs.[13] First, the NGO movement established a basic unity and increased its effectiveness through *networking and coalition building*. Although grassroots work remained the core of their activities, NGOs poured energy into coordinating with other groups to achieve a more complex set of objectives. Noteworthy alliances appeared during this period, among them the Caucus of Development NGOs (CODE-NGO), currently the largest network of networks, encompassing more than three thousand NGOs.

The second breakthrough centered around NGO lobbying and *advocacy for policy reform and social legislation*. Numerous NGO research institutes were set up, mostly outside university settings but with academically qualified staff. They focused their research on the data and analysis NGOs and POs needed for advocacy and organizing.

A third accomplishment was the *professionalizing* of NGOs, making employment with them a legitimate career. More of them set administration and financial management on a sounder footing, built up staff skills through training programs, and committed themselves to adhering to a newly developed code of ethics. Computer and Internet use grew exponentially, greatly enhancing the effectiveness of advocacy and lobbying.

A fourth thrust established *sustainable human development as the vision uniting* NGOs. A fifth focused on NGOs' conviction that political authority had to be located closer to the grassroots for people to participate meaningfully in decision-making. This emphasis on *devolving power and finances* from the national capital to the provinces and municipalities in other regions of the country led NGOs in the late 1980s to lobby Congress for the enactment of the 1991 Local Government Code, which brought decision-making about resource allocations and development strategies closer to the people.

Consolidating the Gains: Civil Society in the Ramos Administration, 1992–98

NGOs' suspicions of a president who had been a key military leader under Marcos were somewhat allayed by Ramos's having turned against the dictator and by President Aquino's having anointed him as her successor. President Ramos's ambitious economic and social program sought "NIC-hood" (Newly Industrialized Country status) for the Philippines among the Asian "tiger economies." Looking to the future, "Philippines 2000" rested on economic growth and empowerment of people.

The NGO community's reaction mixed cautious approval and apprehension. Ramos's decisive resolution of the energy crisis early in his administration earned him accolades. This he achieved by contracting domestic and foreign corporations to supply power, by obtaining international loans to expand the capacity of existing power plants, and by accelerating the development of the country's ample geothermal energy sources. But many worried about his intention to turn large swaths of the country into regional growth areas that would in turn be linked to the economies of neighboring countries. Although foreign investment would create jobs, NGOs feared that forced evictions, tourism projects, and overzealous developers would displace large numbers of ordinary poor people. However, Ramos's determination to bring about a settlement in Mindanao, torn by a Muslim secessionist movement, encouraged NGOs to join confidence-building mechanisms bringing government and civil society together. NGOs also supported his moves to bring the remaining New People's Army rebel holdouts peacefully into the national mainstream.

NGOs collaborated actively but cautiously with government social-forestry and community-based resource management programs, getting POs and themselves into unaccustomed contracts with the Department of Environment and Natural Resources for tree planting and forest rehabilitation. More and more NGOs focused on pushing local government units to rethink budgets and operations to benefit poor people and the environment. POs began merging their planning sessions with legally mandated *barangay* (village or urban neighborhood government administrative unit) development planning, and even began to run for *barangay* positions.

Engagement with government was often contentious. Local government officials complained that NGOs had limited technical skills and little understanding of government procedures; yet, with characteristic arrogance, they continued to make excessive, self-serving demands. NGOs, on the other hand, railed against local bureaucracy, unconscionable delays in the payout of contract funds and delivery of services, and ill-informed, corrupt, uncaring local officials. At the same time, where government and NGOs worked well together, the positive results for poor people were clear.

NGOs operating at the local level have often found themselves in direct confrontations with local elites who, understandably, feel threatened when NGO and PO members build alliances, muster funds and other resources for use by local people outside the control of traditional patrons, and gain the moral high ground in the process. As political scientist Joel Rocamora said, "It is precisely the 'value added' of national NGOs and POs in terms of new ideas, training, financial and other resources, and [their] capacity to mobilize national contacts in the bureaucracy and other NGOs that creates the possibility of a shift in local relations of power."[14]

That conclusion was reinforced by a study of four municipalities showing that people's organizations, with support from NGOs and progressive government officials, have moved from their traditional dependency on elite families and socioeconomic self-help projects to more sophisticated strategies for attaining their objectives in the political arena. Fused political and socioeconomic democracy initiatives have yielded successes, among them significant land transfers to peasants; sugar sharecroppers' victory in lawsuits demanding a greater share of the profits of their work; coalitions stopping or delaying logging and geothermal power projects controlled by elites; and PO members' election to local government posts.[15]

With NGOs pressing hard for accountability, President Ramos agreed to the Social Reform Agenda as his response to institutionalizing the participation of organized poor groups in national policy development. Together with national and local government officials and representatives of NGOs and POs from all regions of the country, Ramos attended a series of basic sector summits. NGOs, conscious as always of the need to avoid cooptation and maintain their stance of critical collaboration or critical engagement, organized networks of POs across the country to identify the key problems they faced and to suggest solutions. The government in turn ordered departments to identify programs that would specifically address those problems.

The massive mobilization POs and NGOs undertook to hold the government to its promises proved an important learning experience for all. Representative groups of small farmers, urban poor, indigenous people, women, and others planned their presentations, articulated their views, hammered out agreements, honed leadership skills, and interacted directly with top officials including the president. Although it ended in disillusionment, since no new money went to basic-sector programs, the process brought POs and NGOs into new kinds of collaboration and networking with each other and with government.

The strengthened networks helped solidify NGOs' support for their coalition partners that were addressing broader national and international issues. The Asia-Pacific Economic Cooperation forum (APEC) was barraged with criticism from NGOs objecting to trade liberalization and the short time interval before its implementation; the ignoring of concerns relating to environment, equity, and social justice; and the failure to hold a parallel NGO session as part of the APEC process. The negative effect of globalization on indigenous peoples' rights over their ancestral domain, food security, and agricultural policy also dominated NGO criticism of APEC. Moreover, on the domestic scene, President Ramos had attempted to engineer a change in the Constitution that would eliminate the single six-year term limit, allegedly so that he could run again. NGOs forcefully opposed the "Cha-Cha," or charter change initiative, in a series of activities culminating in an massive protest march and demonstration reminiscent of EDSA days. The president backed down.

Two knowledgeable observers of the Philippine scene toward the end of the Ramos administration have characterized NGO contributions along three lines.[16] First is the *vibrant public discourse,* both within NGO circles, as divergent opinions are fashioned into some kind of workable consensus, and outside them, when the NGO community must make its views heard and get them adopted by often reluctant partners. Second, NGOs are attempting to *redefine the content of politics.* Topics that would once have been deemed inappropriate for legislation—rape, other violence against women, the rights of indigenous people—have now become subjects of debate and successful parliamentary legislation. Third, civil society is becoming *progressively institutionalized.* Coalitions are structured for greater permanence, while NGOs learn good management and financial practices and professionalize their staff.

Ensuring Accountability to the Poor: Civil Society in the Estrada Administration, 1998–

With the accession to the presidency of Joseph Ejercito Estrada, whose campaign emphasized his commitment to the poor and whose starring roles in films had established his image as a defender of the millions living in poverty, many in the NGO community looked forward to an era in which the principle of equity just might be as central to governance as it was to their own work. Several key figures from NGOs, in fact, had campaigned for "Erap," as Estrada was popularly called, under the slogan "Erap *para sa mahirap,*" or "Erap for the poor."

The appointment of two NGO leaders to cabinet posts as Presidential Assistant on Housing and Secretary of Agrarian Reform gained the administration more support from NGOs. Both departments soon began planning systemic changes that might well have changed the lot of the poor if the administration had backed them. NGOs soon realized, however, that high office was not enough. Although they supported their government friends—and frequently argued with them about what the government should do—the former NGO leaders were dismayed to discover that as government officials they frequently had to make unpopular compromises to retain their power. After angry developers and other disaffected interest groups got the president's ear and forced the resignation of the Presidential Assistant on Housing, any remaining regard for the administration among NGOs virtually evaporated.

At the same time, in some national bureaucracies as well as at the local level, many positive government-NGO partnerships are flourishing and expanding. NGOs and POs find that local government units, being closer to the community level, have a greater interest in improving the lives of constituents, or at least are near enough to the community that organized local groups representing the poor can lobby them and get results.

Disaffection with the Estrada administration set in soon after his inauguration in June 1998. The new president alienated many almost immediately with his support of the Marcos family's request to give a hero's burial to the dictator, who had died in Honolulu in 1989. Yet Marcos's embalmed body, said to be sheathed in wax, still lies on display in an air-conditioned crypt in his Northern Luzon hometown, evidence of the family's insistence on his formal interment in the National Heroes Cemetery in Metro Manila. Civil society coalitions spanning all social classes rallied long and vociferously against President Estrada's position, which they interpreted as a travesty of justice and an insult to the millions who had suffered, died, and disappeared during Marcos's regime. President Estrada eventually backed down, and the impasse continues.

Again in August 1999, President Estrada had to reckon with thousands of peaceful demonstrators, members of NGOs and POs among them, who had been called to defend democracy by former President Aquino, Cardinal Jaime Sin, and civil society leaders. The demonstrators protested the president's argument that foreign investment in the Philippines would accelerate if foreigners were given the opportunity to own land; they also charged that the real purpose behind his Constitutional Correction for Development (CONCORD) was to eliminate term limits on reelection so that current officials, himself included, could perpetuate themselves in office. It was Cha-Cha all over again. Demonstrations in cities and towns across the country also protested against cronyism, inept governance, the drift of the economy, and corruption. Another accusation was that the government was undermining press freedom through an advertising boycott of the *Philippine Daily Inquirer* allegedly initiated at the presidential headquarters in Malacañang. The *Daily Inquirer*, the nation's best-selling newspaper, just happened to be the Estrada administration's strongest media critic.

Stories of cronyism and corruption among influential relatives, friends, and political supporters, disturbing reports of a hard-drinking, influential "midnight cabinet," and allegations about Estrada's personal morality began to circulate through Manila's rumor mills. Erap jokes were now being widely passed from one cellular telephone to another and widely disseminated in email networks reaching Filipinos all over the world. The image of the president as inept and unable to govern effectively became a common topic of discussion anywhere people congregated and in the broadcast and print media.

But the most serious charge that NGOs and POs leveled in late 1999 against President Estrada was that he had betrayed his agenda to help the poor. Little concrete evidence was emerging of antipoverty programs able to reach large numbers of disadvantaged and marginalized people. The National Antipoverty Commission's report on the hundred poorest families in every province and city was discredited by NGOs, POs, and business groups for its tokenism and vulnerability to political favoritism rather than socioeconomic criteria. They further decried the president's apparent lack of interest in encouraging government-NGO-PO partnerships for poverty reduction, and they deplored his tendency to interpret criticism as evidence of plots against his administration. Where, they asked, was the openness to genuine dialogue and constructive engagement implied in the Constitution?

In late 1999, NGOs and POs hoped the message conveyed by Estrada's dramatic 44 percentage point drop in opinion polls would refocus his attention on the agenda for the poor and on improved governance to get it moving. Unfortunately, national and *Metro Manila* polling surveys in January and February 2000 revealed that his net satisfaction rating (the difference between those who approve of his performance and those who disapprove) has plummeted further from minus-9 percent in January to minus-13 percent in February. This disaffection apparently covers all social classes.[17]

By April 2000, public debate centered around the best ways of bringing about the president's departure. The preferred option saw a constitutional process resulting in his resignation or impeachment, followed by assumption of the position by Vice President Gloria Macapagal Arroyo. The scenario most feared by civil society and business, however, was a coup d'état. That alternative would bring back hated military rule, further destabilize trade and investments in an already lackluster economy, and lead to heightened military violence against NPA rebels and civilians. Gone would be the hard-won democracy of the past fourteen years, and NGOs / POs would once more have to mount a supreme effort to nurture the remains of a free society.

Assistance to Civil Society

The prominence NGOs enjoy nationally and locally stems from their success in performing several useful functions. They organize deprived community groups to have a greater say in their lives, improve poor people's economic and social well-being, engage in effective networking, advocacy, and lobbying, and devise innovative ways to reorient institutions or create new ones to serve marginalized groups better. They link up with global alliances and coalitions, promote more equitable and sustainable development, and raise substantial funds for NGO and PO work.

In 1991 alone, their ability to tap donor funding yielded an estimated $102 million, or 7.2 percent of official development assistance, channeled directly to NGOs by foreign donors.[18] From 1980 to 1997, USAID alone allocated $54.6 million in 209 grants or contracts to Philippine NGOs and U.S. private voluntary organizations working in the Philippines. The Agency's Co-Financing Program (Co-Fi), developed along contract lines, required a funding counterpart of at least 25 percent from the recipient NGO. Contractee NGOs generated $26.4 million in cash or kind, an amount well above the 25 percent stipulated minimum for the $54.6 million.[19]

Foreign donors to Philippine NGOs and POs all have their own mandates and specific interests. Donors include countries sending official development assistance to NGOs and private foundations, church organizations, political party foundations, and multilateral agencies, as well as international foundations and NGOs.[20] Given the diversity of the donors and the complex history and activities of Philippine NGOs, one would be hard-pressed to separate assistance that directly aims at promoting democracy from assistance that does so indirectly. Democracy promotion and promotion of economic development are blended together in the activities of Philippine NGOs.

The NGOs that promoted human rights under the Marcos regime later were clearly promoting democracy directly. But NGOs engaged in a mix of activities featuring socioeconomic approaches and community organizing for political empowerment are also promoting democracy. NGOs that carry out mixed programs—and they are the more prominent ones—argue that without political awareness of one's rights relating to social and economic resources in a highly unequal power relationship, and with disadvantaged groups often lacking the determination and knowledge to make successful claims on those resources or to manage them if they get them, people will never experience the full benefits of democracy, directly or indirectly.

Conversely, when NGOs push for good governance, many do so in hopes of enabling POs to pressure local officials into rethinking their distribution of socioeconomic benefits to focus on the poor. "Much of the NGO agenda," assert G. Sidney Silliman and Lela Garner Noble, "is indirectly political, aimed at changing socioeconomic conditions so as to empower ordinary Filipinos."[21] It may be possible to separate the political democracy-promoting elements from the socioeconomic considerations in an industrial country or a dictatorship. But in countries with a modicum of democracy and a highly skewed income distribution that has left large numbers of people poor and powerless, the one is necessarily part of the other.

USAID in the Philippines distinguishes between the work of NGOs engaged in democracy-through-governance and those engaged in democracy-through-development. The latter approach is defined as the strengthening of civil society through socioeconomic activities and community organizing (in the sense of community development). Even the offices are separate, with the Office for Governance and Participation (OGP) handling the former and the Office for Voluntary Cooperation (OVC) the latter.

In 1995, recognizing that "there are issues that cannot be singularly addressed by locally rooted solutions," USAID sought to "open up new arenas for genuine participation in the public policy process by disadvantaged groups with underrepresented interests." The civil society Co-Fi program of the Office for Voluntary Cooperation complemented the governance efforts of the Office for Governance and Participation by supporting coalition-building programs among basic-sector groups like fisherfolk, the urban poor, indigenous people, women and children working in the informal sector, coconut farmers, and microfinance groups. The coalition program will be coming to an end in 2000. OVC's mandate here was to assist groups "that remain marginalized or fall outside the context of the Local Government Code."[22]

USAID officials, however, say the mission devotes less attention to the distinction between NGOs promoting democracy-for-governance and those promoting democracy-for-development than it does to the one between NGOs with a direct-action focus and those with a policy focus. USAID supports both. By strengthening policy-oriented NGOs organized to do research, USAID tries to legitimize NGO participation in policy discussions through their contribution of research-backed data.[23] Moreover, since Philippine NGOs, unlike their U.S. counterparts, can legally engage in political lobbying without jeopardizing their tax-exempt status, USAID need not shy away from supporting the more politically engaged NGOs. All this serves to blur the distinction between democracy promotion and development promotion.

Sustaining Democracy

Although Philippine NGOs are well aware that a democratic framework supports their activities—whether political, economic, or social—they do not consciously think of those activities as "building democracy." That phrasing has a middle-class ring uncommon in NGO and PO parlance. Rather, NGOs speak of empowering people to bring about changes in society that lead to sustainable human development. That in turn implies a society characterized by justice, equitable distribution of resources, environmental soundness, and the participation of currently marginalized groups in decisions affecting them, their communities, and their country. As one Filipino scholar puts it, the main barriers to the affirmation of democracy are a dependency-creating poverty, hierarchical social relations, excessive attention to family ties to the detriment of other relationships, a weak sense of the public good, and the limited discourse in the vernacular on democracy and its meaning.[24]

When and where do development NGOs indirectly promoting democracy become political NGOs directly promoting democracy? One would be hard-pressed to maintain that distinction meaningfully in the Philippines. All indeed work for democracy. But having their organizations categorized as "democracy-building NGOs" (or not) comes uncomfortably close for those involved in those NGOs to the American view of democracy, with its emphasis on elections, voter education, and political parties. Philippine NGOs, on the other hand, equate democracy with overcoming poverty and powerlessness, challenging elite structures of power locally, nationally, and internationally by organizing for more equitable distribution of assets and basic services, social inclusion of disadvantaged groups, participatory processes, and sustainable human development. Commitment to those transformational changes, more than the valued but tangential USAID distinctions around democracy, is what motivates NGOs to do what they do.

To NGOs' way of thinking, the ideal relationship with a donor is one of partnership. That implies a basic agreement on principles of development. NGOs insist that development be rooted in people and the promotion of solidarity around a shared vision for the future. They give top priority to reducing poverty and its impact on vulnerable groups through direct socioeconomic and empowerment interventions, institutional reform, and diminishing the negative aspects of globalization. Donors should "decisively support programs that aim to address the structural barriers to development, avoiding piecemeal palliative programs that do not address the roots of underdevelopment nor the lack of genuine democracy."[25]

NGOs recognize that donors have priorities, but they see those ideally as dovetailing with their own. Usually there is an incipient fit in that an NGO contacts funding partners it believes will be predisposed to supporting its strategy and activities. Donors do the same. Nonetheless, concerns over "donor-driven" programs, the continuing dependence on external grants, and possible loss of autonomy continue to dominate the NGO debate in the Philippines. Rocamora and Aldata comment on these distortions:

> While the funds facilitate significant enlargement of NGO activities, they have also distorted the pace and process of NGO development. NGOs have to devote more time to building their absorptive capacities (sometimes leading to bureaucratic structures); competition over funds has affected NGO to NGO relations; larger NGO budgets have eroded the voluntary nature and "social change" orientation of NGOs.[26]

These concerns, together with the mid-1990s shift in donor priorities to Eastern Europe and other new areas, have triggered a serious reexamination by NGOs of their future without assured funding. One outlook that focuses on autonomy and efficiency issues has encouraged NGOs to form coalitions that negotiate with donor governments or foreign NGOs the turning over of official development assistance or development funds to a local NGO-funding organization created for that purpose or already in existence. Money for activities of Philippine civil society has been channeled in this manner from Australia, Canada, Germany, the Netherlands, Switzerland, the United States, and the World Bank. But even here, NGOs guard against donor tendencies to impose on grantee-partners their own visions of development, sometimes under cover of ensuring sound financial controls.[27]

Other NGO funding initiatives look inward. Organizations have considered and taken up sales of products and publications, fees for services or use of premises, cross-subsidies derived from higher charges to better-off customers for reinvestment in grassroots programs, fundraising events like raffles and dances, contributions from church supporters, government contracts, appeals to local philanthropy, and cost-cutting through streamlining of operations. Several NGOs anticipate setting up endowments after they are accredited by the Philippine Council for NGO Certification, a government-approved institution managed by NGOs. Still others are relying on fostering local government's allocations to POs, making it less necessary for NGOs to search for money to cover POs' needs.

The leaders and staff of NGOs know they need to be accountable not only to the people with whom they work in development and empowerment partnerships but also to those who provide resources and funds for the work. They are constantly seeking to act "between the principled and the pragmatic, between reform and revolution, between honesty and hope."[28]

More than four hundred years of Spanish, American, and Japanese colonization and over fifty years as a republic, fifteen of them under a dictatorship, have made many Filipinos zealous supporters of nationalism and democracy. But the great divide between rich and poor in the country, and the violation of political, economic, and social rights embedded in that distorted social order, calls for political mobilization around the unjust distribution of socioeconomic resources and power as well as around assistance to the poor that would enable them to manage those resources. Philippine NGOs continue to chart a path that confronts inequity and injustice. They invite their partners, domestic and international, to walk with them, so that together they can enter the new millennium with renewed hope and excitement at the challenges ahead.

Notes

1. Angela Stuart Santiago, "Chronology of a Revolution, 1986," in Lorna Kalaw-Tirol, ed., *Duet for EDSA* (Manila: Foundation for Worldwide People Power, Inc., 1995), pp. 15–147.

2. Arsenio M. Balisacan, *Poverty, Urbanization and Development Policy: A Philippine Perspective* (Quezon City: University of the Philippines Press, 1994), p. 26, table 2.4.

3. Paulynn Paredes Sicam, "RP as NGO Superpower," *Manila Times*, February 13, 1999, p. A6.

4. Alan de Guzman Alegre, *Civil Society Resource Organizations and Development in Southeast Asia: Philippines Country Report* (Boston: Synergos Institute, 1999).

5. Michael M. Alba, "Exploring the APIS [Annual Poverty Indicators Survey] Data on the Accessibility of Public Services. A study sponsored by the World Bank," manuscript, Manila, De La Salle University, 2000, p. 16, table 6.1.

6. G. Sidney Silliman, "Transnational Relations of NGOs," in Silliman and Lela Garner Noble, eds., *Organizing for Democracy: NGOs, Civil Society and the Philippine State* (Quezon City: Ateneo de Manila University Press, 1998), pp. 10–11.

7. Silliman and Noble, "Citizen Movements and Philippine Democracy," in *Organizing for Democracy*, p. 306.

8. Much of the following discussion is drawn from Alegre, "The Rise of Philippine NGOs as Social Movement: A Preliminary Historical Sketch, 1965–1995," in Alegre, ed., *Trends and Traditions: Challenges and Choice* (Quezon City: Ateneo Center for Social Policy and Philippines-Canada Human Resource Development Program, 1996), pp. 2–48.

9. Karina Constantino David, "History of NGOs in the Philippines," paper prepared for the Successor Generation Workshop, Caucus of Development NGOs (CODE-NGO) and Community Organizers Multiversity, Quezon City, September 1999.

10. Ibid., p. 11.

11. Marlon A. Wui and Ma Glenda S. Lopez, *State–Civil Society Relations in Policy-Making* (Quezon City: University of the Philippines Third World Studies Center, 1997), p. 3.

12. Ibid., pp. 3–4.

13. Alegre, "The Rise of Philippine NGOs as Social Movement," pp. 27–32.

14. Quoted in Terrence R. George, "Local Governance: People Power in the Provinces?" in *Organizing for Democracy,* pp. 223–53.

15. Ibid., p. 246.

16. Silliman and Noble, introduction to *Organizing for Democracy,* pp. 10–11.

17. Armando Doronila, "Analysis," *Philippine Daily Inquirer,* March 31, 2000, p. 9.

18. Silliman, "Transnational Relations of NGOs," in *Organizing for Democracy,* p. 65.

19. Lynne Cripe and Gregory Perrier, "Evolution of a PVO Co-Financing Program: Lessons Learned at USAID/Philippines" (Office of Private Voluntary Cooperation, Bureau for Humanitarian Response, USAID/Philippines, May 1997), ch. 21, pp. 2–3.

20. Katrina A. Lopa Consuelo and Karel S. San Juan, "NGO Relations with Donor Agencies," in *Trends and Traditions,* p. 129.

21. Silliman and Noble, "Citizen Movements and Philippine Democracy," in *Organizing for Democracy,* p. 307.

22. Cripe and Perrier, "Evolution of a PVO Co-Financing Program," pp. 4–5.

23. USAID officials, author interviews, Manila, June 23, 1999.

24. Fernando N. Zialcita, "Barriers and Bridges to a Democratic Culture," in Maria Serena I. Dioko, ed., *Democracy and Citizenship in Filipino Political Culture: Philippine Democracy Agenda,* vol. 1 (Quezon City: Third World Studies Center, 1997).

25. Eugene M. Gonzales, Consuelo, and Alegre, in *Trends and Traditions,* p. 185.

26. Joel Rocamora and Fernando Aldaba, introduction to *Resource Manual on NGO-Managed Fund Mechanisms* (Quezon City: Caucus of Development NGO Networks and Transnational Institute, 1997), p. i.

27. Caucus of Development NGO Networks (CODE-NGO), Association of Foundations (AF), and Philippines-Canada Joint Committee for Human Resource Development (PCHRD), *NGOs in a New Arena: Initial Reflections on Managing Fund Mechanism for Development* (Quezon City: CODE-NGO, AF, and PCHRD, 1997), p. 85.

28. San Juan and Alegre, "Summary and Conclusion," in *Trends and Traditions,* pp. 207–10.

Part Four

Eastern Europe

7

Lofty Goals, Modest Results:
Assisting Civil Society in Eastern Europe

Kevin F. F. Quigley

DURING THE 1990S, the United States and many countries in Western Europe gave aid to promote the development of civil society in Eastern Europe, as part of the broader Western effort to facilitate transitions to democracy in the region. These efforts to assist civil society in Eastern Europe fell far short of their lofty goals, for reasons having to do with donors' and recipients' assumptions, the aid programs themselves and the settings in which they operated, and the institutions assisted. Western European and North American donors harbored different assumptions about civil society and its relationship to democracy than did the Eastern Europeans they were attempting to assist. Donors also had unrealistically high expectations for their aid, even considering that many overstated what they could deliver.

The aid programs for civil society had to keep their balance in the midst of a rapid double transition in the societies around them—away from a communist monopoly on power and centrally planned economy and toward a democratic polity and market-oriented economy. Making program design and implementation even tougher, the countries of Eastern Europe had had divergent experiences with civil society and possessed varying human resources on which to build a civil society. And finally, donors complicated the job of those implementing the programs with dramatic shifts in the geographical areas and institutions they targeted, as well as in the substance of the programs.

As for targeted institutions, most of the international community's money and efforts have gone into establishing market economies rather than building civil society. The assistance began in Central Europe. Gradually, as political openings took place in neighboring countries, aid flowed north to the Baltics, south to the Balkans, and east to Russia and Ukraine. From 1989 to 1996, 90 percent of the approximately $108 billion the international community provided was intended to help free markets develop, primarily by encouraging stabilization, liberalization, and privatization of the economy. As economic reform took hold and most East European countries made progress in privatizing and consequently experienced modest growth, aid programs gave greater attention to democracy. The remaining 10 percent of assistance supported democratic development, broadly defined. Despite the high-flown rhetoric, the merest fraction of Western aid overall—probably no more than 1 percent—went to civil society.[1]

Aside from the modest amounts spent on them, one reason civil society programs have produced limited results is that donors generally have allocated funds only for short periods. In Estonia and the Czech Republic, most aid programs were phased out by the mid-1990s because of those countries' perceived economic success. Both public donors such as the U.S. Agency for International Development (USAID) and private donors including various foundations shifted their programs to other countries or terminated them.[2] If, as it was broadly understood, civil society takes at least a generation to build, programs operating a mere five or six years were unlikely to significantly affect civil society or democracy.[3]

Another problem with the programs in Eastern Europe was that aid officials did little to adapt them to local circumstances.[4] Although political and economic conditions were generally similar throughout the region, each country presented different opportunities and dilemmas for civil society and democratic development.

Moreover, the international community changed its mind several times about institutional partners. At first, donors worked closely with national governments to strengthen democratic institutions such as parliaments and judiciaries, as well as striving to bolster procedures for free and fair elections. Later, they de-emphasized work with national governments, teamed up increasingly with regional and local governments, and sought new partners in civil society. Key to their strategy for civil society was partnership with nongovernmental organizations (NGOs). But since donors never decided what kind of NGO sector, made up of what kinds of NGOs in what quantities, would be most beneficial in strengthening civil society and building democracy, identifying the appropriate local partner was sometimes difficult.[5]

Efforts to assist civil society in Eastern Europe have been under way at least a decade, and now is a natural juncture to look at what they have accomplished and how they might be improved. Such an assessment must begin by noting that the state of civil society varies widely within the region. The range of projects implemented, countries and institutions aided, and donors and agendas at work makes for a busy canvas. In Central Europe, civil society has progressed relatively well, though the rate and extent of development vary. In the Czech Republic, Hungary, and Poland, for example, a relatively healthy civil sector mediates effectively between the state and its citizens.[6] In Slovakia, however, civil society did not fare as well until recently because of opposition from then-prime minister Vladimir Meciar's government. In southeastern Europe, for instance in Romania and Bulgaria, civil society is less robust. In Serbia and Kosovo, and at least until recently in Croatia, civil society is threatened or under siege. An assessment is especially timely now, when donors are working with NGOs all around the world as an approach to strengthening civil society and searching for programs with greater impact.

This chapter examines how differences in mindsets and changes in program emphasis and targeted institutions have hurt civil society assistance efforts in Eastern Europe. It focuses primarily on Central Europe, since that region received the greatest attention and aid. The chapter begins with a discussion of premises about the relationship among NGOs, civil society, and democracy.[7] It then considers attempts by public and private donors, including Europeans and North Americans, to support NGOs and thereby strengthen civil society. It concentrates on the democracy programs of USAID, especially the Democracy Network Program (DemNet), and on the Civil Society Development Program, part of the European Union's overall aid to the region organized as the PHARE program. Some generalizations about these programs and their effectiveness follow. Crucial questions for any assessment are to what extent civil society assistance programs have affected the development of civil society and which programs were especially effective in which contexts. After discussing the overall impact of work with NGOs to strengthen civil society, the chapter concludes with ideas for improving civil society assistance programs.

Two Mindsets

When a group of people with one set of ideas about problems and solutions attempts to help a group of people with a very different set, the differences between the two mindsets often impede progress. Eastern Europeans, because of their history, viewed civil society and its relationship to democracy quite differently from donors in Western Europe and the United States. Subtle but important differences on these issues also divided Western Europeans and Americans.

For Eastern Europeans, the fall of the Berlin Wall in 1989 and the subsequent collapse of communism engendered dreams of rejuvenating society in the region. After more than forty years of socialism, during which government had exercised a virtual monopoly over economic, social, and political life, Eastern Europeans believed they had a unique opportunity to construct political and economic systems that offered more choice and was more responsive to citizens' concerns.[8]

Movements such as Solidarity in Poland, Sajudis in Lithuania, and Civic Forum in Czechoslovakia, which had widespread popular support and were instrumental in sparking fundamental political change, convinced Eastern Europeans that building civil society was vital for their new democracies. Solidarity counted ten million members, more than a quarter of the population of Poland. In 1989, Sajudis was a leading organizer of one of the most moving demonstrations in history, in which people formed a human chain across the Baltic republics that could be seen from space. Later that same year, Civic Forum orchestrated Czechoslovakia's Velvet Revolution, a peaceful transfer of power by one of the region's most repressive regimes.

Eastern Europeans and their supporters mistakenly assumed that the mass movements could readily be transformed into effective, representative political parties and civil society, a rich set of institutions and associations mediating between citizens and government. They dreamed of civil society replacing the highly coercive and atomized politics of the communist era with a politics of choice and opportunity. Unfortunately, as a freer political life opened, each of these mass movements became factionalized and highly politicized. Colleagues at the barricades became embittered political foes. Competing visions and approaches splintered the movements' unity. This stalled Eastern Europeans' hopes for a new society rich in associational life characterized by a more humane politics.

Nor had Eastern Europeans defined what they meant by civil society or thought much about the role of NGOs in it. In the late 1980s and early 1990s, they were too busy doing away with the old to articulate what institutional arrangements and processes they wanted to end up with, other than that these would be market-oriented and democratic. Because of civil society's strong association with movements like Solidarity, Sajudis, and Civic Forum, people saw it in a highly positive light, as a collection of organizations operating outside government to protect citizens' interests. They did not spend much time thinking about NGOs per se.

U.S. donors, on the other hand, tended to view civil society as a generalized "good," and their aid reflected that. U.S. programs intended to assist civil society in Eastern Europe were heavily influenced by the historical experience in the United States with civil society and democracy. Donors were driven less by ideological aspirations for the achievement of a special condition of "antipolitics" (a favorite concept of East European dissidents) than by pragmatic notions about civil society's fulfilling of societal needs unmet by either the market or the state.[9]

Relatedly, U.S. programs were predicated on a strong causal relationship between the development of NGOs and development of civil society and democracy. Aid officials believed that a robust, highly independent NGO sector is a prerequisite for civil society, which in turn is essential for a working democracy. In effect, the programs attempted to re-create Eastern European civil society in the American image—another instance of the "be-like-us" syndrome afflicting the U.S. approach in other parts of the world, which has drawn so much criticism. The approach, however, has perhaps been motivated less by arrogance than by a desire for others to share the political and social stability and prosperity the United States has enjoyed.

Attempts to make civil society in Eastern Europe mirror the American version were unlikely to succeed. Although aid administrators never claimed to be trying to do such a thing, in practice the American experience with NGOs and civil society shaped their approach and programs. That experience, however, is an unusual one, and should not be allowed to influence thinking about other countries nearly as much as it does. There are approximately two million NGOs and a range of other independent organizations of civil society in the United States, from independent media to countless community and neighborhood voluntary organizations. That makes the United States' NGO sector the largest and most robust anywhere.[10] Although American NGOs must register with the government if they wish to receive tax-related benefits, they tend to be fiercely autonomous; the NGO sector is often called the independent sector. Religious organizations are the sector's largest component, although educational associations and medical organizations also are significant categories.

Western Europeans' views on NGOs, civil society, and democracy have been similarly affected by their experiences and regional history. In Europe, the NGO sector is much less robust and the fabric of civil society is thinner than in the United States. There are far fewer NGOs, and these tend to have much closer relationships with government. In many cases that may involve receiving substantial government funding, as well as accepting officials' involvement in the governance of NGOs. The media, especially the electronic media, is heavily regulated, if not owned, by the state. Given these close ties, NGOs in Europe tend to work cooperatively with government more than many American counterparts.

Not only were there conceptual differences over NGOs and civil society, but Eastern Europeans and their donors did not share a definition of democracy.[11] The United States seemed to have its own version of a liberal democratic system in mind, as did Western European countries. Eastern Europeans had inchoate notions about democracy. While generally in favor of some form of liberal democracy, they tended to equate democracy more directly with material prosperity.

Moreover, there was certainly no understanding between Eastern Europeans and their donors about the best way to build democracy. Nor was there a clear sense of what type of NGO sector was required. Should the sector have a large number of NGOs highly independent of the government pursuing multiple agendas, or should it be relatively small, with close ties to government, focusing on a modest number of issues—or should it be a hybrid? Lack of clarity about these basic concepts held back efforts to strengthen civil society in Eastern Europe.

Despite the differences in assumptions in Eastern Europe, Western Europe, and the United States on NGOs, civil society, and democracy, donors and their partners all recognized that NGOs were a vital part of civil society. Furthermore, it was generally understood that democracies tend to have vibrant civil societies. There was much less consensus, however, on the premise behind the U.S. program: that support for NGOs strengthens civil society, which in turn helps democracy develop.

USAID Democracy Program

Perhaps the most important democracy-related program in Eastern Europe—at least the most touted in official pronouncements—was that sponsored by the U.S. government as one part of the overall U.S. aid program for the region, and principally administered by the Agency for International Development (USAID). Authorized by the Support for East European Democracy (SEED) Act of 1989, from 1990 through 1997 the U.S. government provided approximately $12.2 billion of aid to the region, an amount roughly comparable to that from the European Union (EU).

The U.S. aid program, designed as a short-term boost for the transition under way in Eastern Europe, had three broad goals: development of a market economy, improvement of the basic quality of life, and support for democratic development. Support for the market economy accounted for just over 70 percent of allocations, projects improving the quality of life 21 percent, and democratic development projects less than 9 percent. Thus although projects addressing any one objective may affect progress on another objective, projects explicitly for democracy-promotion purposes represent a modest amount of the overall support. And assistance to civil society accounts for a mere fraction of that.[12] Any assessment of U.S. efforts to strengthen NGOs must place them against the backdrop of both broader U.S. democratization efforts in Eastern Europe and the much larger effort to develop market economies and improve the quality of life.

To bolster democratic development, the United States sought to strengthen democratic processes, support the institutions that make democracy more durable, and encourage the development of civic values and virtue that underlie democratic practice.[13] U.S. aid officials, working with U.S. democracy promotion groups such as the National Democratic Institute, the International Republican Institute, and the International Foundation for Election Systems, designed projects to meet these concerns, and the program was implemented throughout the region, with only slight modifications from country to country. They focused on improving public administration, promoting decentralization, fostering independent media and judiciary, and strengthening NGOs and other similar concerns.

Despite the relatively small amount of funding that went to projects to assist NGOs, those efforts deserve further scrutiny because both host countries and donors considered them important. They were important to host countries as the most direct responses to the calls for strengthening civil society in Eastern Europe. And donors regarded them as important since they involved a new emphasis and, consequently, new sets of institutional partners.

When the U.S. government began its efforts to strengthen the NGO sector in Eastern Europe, there were few NGOs there—at least according to the American definition of independent, voluntary nonprofit organizations. Communist regimes had generally not tolerated such organizations. The associations that most resembled NGOs were closely tied to the government and were primarily concerned with culture, sport, and youth issues.

Broadly speaking, there are two types of NGOs: policy-oriented and service-delivery. Policy-oriented NGOs seek to affect government policy, usually through advocacy methods, and can operate at various levels— internationally, nationally, regionally, and locally. Service-delivery NGOs provide citizens with essential social services including health care, education, and other forms of humanitarian assistance. They work in conjunction with governments or in lieu of them. Although they may operate at the national level, they tend to be most active and effective at the grassroots, in the community.

At a time when Eastern European NGOs were either nonexistent or embryonic and the sector could have been encouraged to develop in any of several directions, the United States decided to focus its program in the region on public policy-oriented NGOs advocating constructive change in a small number of substantive areas. The most common of these issue areas were democracy, the environment, economic growth, and support for improvement in social safety nets.

Although NGOs oriented toward public policy were likely to be a very small segment of the NGO sector in Eastern Europe, focusing on them made considerable sense. With the American model before them, designers of U.S. projects believed that a blossoming NGO sector would soon present them with virtually unlimited potential partners. If their projects were to make a difference, they would have to concentrate USAID resources on a narrow set of institutions.

Although NGO statistics from Eastern Europe, as from many regions, are imprecise and unreliable, Poland's experience provides perspective on both the growth of the sector and the breakdown between policy-oriented and service-delivery NGOs. In 1989, Poland had some five thousand nationally registered "independent organizations." The vast majority were youth or cultural organizations. Less than a decade later, in 1997, approximately thirty thousand NGOs had registered. Among these, the bulk were service-delivery NGOs, generally funded by small individual contributions; many were run by three or four people. Probably no more than five hundred were policy-oriented NGOs.[14]

In its efforts to strengthen NGOs, USAID employed two basic approaches: technical assistance and other forms of training, and grants to policy-oriented NGOs.

During the first few years of its program in Eastern Europe, USAID relied heavily on training and technical assistance projects. The former included workshops and seminars on NGO-related topics, as well as study visits to NGOs in the United States. Perhaps the most common form of assistance was the provision of technical advisers who helped legislatures draft new legal frameworks for the NGO sector, as with the work by the U.S.-based International Center for Non-Profit Law. Such advisers sought to develop appropriate legal arrangements for NGOs to ensure that they were free of government interference.

Advisers also worked on other NGO-related issues, such as capacity-building, advocacy, and outreach. The focus here will be primarily on technical advisers' role in the development of legal infrastructure because such activities were especially visible and serve as a foundation on which to build other NGO-related activities.

Although providing technical advisers to support the construction of the legal infrastructure for the NGO sector both satisfied a real need and was a sensible use of USAID resources given the agency's democracy-promotion goals, two factors limited the projects' impact. These were the knowledge and experience of the technical advisers and the prevailing political conditions.

Many of the advisers had scant knowledge of legal systems outside the United States, and their advice relied excessively on American models. Although freedom of association is clearly essential to the functioning of an NGO sector, principles that are central in the United States— tax-free status and the deductibility of charitable contributions, for instance—are less so elsewhere. The idiosyncratic NGO sector in the United States heavily influenced how USAID-supported advisers conceived of the NGO sector. Thus these advisers often pushed for arrangements regarding tax status and the independence of NGOs that were likely inappropriate for the political culture and economic conditions of the country they were advising.

In addition, many of the legal efforts encountered considerable political difficulties. The new constitutions that came out of the first wave of constitution drafting that swept the region provided for greater freedom of association and thus enhanced legal authority for NGOs. But a series of well-publicized abuses brought discredit on any type of special treatment for NGOs. One so-called NGO in Bulgaria used its tax-free status to import duty-free liquor, which was sold at substantial profits. Leaders like former Czech prime minister Vaclav Klaus, echoing a common sentiment, questioned why a small interest group should receive preferential tax treatment at the expense of the larger society. In his view, the government was abdicating its decision-making role in the allocation of resources.

The abuses coupled with the substantive arguments against preferential treatment rendered problematic the crafting and passage of new legislation for the NGO sector. Projects involving technical advisers had less effect than USAID had envisioned. Despite these difficulties, all the countries in Eastern Europe now provide greater legal protection for the NGO sector than they did before 1989. Technical advisers and other training projects made some contributions to this.

In the second half of the 1990s, USAID shifted its efforts away from developing the formal institutions of democracy (the legislature and the judiciary, for example) toward helping people organize to develop creative solutions to problems facing their societies. Institution-strengthening grants to policy-oriented NGOs have been a key element of this strategy.

Both in projects providing technical advisers and in its institutional grants, USAID has entrusted the execution to intermediary organizations. These have included political foundations such as the National Endowment for Democracy and its affiliated organizations (the Center for International Private Enterprise, the Free Trade Union Institute, the International Republican Institute, and the National Democratic Institute), along with a variety of U.S.-based NGOs. These intermediaries, some of which were active in the region before USAID arrived there, provide much-needed financial and technical resources to Eastern European NGOs.

U.S. Government-Sponsored Programs

The Democracy Network (DemNet) Program, which channeled small grants to Eastern European NGOs through U.S.-based intermediaries, was the leading example of the U.S. effort to help NGOs so as to strengthen civil society in the region. President Bill Clinton announced the initiative during a visit to Prague in January 1994, and DemNet was formally established the next year. The program provided $30 million for an initial three-year period to a group of American NGOs that funneled the funds to NGOs in eleven countries in Eastern Europe (the entire region except the former Yugoslavia). DemNet also provided two regional grants—one to support the development of the legal infrastructure for the NGO sector and the other to encourage training and networking among NGOs throughout the region.

DemNet's approach was an innovative break with USAID's usual practices. It involved greater coordination and cooperation between USAID and the NGOs that were implementing the DemNet projects, and other related measures designed to fit the aid to the local context. In fact, in a virtually unprecedented move, USAID participated in a series of meetings with the NGOs held at the Rockefeller Brothers Fund's conference facility in Pocantico, New York. There, even before some of the cooperative agreements were finalized, the participating NGOs discussed strategies and how to enhance cooperation. Another Pocantico meeting, held approximately a year after DemNet started, offered an opportunity for assessment and adjustment.

Participating U.S.-based NGOs were selected through a competitive process. All had previously worked in the region or with similar projects in other parts of the world. Among the eleven that received funding, some, such as the Foundation for Civil Society and the U.S.-Baltic Foundation, had been active since the political transition began (in Czechoslovakia and the Baltic states, respectively). Other organizations, such as the Academy for Educational Development—which implemented the largest program in Poland—had been a partner of USAID's in other parts of the world for many years.

American NGOs involved in DemNet were responsible for establishing country-specific strategies and priorities, consistent with the program's basic guidelines of supporting policy-oriented participatory NGOs. Those NGOs hope to affect policy, generally at the national level, and to engage memberships of some size and significance. The American NGOs administering DemNet also selected a local advisory committee and developed grantmaking guidelines and procedures. Political sensitivities in many of the host countries, coupled with the numerous reporting and accounting requirements mandated by the U.S. government, made these procedures more complicated than those followed by private foundations such as the Soros network of foundations. In addition, grants had to be approved by the U.S. embassy in the country in question, adding a significant layer of bureaucracy and control. Consequently, some of the country programs were slow in getting started. Bureaucratic politics hindered the cooperative agreements and impeded the quick disbursement of USAID funds. Also, given the fact that DemNet was launched with presidential fanfare, it raised expectations that were difficult to meet. Although initially designed as a three-year program (with the exception of the Czech Republic and Estonia—which were "graduating" and the programs being phased out due to their perceived "success" after a two-year effort), DemNet was extended. This extension dealt with a major downside of the initiative—the limited time frame effectively precluded institutional learning and program improvement critical to the development of viable NGOs.

DemNet's complicated and layered approval processes also occasionally resulted in bureaucratic struggles—between USAID in the recipient country and headquarters in Washington; between USAID and the State Department; as well as occasional differences between the host country advisory committee and the USAID mission. In one case, the entire advisory council resigned after a first round of grant-approval letters was sent to NGOs' directors and then revoked—apparently because the embassy's approval process had not been followed in full. Many of the directors were reportedly incensed by what they perceived as U.S. officials' cavalier treatment of them, comparing it unfavorably with their treatment at the hands of Soviet officials. Clearly, this was not an auspicious start for a democracy-promotion project.

The above example illustrates the importance of appropriate implementation. The design of projects intended to strengthen democracy should ensure that the project's operational modes promote its goals. With DemNet, the U.S. government's modus operandi undercut the transparency and accountability that lie at the heart of democracy and that they were designed to foster.

USAID's efforts were also hampered by bureaucracy, especially the relationship with the State Department and procedures developed in response to congressional concerns about financial accountability. DemNet was not the only important U.S.-administered regionwide program supporting indigenous NGOs in Eastern Europe. The other was the Democracy Commissions at U.S. embassies across the region. Comprised of the U.S. ambassador and other senior embassy officials, the commissions sought to build the social and intellectual foundations of democracy and encourage democratic resolution of common problems. One way they did this was by providing small grants to NGOs of up to $25,000. Recognizing that many NGOs have limited institutional capabilities, these grants were designed to be easy to apply for and to have a relatively quick response time—three to six months as opposed to a year or more for a standard USAID grant.

The existence of two parallel U.S. programs to assist NGOs, with comparable procedures and similar grantees, complicated execution for DemNet. A critical issue was control: the U.S. ambassador headed the Democracy Commission in each of the region's countries, while USAID's country mission director was the nominal head of DemNet there. In both cases, however, the Democracy Commission made the final decision; both programs were effectively under embassy control. One of the problems that created was the perception that the democracy-building grants for NGOs were politically motivated, their primary purpose being to promote specific U.S. political objectives.

European Union Program

The European Union also mounted a major effort in the 1990s to strengthen Eastern Europe's NGO sector, to promote democratic consolidation in the region's countries consistent with their integration into the EU at some future date. While similarly targeting NGOs as instrumental in building up civil society, the EU adopted a markedly different approach than the United States did with DemNet. Rather than using external NGOs as intermediaries, it chose to channel financial and technical support to Eastern European NGOs through a locally constituted organization governed and staffed by local citizens. In each recipient country the EU established a Civil Society Development Foundation

(CSDF). These foundations required the approval of the government of the country in question. The government of that country also had to agree that a portion of its EU funds would be used for promoting civil society.

The foundations' mandate was much broader than DemNet's, which gave them much greater flexibility when deciding which projects and NGOs to support. Unlike DemNet, they did not exclude service-provider NGOs in favor of policy-oriented organizations. Among their many fields of activity, NGOs in CSDF projects worked for greater governmental transparency, promoted more pluralistic media, improved human rights education, and addressed environmental issues. Hundreds of NGOs received support.

The EU program had its drawbacks. Sometimes local government approval was a problem. In Romania and Bulgaria, for example, the leaders in the mid-1990s were opposed to strengthening civil society, and created roadblocks that delayed the establishment of the foundations in their countries. Moreover, the NGOs that received grants under the program tended to be the larger, urban-based, more cosmopolitan ones. Nor did the relatively small amounts and short funding periods of most grants allow for the development of sustainable institutions.

The program's flexibility came at a cost: it dissipated relatively scarce resources, a dilemma common in other grantmaking contexts as well. The CSDF in the Slovak Republic, for example, dispensed approximately $3 million a year. With grants averaging $10,000 to $20,000—very small, by the standards of the grant world—the locally administered foundations awarded hundreds annually. While that supported a relatively large number of NGOs, it did not in and of itself create a more robust civil society. Given the limited resources and the embryonic state of civil society across much of the region, expectations that a lot of small grants would create civil society were inflated or naïve. The grants did, however, boost the morale of civic activists and encourage the creation of many NGOs active at the national and the local level.

Partners in Democracy

A decade after the collapse of the Berlin Wall, the NGO sector in all the Eastern European countries is much more vigorous and pluralistic, but international donors played only a modest role in its development. The bulk of the region's NGOs did not benefit directly or substantially from foreign assistance, nor did donors have a major impact on civil society or democracy. In fact, some NGOs that received aid have actually impeded the building of democracy with their pursuit of highly personal agendas. Whether a particular NGO will help build democracy in a particular country depends on the political conditions in that country, the organization involved, and how the activities are carried out, among other variables. Similar rules hold true for an NGO sector as a whole. Donors' choice of partners is thus a crucial decision.

Very different conditions confronted NGOs and the donors intending to assist them in different countries of the region. In Poland and Slovenia, for example, the government was generally receptive to the NGO sector and gave it considerable space within which to operate. In Slovakia and Serbia, on the other hand, the government provided no space or limited space for extragovernmental activities. In the more restrictive countries, NGOs tended to operate in a highly politicized environment and the government generally regarded them as opponents. For example, one of the leading figures in the NGO community in Slovakia, the founder of a major NGO resource center there, was also the foreign policy adviser to President Jan Kovacs, who was engaged in a bitter struggle with Vladimir Meciar, then the prime minister. People were often confused—understandably—about whether the adviser was speaking as an advocate for civil society or a political opponent of the prime minister. In countries where NGOs had little room to operate, it was very difficult for them to broadly promote civil society. The NGO sector was, however, one of the few places in which some form of oppositional politics was practiced, and thus served a useful purpose.

Donors must carefully calibrate programs to take advantage of political conditions. In a relatively closed setting, support for a few narrowly targeted sectorwide initiatives such as strengthening the legal framework for the sector and developing NGO resource and training centers makes programmatic sense. In a more open setting, assistance should be targeted to address weaknesses of the NGO sector and specific issues identified by local citizens. Donors, however, should not think or say that the first kind of aid "strengthens civil society," since political conditions do not permit a vigorous civil society, at least in the short term.

What kind of NGO the donors choose as the institutional partner, who the leaders there are, and what activities donors support are three other key factors determining the impact of civil society assistance. Many of the NGOs in Eastern Europe created since the collapse of communism have not been effective vehicles for promoting civil society. In numerous cases, NGOs were founded by political figures who had been elected in the first round of elections but then defeated in subsequent elections. Many of these leaders, while in office, developed relationships with foreign donors that they effectively parlayed into resources for their new organizations. These new organizations, generally policy-related research institutions or think tanks focusing on economic issues, often had highly personal or political agendas. They attracted resources from abroad since think tanks had been relatively successful in opening and pluralizing the policy-making process in the United States and some parts of Europe.[15] All too often, however, they became platforms for launching their leaders back into power. In some cases, they lost touch with broader elements of their own society, ending up either irrelevant or discredited.

Throughout Eastern Europe in the 1990s, policy-oriented NGOs were good at getting grants but much less successful at embodying democratic values like transparent governance and accountable leadership. Many of their leaders operated in a high-handed, even authoritarian, manner. Often they were intolerant of individuals and institutions espousing contrary views. Moreover, because of the relatively strong growth of policy-oriented NGOs focusing on economics and politics, other types of policy NGOs, as well as highly participatory service-oriented NGOs, lost out in the competition for donors.

The NGOs that rely on external funding—a relatively small but visible group—appear somewhat disconnected from the society around them. It may be that others resent them because of their access to foreign funding, which might provide generous salaries and opulent, well-equipped offices—at least compared to their counterparts. These NGOs may also lose their connection with society because their leaders, preoccupied with maintaining their foreign funding, spend a large proportion of their time traveling and responding to their foreign donors.

The experience in Eastern Europe strongly suggests that NGOs, civil society, and democracy are only loosely related. In some circumstances, certain kinds of NGOs, under the right leaders, can promote civic virtues like openness and tolerance that are essential to nurturing civil society. The development of such virtues, along with the experience of certain practices that promote participation and accountability, may also give a boost to democratic development. Assuming that this is true in all circumstances, however, is risky. Suffice it to say that there is no inevitable connection between NGOs, civil society, and democracy. It is also clear that the relationship is complex and neither causal nor linear.

Aid's Impact

Assessing donor efforts to strengthen civil society in Eastern Europe via aid to NGOs is a difficult task. Since both donors and recipients were fuzzy about goals—there was never any consensus on what kind of NGO sector might be most beneficial in the various countries—it is hard to say how much the assistance accomplished. Further complicating any attempt at evaluation, the NGO sector in Eastern Europe now comprises myriad organizations addressing a range of social and political issues and operating from the national level down to the village level. Most of these organizations did not benefit from civil society assistance at all, at least not directly. And since explicit political development assistance, and especially projects targeting the NGO sector, is relatively new, no precise measures are available for assessments nor do experts agree on what constitutes success. For assistance projects with complex objectives like strengthening civil society, quantitative yardsticks are clearly insufficient, as are purely qualitative ones. What follows is an attempt to glean from the experience in Eastern Europe some useful criteria for civil society assistance, suggesting the types of projects, operating styles, and substantive focuses likely to advance democratization most.

The general impact of aid projects can be gauged from their effects in three interconnected arenas: individuals, institutions with which those individuals are affiliated, and the ideas that have currency in a society. In addition, procedural indicators including flexibility, efficient administration, and high citizen participation signal effective projects. All these factors affect sustainability, which for many Eastern Europeans is the most concrete measure of an NGO's success.[16]

After hundreds of technical advisers and training projects have done their bit in the region's NGO sector, there is considerable evidence that Eastern Europeans, especially urban elites, are much more knowledgeable today than ten years ago about NGOs and what those organizations can contribute to society. In addition, thousands of organizations throughout the region have benefited from civil society programs; without the assistance, they would not be nearly so mature today. They are helping pluralize the institutional landscape—a healthy development after the long communist monopoly on power. Such pluralization, however, is not synonymous with a more democratic system, although it may eventually provide the foundation for a strong democracy.

It is on the level of ideas affecting society that evidence of aid's effect is thinnest. Some policy-oriented NGOs have contributed to the public debate on crucial issues, particularly the pace and course of economic reform. Others have added their voices to discussion of the environment and its importance to a society's long-term sustainability. As is true for their West European and North American counterparts, very few NGOs in Eastern Europe can prove that their activities have had a positive effect on public policy.

On projects' operational side, flexibility is a primary concern since transitional countries are by definition in flux. Thus administrators should get funds into the hands of local NGOs quickly so that they can get started before the motivation evaporates. Civil society assistance projects such as DemNet, to their credit, tend to disburse money faster than many other types of programs. Far too much time, however, elapsed between President Clinton's announcement of DemNet and the actual release of funds to Eastern European NGOs.

Another major concern is whether projects are participatory. Many assistance efforts for civil society are described as participatory. What that usually means is that NGOs are involved in the execution of a project; rarely are they involved in the problem identification, project design, or evaluation stages. Participation at all stages would enhance participatory skills and attitudes—a goal that all civil society assistance professes to have.

The most participatory projects have tended to be the most empowering at the grassroots, giving citizens the confidence they need to extend participatory practices to other spheres of their community. But there are far too few examples of such programs. The most participatory have tended to be on the environment, like the Environmental Partnership for Central Europe established in the early 1990s. That project and similarly successful ones mobilized broad segments of the population to address widely held concerns. The partnership had identifiable goals, and there was a clear correlation between the stated objective and project activities. The partners operated primarily at the local level, in a highly decentralized and transparent fashion, and their accomplishments and failures were readily apparent.

As mentioned above, another measure of success that has emerged from experience is sustainability. Sustainable NGOs have the ability to secure the resources—political, economic, and human—necessary for continuing when donor support recedes, as it eventually will. Very few NGOs in the region have reached that point.[17] Policy-oriented NGOs in particular face an uncertain future since few alternative sources of support beckon. And the NGOs that have received the most money from the international community appear to be at greatest risk. Few of these are likely to survive once external donors withdraw funding, unless they establish cooperative links with the government, business, or both.

The decade-long attempt to strengthen civil society in Eastern Europe has also shown that such assistance projects have only limited effects on a country's political development. Factors beyond the control of any donor, no matter how extensive the donor's resources, heavily influence countries' chances of success in building civil society. Even the strongest project, for instance, is likely to yield only modest results in a country hit by an economic depression or war.

Room to Improve

A decade after civil society assistance began in Eastern Europe amid fanfare and high expectations, it is important that donors commit themselves to improving such efforts going forward. Although civil society aid and democracy assistance generally continue to command broad support, the programs are coming under scrutiny. Both donors and recipients are asking hard questions about what they have achieved. In the new political context, programs' easy acceptance is no longer assured. With international aid dwindling, donors and recipients must develop projects that help civil society organizations take root in the local soil and thus become more self-reliant.

At the start of the 1990s, the U.S. government and other donors faced a strategic decision on what would be the most effective approach for them to follow in strengthening civil society. Instead of working with the embryonic NGO sector, donors could have chosen to rely on long-term economic forces or to work only with governments. Given these three broad choices and the modest resources allocated for the job, focusing their attention on the NGO sector was a good idea for donors.

If the donor and the local partner agree that working with an NGO sector is their preferred approach for strengthening civil society and inculcating civic values, they must then agree on the characteristics they are trying to foster in the sector and the methods they will use. The approach will vary depending on local circumstances, including the government's attitude toward the NGO sector. A more precise delineation of the donors' approach will enable donors and their local partners to set more appropriate goals for the program.

Setting aside the question of whether strengthening civil society was the best way to promote democracy, donors could have chosen to strengthen civil society by means other than working with NGOs. They could have zeroed in on labor unions, although many unions had unsavory pasts, or concentrated much more than they did on using the media to educate and engage the public.[18] Similarly, donors could have made a more concerted effort to enhance civic education so as to encourage values conducive to civil society. Relying more on media or civic education would likely have allowed for broader engagement than did working with mainly policy-oriented, urban-centered, elite-led NGOs. Those approaches too, however, were likely to produce only modest advances in civil society given the political and economic circumstances in Eastern Europe and the ambitiousness of the goal.

The institutions that donors took as partners in trying to reach that goal also constrained the reach and impact of assistance programs for civil society. The choice of policy-oriented NGOs as the chief partner seemed as much driven by donors' preference for "professional NGOs" as by calculations of the most efficacious means of strengthening civil society. These "professional NGOs" tended toward conventional institutional forms, involvement with public interest advocacy, and a focus on issues perceived as directly related to democratic development, such as election monitoring, voter education, governmental transparency, political and civil rights, and on down a familiar list. Donors thus restricted assistance to a narrow band of the NGO spectrum whose organizations were likely to have difficulty taking root in Eastern European societies because of government resistance and the perception that they were remote from the concerns of ordinary people. Such an approach also guaranteed that relatively little attention goes to problems that most people deem more urgent, such as unemployment and environmental degradation. Policy-oriented NGOs also had many structural impediments that made them a less than perfect tool for building civil society, including a lack of adequate legal infrastructure; too few, and poorly trained, staff; inadequate funding; and in some countries, sustained opposition from government. Another drawback of relying on policy-oriented NGOs to foster civil society was that many of their relations with other segments of society were problematic. Few elite-led, urban-based institutions were adept at encouraging civic participation. Their narrow focus on policy was often inconsistent with the goal of broad citizens' participation. They were sometimes resented because of their international support. Such perceptions resulted in sharp conflict between many such NGOs and government, severely limiting the NGOs' effectiveness. Add to those impediments some NGOs' highly individualistic agendas and high-handed if not autocratic leadership, and one sees why NGOs were not ideal for strengthening civil society.

In the late 1990s, however, USAID and other organizations involved in civil society assistance in Eastern Europe adjusted their programs in important ways. Increasingly, they began to emphasize a local focus that allows local citizens to play a larger role in project design and execution. In addition, USAID and other donors are shifting attention away from NGOs in the major urban centers toward smaller, less Westernized organizations working locally or regionally rather than nationally. That shift can contribute to decentralization, which is essential to democratic development—especially in Eastern Europe, because of the region's recent past. Donors have also made strides in building flexibility into program design and in disbursing funds more quickly. Establishing self-sustaining NGOs remains a major challenge for the region's people, and for the donors assisting them.

Besides the difficulties associated with NGOs, problems with the donors have held back civil society assistance. A major problem was conceptual. Donors tended to have a monochromatic view of civil society. Many idealized it, envisioning a homogenous entity extending throughout the region. They also expected that the NGO sector everywhere in Eastern Europe would become a repository for civic values and practices. Moreover, in donors' wishful thinking, strengthening the NGO sector would automatically build civil society and ineluctably lead to democracy. If they want to strengthen civil society, donors must begin cultivating a more nuanced understanding of what kind of NGO sector is most conducive to that under what particular circumstances, as well as of precisely how to fulfill their limited role in civil society development.

Another shortcoming of assistance programs for civil society was that many designed to assist democratic development created dissonance between means and ends. As discussed above, projects were not as participatory and transparent as they might have been. Nor did they convey in their practices the full meaning of accountability. Greater convergence between the objective of building democracy and the use of quintessentially democratic means would have enhanced the effectiveness of civil society assistance considerably.

The frequent shifts in program emphases, direction, and partners ensured that building a strong civil society in the region would remain an elusive goal. The resources allocated—time, money, personnel, and so on—were not nearly enough for achieving projects' lofty ambitions, even allowing that some of the loftiness was political rhetoric calibrated to win congressional (and taxpayer) support. Expectations could not be met, which struck a blow to some democracy promoters' morale and to political and popular support, whether or not the expectations were realistic.

If a donor decides that strengthening civil society and democratic governance is important enough to pursue, it must be pursued assiduously, with considerable investment of time and money. Although the effort will fail if a country is "graduated" from the program in a few years, Congress decreed that the USAID assistance would run no more than five years. Further, the approximately $1 billion the United States provided for democracy promotion in Eastern Europe could not conceivably build democracy there, nor could approximately $100 million noticeably strengthen civil society.

Donors, intermediaries, and recipients must supplement their work with NGOs with other approaches. NGOs do not automatically strengthen civil society and bolster democracy. They can encourage democratic attitudes and practices—what de Tocqueville called democratic "habits of the heart"—or serve, as others have said, as "schools for democracy" or democratic DNA.[19] Whatever the metaphor, it is clear that NGOs have the potential to help promote democratic tendencies, but equally clear that neither schools nor DNA by themselves necessarily produce the desired outcome of a robust civil society.

In the long run, economic reform leading to broadly distributed economic growth is probably the most effective way of developing civil society. In the short run, NGOs have a useful but not determinative role to play in shaping civil society. They will perform better in the role to the extent that they harness the powers of the state and market without losing their autonomy. Success requires, in addition, a considerably larger investment in time and money than has been committed up to now. Without it, civil society assistance programs lack the means to achieve their lofty goals.

Notes

1. Assessing exactly how much aid was provided by whom for what purposes is extremely difficult since there were multiple donors, public and private, dispensing a mix of grants and loans for a wide variety of often overlapping purposes. These estimates are based on sources including U.S. Agency for International Development, *Scoreboard of Assistance Commitments to the CEEC* (Washington, D.C.: USAID, 1996); Krzysztof J. Ners and Ingrid T. Buxell, *Assistance to Transition Survey 1995* (Warsaw: Institute for East West Studies Policy Education Center on Assistance to Transition, 1995); reports from international institutions active in the region, such as the European Bank for Reconstruction and Development and the World Bank; and the author's own research.

2. Virtually all donors, public and private, interested in civil society assistance shifted their geographic focus. For example, by the mid-1990s, USAID had terminated its programs in the Czech Republic and Slovenia so that it could concentrate on other countries. The European Union engaged in a similar shift. Among private donors, some, such as the Pew Charitable Trusts and the Andrew W. Mellon Foundation, announced in 1995 that they were closing their programs in Central Europe.

3. In fact, in his prescient *Reflections on the Revolution in Europe* (New York: Random House, 1990), the sociologist Ralf Dahendorf suggested that while building a market economy would take six years, developing civil society would take sixty years—considerably longer than a generation.

4. See Thomas Carothers' discussion of this generally undifferentiated, or "checklist," approach, *Assessing Democracy Assistance: The Case of Romania* (Washington, D.C.: Carnegie Endowment for International Peace, 1996).

5. For a discussion of some donors' shifting strategies, see Kevin F. F. Quigley, *For Democracy's Sake: Foundations and Democracy Assistance in Central Europe* (Washington, D.C.: Woodrow Wilson Center, 1997).

6. There is a rich literature on the mediating role of civil society. Alexis de Tocqueville's *Democracy in America* presents a classic discussion of this.

7. Although there is a burgeoning literature on links between markets and democracy, including classics such as Charles E. Lindblom, *Politics and Markets: The World's Political Economic System* (New York: Basic Books, 1997); Seymour Martin Lipset, *Political Man: The Social Bases of Conflict*, 2nd ed. (Baltimore: Johns Hopkins University Press, 1981); and Joseph A. Schumpeter, *Capitalism, Socialism, and Democracy* (New York: Harper and Row, 1950), there is as yet a scant literature regarding how and under what circumstance civil society links with democracy.

8. There are numerous superb books on the fall of communism and the attempt to develop open political and economic systems in Eastern Europe including Timothy Garton Ash, *The Magic Lantern* (New York: Vintage Books, 1993), Andrew Nagorski, *The Birth of Freedom* (New York: Simon and Schuster, 1993), and Vladimir Tismaneanu, *Reinventing Politics: Eastern Europe from Stalin to Havel* (New York: Free Press, 1992).

9. One very articulate and forceful proponent of this was philanthropist George Soros. See his *Underwriting Democracy* (New York: Free Press, 1990).

10. For a comparative perspective on the state of civil society, see the work done by Lester M. Salamon and his colleagues at the Institute for Policy Studies at Johns Hopkins University in Baltimore, Md.

11. Although there is considerable discussion about what democracy is, one of the most effective and persuasive discussions recognizing its inherent complexity occurs in Robert Dahl, *Polyarchy: Participation and Opposition* (New Haven, Conn.: Yale University Press, 1971). Dahl argues that democracy has a tripartite structure linking institutions and processes that are formal and informal. These in turn are buttressed by supportive values. This functional, as opposed to normative, understanding is useful for those engaged in civil society assistance efforts who wish to avoid a cultural bias in their efforts.

12. The discussion in this section is based primarily on U.S. Agency for International Development, *Scoreboard of Assistance Commitments to the CEEC* (Washington, D.C.: USAID, 1996).

13. This discussion of USAID's civil society and democracy promotion objectives draws on "Building Democracy: AID's Strategy," in AID Documents (online gopher site), as well as SEED Act Implementation Report (Washington, D.C.: U.S. Department of State, 1995–97) and various other materials.

14. There are no precise data on numbers of NGOs since many civil society organizations do not formally register with governments and ones that do may

not be active. These numbers, however, do suggest a dramatic trend—a proliferating NGO sector. They are based on KLON, "Basic Statistics Concerning the
Scope of Activities of Nongovernmental Organizations in Poland" (KLON,
Warsaw, 1995 photocopy) and are mirrored by comparable trends in virtually
all the countries of Eastern Europe.

15. For a discussion of how think tanks can impact the policy-making process in the United States, see James A. Smith, *The Idea Brokers: Think Tanks and the
Rise of the New Policy Elites,* rev. ed. (New York: Free Press, 1993). For a global
discussion, see Jeffrey Telgarsky and Makiko Ueno, eds., *Think Tanks in a Democratic Society: An Alternative Voice* (Washington, D.C.: Urban Institute, 1996).

16. These criteria are discussed in greater detail in Quigley, *For Democracy's
Sake,* chapter 8.

17. Relatively early, NGO leaders from Eastern Europe saw sustainability as
the key challenge confronting the embryonic civil society in the region. See Kevin
F. F. Quigley, *Conversations on Democracy Assistance* (Washington, D.C.: East European Studies, Woodrow Wilson International Center for Scholars, 1996).

18. Although donors paid some attention to media development, the efforts
tended to be modest or short-lived. One of the more promising initiatives was
the International Media Fund whose mission was to promote independent media in Eastern Europe. But the fund was given too short a time frame; by 1996, it
was closed.

19. Miklos Marschall, executive director of Civicus, and Michael Zantovsky,
Czech ambassador to the United States, suggested this at a June 5, 1996, workshop at the Woodrow Wilson Center in Washington, D.C.

8

Civil Society in Romania: From Donor Supply to Citizen Demand

Dan Petrescu

ROMANIA SUFFERED FOR DECADES prior to 1990 under one of the most repressive, absolutist communist regimes, that of Nicolae Ceausescu. The transition to democratic government that began at the end of 1989, though along the lines of those in the other Eastern European countries (with "free and fair" elections, a new constitution, and the establishment of political pluralism), has been shaped by the abruptness of the change. During his twenty-five-year rule, Ceausescu did not allow any organizations not completely controlled by the Communist Party, and dissident movements were promptly smashed by the infamous secret police, the Securitate. Romanians had no "Charter '77" movement as in Czechoslovakia or Solidarity as in Poland, which even under communism managed to show citizens what an active civil society could do and prepared civic activists to take over the administration of the country after the regime's fall. The abrupt and violent nature of the Romanian revolution,[1] which set it apart from the more gradual political openings in most other states behind the Iron Curtain, allowed second-tier communist apparatchiks to grab power, pushing aside, gently or not so gently, the revolution's overnight heroes.

Only then, protesting the "stealing of the revolution's gains," did Romanian civil society come to life, through its first, somewhat disorganized, but vocal groups. At that important juncture a number of foreign organizations, including the U.S. government and a handful of American private foundations as well as the European Union and several West European governments and foundations, stepped in to support the forces for democracy, consistent with the emerging Western policy of support for civil society in all the newly post-communist countries of the region.

The development of civil society in Romania through foreign assistance has been supply-driven. According to the donors' theory, as citizens were taught and saw for themselves what the organizations of civil society can do, popular demand for them would be created. In practice, demand has indeed been created, but mainly among those who would like some grant money and made a business out of obtaining grants. Following the same Western paradigm, donors concentrated civil society support on the fostering and funding of associations and operating foundations. Unions, religious organizations, and other forms of civil society institutions were, if not totally neglected, left far behind in the level of support and attention. This trend has continued and increased until, by "civil society support," donors in Romania refer to assistance provided to nongovernmental organizations (NGOs) dedicated to a few, core activities related to the fundamentals of democracy (that is, election monitoring, human rights, advocacy training). Therefore, the present study tracks this pattern by focusing its analysis mainly on the development of NGOs. Romanian unions, media, and religious organizations have followed a more "natural" development since 1989, influenced mainly by domestic factors (such as political developments, labor supply and demand, and economic contraction).

An unhappy combination of donor stress on rigorous financial management combined with weak programmatic governance within many NGOs has in many cases estranged those organizations from the community they are supposed to serve. The combination of economic woes at home and ready aid from institutions from abroad has driven NGOs eager for resources and issues to look, not to the Romanian people, but to the foreign suppliers, with their foreign perceptions and assumptions. In the past several years, however, steadily decreasing aid flows have led some NGOs to discontinue some democracy programs and cut back on others, to search for new foreign benefactors, or, at well-managed NGOs, to rethink both their mission and their approach.

Civil society assistance from Western donors has neglected institution-building, concentrating instead on programs that deliver services—from public health to education—which are the ones that make headlines. Thus few projects ever become self-sustaining. At the same time, independent of or only indirectly inspired by the West's work in the country, a new breed of NGO is appearing—leaner and better adapted to the setting, with stronger links to the community and better access to available resources.

This chapter discusses several problems that foreign assistance efforts encounter in Romanian civil society and assesses its success in dealing with them. It begins with a brief description of the environment and the actors. It goes on to describe the philosophies behind the aid, the evolution of aid efforts, and some of the realities on the ground in implementation. The final paragraphs sketch the most recent trends in the NGO sector and suggest possible new goals.

The Climate in Romania

Assistance providers must take into consideration the environment in which any activity they fund is going to take place. Knowledge of historical, social, economic, and geographical conditions should always play a major role in donors' decisions about strategy, especially in an unstructured field like civil society. In Romania, those conditions vary widely from region to region, and such differences must be factored into aid if it is to be really useful.

Romania's three historical regions, Transylvania, Muntenia, and Moldavia, comparable in size and population, have been subject to different religious and cultural influences that have molded organizational forms and community response. Where the influence of Protestant Saxons and Hungarians (whose ancestors began arriving in the twelfth century) has been strong, particularly in Transylvania, the society has developed much more autonomously, due to local associative institutions and greater entrepreneurial activity and philanthropy. Community-based organizations, from the village band to guilds, abounded in Transylvania, where they served as a model and created a competitive environment for ethnic Romanians.[2] Muntenia and Moldova, under the influence of the Orthodox Church, which was less concerned than Protestantism with the material well-being and social values of its followers, developed advanced social institutions and associative forms only when exposed to the modernizing Romanian state in the latter half of the nineteenth century. Even then, the Jacobin model of the state held sway, and the government kept the institutions of civil society under extremely tight control. The old regional cultures are still relevant today, as the figures on nongovernmental organizations show: 32 percent of Romania's NGOs are in Moldavia and Muntenia, 45 percent in Transylvania, and 23 percent in Bucharest, which, as the capital of the country and its main industrial, cultural, and academic center needs to be considered separately. In view of the comparable size and population of the three regions, the disparity in the proportion of structured citizens' groups is alarming.

As for the political and economic conditions with which aid for civil society must contend, Romania fell under communist rule after World War II and lived through more than four decades of totalitarianism that effectively eliminated, at first by brute violence and later through legislation and oppression, all organizations not inspired and controlled by the Communist Party. In the immediate aftermath of Ceausescu's ouster, former second-tier communists took over the government, skillfully manipulating nationalistic sentiment, satisfying Romanians' immediate demands for basic freedoms while proposing a gradual political transition. They played the job-security card rather than undertake tough economic reforms, and brought an already sick economy to the brink of collapse by catering to the vested interests of powerful individuals. Numerous weak parties made up the opposition, which centered around two traditional parties from the pre-World War II era. Infighting along with weak organization and political leadership prevented any threat to the neo-communist regime. Not until the mid-1990s did the democratic opposition coalesce sufficiently to play a significant role. In the 1996 national elections, Romanians, dissatisfied with the slow pace of reform and disgusted by corruption in the administration, gave the democratic coalition a landslide victory that surprised almost everyone.

The communist regime had done something else to Romanian society: instilled distrust, fear of, and contempt for the state. The performance of state institutions even after the dramatic changes ushered in by the 1989 revolution has not led to a marked increase in citizens' trust of government: Parliament and the justice system are the least trusted institutions in the country, while the Orthodox Church and the army are the most trusted.

With the decompression of politics after 1989, the alternative realm of civil society blossomed, though not without conflict between it and the government. The number of civil society institutions, broadly defined, grew spectacularly in the early 1990s. In the space of a few months, hundreds of political parties and unions and thousands of NGOs sprang up. Organized by cranks or geniuses, based on real grievances and pressing social issues or on strong personalities and momentary enthusiasm, the forms of social organizations outside the domain of the state began to develop. But the political conditions of the early 1990s, including extremely violent forms of control (such as the infamous incursions of miners to subdue opposition forces in Bucharest), disregard of human rights, and disrespect for state institutions, created antagonism between the state and the institutions of civil society. Gradually, open conflict abated, and a tentative dialogue began, with prodding—to give Caesar his due—from Western governments and other Western actors.

The democratic opposition's victory in the 1996 elections—due partly, as the winners acknowledged, to help from institutions in civil society—improved relations between the state and civil society. However, the wildly optimistic declarations of late 1996 and early 1997 about a "partnership" between the two have been moderated lately, as neither side has entirely lived up to its obligations or the other's expectations. Although there has been definite progress on the legal framework for state-NGO collaboration and communication, and advocates can point to numerous examples of partnering, state funding of nongovernmental projects, and so on, more must be done to build the trust necessary for the two realms to cooperate in renovating Romania.

The Actors and Their Evolution

Foreign assistance has come into Romania, as into the other Eastern European countries, in many forms, from many sources, for many recipients. But this chapter deals only with the small portion of that aid going to programs explicitly intended to develop civil society. Other programs directed at NGOs but under social and economic rubrics—for instance, training for environmental NGOs and a family planning project implemented through an NGO—have helped build up the institutional capacity of particular NGOs but are not explicitly aimed at the task of fostering civil society.

I confine the discussion here to the major donors. The two main players have been the U.S. government, acting mainly through the United States Agency for International Development (USAID), and the European Union, which has sponsored the PHARE programs. Several dozen U.S. and European private foundations have played an important role as well, and their approaches also merit examination.

As for the recipients of the aid to civil society, if at first most of the money went to unions, political parties, and even businesses such as newspapers and television stations, after the first few years it went primarily to NGOs—and, at least in the case of official U.S. aid, to a particular narrow type of NGO, strictly concerned with civic, later with advocacy, programs. Donors required that the organizations be politically neutral, or behave as if they were; teaming up with a political figure meant certain disqualification from any future program. The host, the post-1989 Romanian government, was very patient, if one looks at it from the government's perspective. Its leaders saw no need to develop NGOs for alternative viewpoints, civic engagement, or other supposed democratic benefits. They were believers in the communist credo *Who is not with us, is against us*—thus all NGOs were enemies.

And most NGOs *were* in a sense enemies or at least opponents of the government, because they sought to challenge the government's weak human rights performance and apparent tepid commitment to democratic norms. U.S. and European authorities, who could not support Romania's democratic opposition parties openly, supported them indirectly, by helping NGOs promote democratic values that were opposed to what were generally perceived to be the ruling parties' values. Although the government could have cited outdated but still valid legislation and tightly controlled the NGOs, it did not. While not forthcoming or helpful, officials allowed domestic NGOs to set up and operate and looked on while foreign donors spread money around that was used to criticize and monitor them. Some circles were driven to paranoid flights of fancy, imagining the assistance was much heftier and more ambitious than it actually was.

But the pre-1996 administration had some sophisticates among its policy-makers who understood that a restrictive policy toward NGOs would tarnish Romania's image abroad and have a negative economic and political impact. In the early 1990s, the Romanian government avidly sought a resumption of "most favored nation" (MFN) trade status with the United States (it had been suspended in the late 1980s), and the U.S. administration and Congress were judging the issue in terms of whether Romania really was democratizing. Top officials at the State

Department and White House, as well as some key congressmen, were deeply skeptical about the democratic bona fides of President Ion Iliescu and his ruling circle. Restricting NGOs would have been fatal to Romania's hopes for MFN. Also in the early 1990s, European officials demonstrated Europe's commitment to NGO development and democratization, through both diplomatic measures and aid programs.

In these circumstances, Romanian leaders accepted NGOs as a necessary nuisance, drawing the line, however, at any serious attempts to involve NGOs in significant projects. The World Bank's efforts to bring domestic NGOs in on health projects, for example, were resisted by the relevant ministry. The government tolerated civic movements so long as they did not enter the political fray, but as soon as they did they were treated as an opposition party, as in the cases of the Civic Alliance and the Romanian Foundation for Democracy. This meant being on the receiving end of political bullying, intimidation, and efforts to block access to resources. Unfortunately for such groups, most Western funding organizations applied the same test and ruled them out as possible recipients.[3]

How the United States Does It

In the beginning, the feeling among many Romanians about U.S. assistance was extremely positive. Aid for democracy-oriented NGOs flowed into Romania rapidly, without obstructive bureaucracy or narrow guidelines. The staff of domestic NGOs found that U.S. aid officials listened to and helped them, which boosted their self-confidence. Moreover, the "limited government" philosophy of American democracy appealed to Romanian civic and democracy activists after decades of authoritarianism.

The first, heroic days of democracy assistance often involved finding an active group or person ready to promote universal democratic values and struggling to put out a newsletter or hold a conference or something of that sort. The proposal and the contract would be drawn up in a few minutes and the funds wired soon after—or if that were impossible, cash would change hands, computers would be sent by post, and so on. Cloak-and-dagger style operations were not unknown. To avoid the new government's devious scrutiny, the volume was, of necessity, small: a few dozen grants, most to recipients in the capital and a few other large cities. Most of the grants were made directly by the National Endowment for Democracy (NED), a public-funded, privately run U.S. organization, or by the Institute for Democracy in Eastern Europe, a U.S. group that received NED funds for distribution in Eastern Europe.

These first small grants had a decisive effect. They helped establish the credibility of a few NGOs, set them up as institutions, and formed a set of "traditional recipients" of grants. Many of these organizations are now well-established institutions with a defined niche; a number are on the point of becoming self-sustaining.

The next phase of civil society assistance was a strategic extension of the U.S. effort in Romania's 1992 elections. Attempts to level the playing field for that election had included organizing or assisting domestic election observers and aid for civic and voter education. Financed by USAID and NED, U.S.-based organizations like the National Democratic Institute and the International Foundation for Election Systems sent in resident teams to provide technical and financial assistance for civic groups working for a free and fair electoral process. Although they did not provide direct financial assistance to domestic NGOs, and although the fairness of the election was unclear, the U.S. groups achieved something that lasted. They helped build a few stable institutions, which became models, and later played a support role in the NGO sector, such as Pro-Democracy and Centras. The U.S. programs' far-reaching goals, including creation of parliamentary transparency, introduction of advocacy for NGOs, and formation of a nationwide, effective umbrella organization for NGOs, could not be achieved under the conditions of 1990–92. But the seed had been planted, and at the end of the decade, with other actors and in other programs, definite action is starting to take shape even though aid levels are declining.

In the mid-1990s, with more NGOs up and running and the political situation relatively stable, the United States moved to the logical next step: direct financial and technical assistance to Romanian civil society through the regional Democracy Network Program, sponsored by USAID. Both generosity and a strategic purpose motivated U.S. policy-makers. The program signaled a shift from an exclusive focus on elections and support for the democratic opposition to a long-term program for the sustainable development of civil society as a basis for democratization and social and economic development. As such, it had provisions for several million dollars worth of technical as well as financial assistance to advocacy NGOs through small and medium-size grants. The program was to encompass the whole of Eastern Europe, fostering civil society in all the region's countries at the same time that it encouraged cooperation between NGOs across borders.

In Romania, at least, the program had some negative features. It started "just" two years late because of bureaucratic delays, and at nearly the same time as the EU's PHARE program for technical and financial assistance to NGOs, which guaranteed much duplication of effort. The contractor for the Democracy Network was World Learning, an American nonprofit corporation with very limited experience in Romania. The National Democratic Institute served as a partner to World Learning in the project, providing some of the training.

On the technical side, implementation of the Democracy Network program was rigid. Candidates for grants had to endure a drawn-out, bureaucratic process with compulsory theoretical and practical training in advocacy skills and in evaluation before they could obtain funding.[4] Such a process was not a bad idea in itself, but it should have been adapted to local conditions. The evaluation mechanism was adopted nearly wholesale from the United States, despite obvious contextual differences. The advocacy training, too, was based on the U.S. model, which assumes lawmakers are more sensitive to their constituents than to their party leaders—not the case in Romania, where election to Parliament is by proportional representation from party lists.

Further complicating the process, projects had to receive final approval from the U.S. embassy, which was far from automatic. The fate of a model proposal to advocate the passage of clean air legislation is still pointed to as a case study in the politics of grant-giving. The applicant, an NGO from one of the smaller cities in Romania, asked for support to work for the approval of a law protecting nonsmokers from passive smoke. The NGO's staff dutifully went through the Democracy Network training, having their proposal all but spelled out for them by the trainers. The trainers held up the final proposal as an example to other trainees. Yet the embassy's Democracy Commission rejected the proposal—because, according to some observers, powerful American tobacco companies operating in Romania had the ear of embassy officials, and a lowly Romanian NGO could hardly compete.

The grant-making thus was supply-driven—the applications were actually framed and worded by the supplier during the training classes. Little wonder the Democracy Network Program failed in Romania. Some of the public relations techniques the trainers taught were useful, as were parts of the booklets on management issues that the trainers distributed. But of the program's $3.5 million budget, only a dozen grants were disbursed, totaling a few hundred thousand dollars, and those went to the best "performing bears" among the Romanian NGOs. USAID was deeply disappointed with the management of the program and finally decided to stop the grant-making part of the program. Approaching the end of its five-year mandate, the program now has a strategy diametrically opposed to its old one, attempting to start at the grassroots in traditional fashion by training activists to assess needs in the community and identify and train leaders for work at that level.

The USAID approach to democracy assistance and civil society development, as embodied in the Democracy Network Program and other efforts, has been based on three assumptions that do not hold true in Romania. The first is that advocacy organizations, unlike the church or organizations providing social services, are at the core of civil society and are capable of giving it direction. That assumption reflects the experience in the United States, where civic organizations have persuaded state legislatures and Congress to institute major changes and have become efficient forms of expression for civil society. The second assumption is that various interest groups' influencing of legislation is intrinsically democratic, more democratic than elected representatives acting through established processes for drafting legislation. The agency's final assumption is that NGOs that aim to promote the public interest are far more important for strengthening civil society than the informal groups of citizens that aim to bring about change in public policy because of a special, local interest.

Romanian political culture, however, is a somewhat different proposition than the American version. Client-oriented under communist rule, it remains so today. Clients lobby behind closed doors for high economic stakes, and their patrons take care of them. Both the administration and members of Parliament tend to obey their political masters rather than heeding their constituents, and they are jealous of their prerogatives. They may view an NGO aiming to "represent" as a threat. On the other hand, few NGOs have achieved the structure and sophistication necessary in a representative force for a large interest group. It is unsurprising that World Learning, faithfully applying USAID's narrow standard for NGOs (a particular kind of nonpartisan advocacy group), found few it considered eligible for the Democracy Network. Most of the organizations that obtained grants under the program were technical, and some had a strictly economic aim: a meat processors association, a group of energy experts, and so on.

European Union Support

All Romanian governments since 1989, whatever their political bent, have pursued the goal of membership in the EU. To support the accession process, the EU's executive body, the European Commission, began giving significant amounts of aid to Romania through the PHARE program. Among the fields covered by PHARE is development of democracy, and support for civil society comes under that heading.

PHARE is the largest source of aid, public or private, for the development of civil society in Romania providing over 7 million euro over the last ten years. The assistance comes in several forms: so-called macro, or large, grants (up to 500,000 euro) administrated from Brussels by an outside contractor; small direct grants (up to 10,000 euro) managed by the local European Commission delegation; and the biggest component, the 5 million euro Civil Society Development Program, managed by the independent Foundation for the Development of Civil Society. The last program started rather late, in 1995, because the Romanian government was reluctant to accept it; EU officials patiently negotiated with government representatives for two years before they got the go-ahead.

The European Commission had no strategy, in the strict sense of the word, for the development of civil society in Romania. The programs of PHARE espouse broad goals based on the commission's published strategy document for the accession of Central European states,[5] which is rooted in the "European" philosophy of civil society and democratic development. That philosophy is much broader and more inclusive than the American one, envisioning close cooperation between the authorities and social services NGOs as well as civic NGOs and professional associations, beginning at the local level and continuing up through the central government, as the path to the consolidation of democracy and future integration into the EU. Thus PHARE allocates money to NGO projects having to do with transparency and management of Parliament and local government, independent, politically diverse media, conflict resolution, and education in and monitoring of human rights and minority rights. In addition, PHARE is committed to financing "development of NGOs and representative structures," which it defines broadly to include unions, political parties, consumer associations, and more.

The macro program functions surprisingly poorly. The contractor manages it from Brussels with no active representative in Romania, and is highly bureaucratic about it into the bargain. The partnership conditions included the requirement that one organization be from an EU member country and at least one from the associated countries of Romania Hungary, Bulgaria, etc., and that a 25 percent financial contribution to the project budget be from the applying organization; these conditions shut out all but a few well-connected organizations. The time frame for application, response, and contracting of a project, sometimes as long as two years and seldom less than nine months, makes it hard for the applying NGO to plan and manage.[6] Finally, complex reporting requirements have NGOs questioning the wisdom of applying. The program administrators are themselves frustrated by the program dynamic and the slow progress of projects but make no serious effort to improve communication and procedures. They also complain about the quality of the Romanian proposals.

The small-grants program, managed out of the local resident delegation of the EU Commission, has a much more hands-on approach. The EU staff did a lot of outreach work to publicize the program, which has clear deadlines, easy-to-meet conditions, and very reasonable reporting requirements and also uses local independent evaluators (rather than foreign consultants with little idea of the local scene). NGOs appreciate the program because it provides an accessible (though highly competitive, with about one in fifteen proposals selected) source of funds for small-scale projects. The program is still running successfully.

By far the largest public program supporting the development of civil society in Romania is run by the independent Foundation for Development of Civil Society (FDCS) funded through PHARE. Wholly Romanian-administrated and -managed, the foundation had an ambitious agenda of training, research, and funding of NGO projects. Open to proposals from NGOs in nearly all domains, keeping application fairly easy but financial controls tight, the foundation at first tried to finance nearly every plausible proposal. It awarded about five hundred grants for projects ranging from NGO public relations campaigns and institutional strengthening to art shows and shelters for the homeless. Most of these grants were small but adequate for a short program. The larger grants, however, for NGO Resource Centers intended to strengthen the capacity of NGOs at the local level, imposed detailed guidelines for applying that greatly restricted the circle of applicants. Evaluation of this aspect of the project indicated a low success rate.

The training the foundation conducted covered the basic knowledge needed to start and run an NGO. Developed with the help of Western consultants, it was adapted to local conditions and run by local trainees through extended classes and one-time seminars at locations nationwide.

The foundation's future is uncertain, however, as the EU Commission has suspended financing of its operations pending audit and review. This is bad news for Romanian NGOs, which have seen their windows of opportunity close one by one. Even more alarming are the EU's lack of a strategy for NGO development and lack of an exit strategy that takes account of the problem of sustainability, reflecting confusion high in the commission bureaucracy about what attitude to take toward NGOs.

Comparison of the results and modus operandi of the FDCS, the EU's foundation for civil society, with those of World Learning, the USAID contractor, may be instructive. The FDCS and World Learning had comparable aims, budgets, and administrative expenses. But the FDCS became the most important institution in civil society development in Romania, while World Learning now has only a small, not very active office in the country. The former has given out more than five hundred grants, the latter around twenty. The foundation has trained several hundred NGO activists, World Learning fewer than a hundred.

Operationally, the differences are also significant: the FDCS is a Romanian-registered organization with a Romanian board and executive, and PHARE oversight is limited. World Learning, based in the United States with an office in Romania, has American managers and professional staff, and Romanians work there only as assistants or support staff. U.S. officials' involvement is heavy. The FDCS has entered into cooperative arrangements with many American and European institutions—among them the Soros Romania, The International Center for Non-Profit Law, and British Charity Know-how Fund—and is free to take part in others. World Learning, on the other hand, has worked closely with the National Democratic Institute, its joint partner from the beginning, and almost no one else.

Paradoxically, while the FDCS is in dire straits after the EU's stoppage of its funding, World Learning is again in line out on the playing field, waiting for the next installment from USAID. Which is better, to do it by the book or to do what needs to be done?

Private Donors

Aside from the official U.S. and European support, some private Western foundations have helped NGOs in Romania, as elsewhere in Eastern Europe. The German *Stiftungen*, or foundations of the major political parties, and a handful of Dutch and American private foundations have played an important role. I am concerned here, however, with the activities of foundations that have sought to foster civil society development in and of itself, not those that have worked with civil society organizations for other developmental purposes.

The philosophy of private donors does not differ fundamentally from that of public donors, and one sees the European and the American school of thought at work in this domain, too. Private European foundations tend to fund social, environmental, and cultural NGOs, generally finding a good organization and keeping up the relationship for years. Development of civil society and democracy per se is often the goal of the U.S.-based foundations, which concentrate on what they consider the spearhead of civil society, the civic NGOs; the American foundations do, however, insist on a closer tie in their programs to the community.

Most Western private sources assisting the development of civil society approach operations differently from their public counterparts. Rather than elaborating guidelines and launching requests for proposals, the foundations have gone out and looked for the right organization, one whose goals match their own. They then help build up the adopted organization and its work. The private donors should be applauded for their sensitivity in avoiding giving directives to the local NGOs. Most of the grants are generous by local lights, in size but also in the spectrum of activities and expenses allowed, and reporting requirements are quite reasonable for organizations with an adequate financial management system. The customary "challenge grant" provisions keep organizations busy trying to diversify their resources, through income-generating activities or local fund-raising. The few happy NGOs that have been selected have grown into fairly stable institutions, staffed by quasi-professionals from the NGO sector. There is only one drawback to private foreign funding; there is not enough of it to make a real difference. With the exception of the Charles Stewart Mott Foundation and the German Marshall Fund,[7] large private organizations have halted their southeastern advance in Hungary; for the region's other countries, there are only minor activities through regional programs.

A few words on the Soros Foundation for an Open Society—Romania (the Romanian organization in the Soros foundations network) are imperative. With Romanian registration and a Romanian board and executive, and spending between $8 million and $15 million annually on programs in areas ranging from education and publishing to legislation and public administration, the foundation occupies a very special position among donors operating in Romania. In the first years after the revolution, it was constantly criticized from nationalist forces, reflecting nationalists' suspicions about an organization funded by a prominent American of Jewish and Hungarian origins. But it plowed ahead and soon became the major player in democracy assistance efforts in the country. It opened the first grant-giving facility for NGOs, providing money for projects in civic and political culture, ethnic issues, education, and the media, among other areas. In the late 1990s foundation officials spent a year reorganizing from top to bottom, spinning off some departments as independent organizations, some as for-profit institutions or independent foundations, and rethinking the organization's mission. Grants to NGOs are way down; resources are instead being channeled into strengthening public administration, assistance for Parliament, and ethnic relations. It is too early to comment on the restructuring, but critics warn that the concentration on support for public administration may not be efficient. Various donors have committed more than a billion dollars to make government in Romania work better, and the state implements at a crawl, so there is a tremendous backlog in aid efforts in this domain. Overall, the activity of the Soros Foundation has been extensive rather then intensive, covering an extremely wide field. It has left behind several strong institutions. Its recent evolution, however, tends to support public institutions rather than civil society.

What Aid Has and Has Not Done

The results of programs mentioned above and of initiatives of the United Nations Development Program and other donors, expressed in grants awarded, seminars held, people trained, and so on, may be impressive or not. I want to inquire here into the degree of real progress Romanian civil society has made as a consequence of foreign assistance.

The main point, which takes precedence over all criticism, is that aid from abroad has been a major support in building what has become an important network of NGOs. When Ceausescu fell, there were no NGOs in Romania. Ten years later, Romania has hundreds of strong NGOs capable of entering into contracts with the state to provide social services, monitoring environmental issues and assisting the government in ameliorating environmental problems, caring for orphans and street children, running microcredit programs, influencing state policies on economic issues, and on and on. Because of the advance work of these assistance organizations, the World Bank can now safely present to its board a project for Romania to be implemented mainly through NGOs. Moreover, the role the new, self-confident civil society played in the 1996 elections helped drive home to Romanians the deficiencies of the governing coalition, including corruption and unwillingness to change an economic system that was terminally ill.

In 1990, Romania had no legislation concerning NGOs on the books aside from a forgotten 1924 law on associations and foundations. Today, due largely to the indirect and direct influence of aid from abroad, the creation and growth of NGOs is protected and encouraged by law. A body of laws allows for the development of independent NGOs and their partnership with foreign and Romanian public and private organizations.

Civil society has been reborn in Romania and grown to be an actor, and foreign assistance midwifed the birth and helped the young sector gain influence. However, various issues and problems remain to be addressed, some of them inherent in civil society assistance, others particular to the nation.

First, if civil society's purpose is to serve as a link between community and government, to crystallize the will of a community and then advocate it to advance the common good, let us examine the ties that NGOs in Romania have with the authorities and with the community. There is no question that the continuous advocacy for transparency in public institutions and for partnership between government and people has borne some fruit. Because of pressure from NGOs, most central and local institutions of the state now have an office designated to provide information to and serve as a liaison with NGOs. Today NGOs command attention and make their voices heard; they are sometimes called on to testify in Parliament, even if what they say is not always paid attention to.

But what about the relationship with the community, and with the voter? There has been a longstanding assumption that NGOs—for the sake of the discussion, let us say civic NGOs—are an emanation of their communities' will. If true in the past, does the work of civic NGOs nowadays still reflect what their communities want and need? The evidence suggests that the answer is no. Faced in the political world with their representatives' corruption and indifference or inadequacy and indecision, citizens tend not to look or ask for the accountability that civic NGOs push for. They simply begin to ignore and despise politicians and politics. A country in which voter turnout always topped 70 percent in the various elections in the first half of the 1990s now sees turnout of only 54 percent, according to the latest data. Romanians rate the fundamental institutions of the rule of law, Parliament and the Justice Ministry, lowest among their country's major institutions for trustworthiness and relevance—and the trend is toward further decline. And for the first time since 1989, a majority of Romanians declare that they were better off under communism. The main cause of all this is the poor performance of politicians on both sides of the spectrum, but still, understanding of democracy does not seem to have risen one iota, and the citizenry seem as estranged as ever from their elected officials, if not more so. A possible, and distressing, conclusion is that civic NGOs over the years did the kind of projects that donors trained and funded them to do—advocacy targeting politicians—rather than educating the community, especially the less educated among its members. They took the community for granted, or if they didn't, they lacked the resources and training for what needed to be done: work with citizens.

Environmental NGOs provide another example of letting down the community. In the early 1990s, they were the example of a well-trained, fairly well-funded sector, with the best network; unsurprisingly, USAID at the time was sponsoring a generously funded national training program for the sector's NGOs. Now, most observers agree that, with a few exceptions, environmental NGOs have lost their tie to the people, using up most of their energy looking at internal organizational issues or squabbling with the relevant ministry or among themselves. In current NGO parlance, "doing a project" means writing a proposal that will bring in grant money for salaries and the office rent, rather than organizing a protest rally at a polluting factory to raise people's awareness or cleaning up a river. Fatigue with the overall idea of environmental advocacy seems to have set in.

Another field in which NGOs should have done much more and in which donor agencies could have encouraged them is in leveling the social, economic, and political disparities between regions of the country. Although almost everyone agrees regional inequality is a problem and is beginning to have serious repercussions, no one has made any apparent effort to solve it. Have NGOs not proposed projects in the less favored provinces, or are conditions so bad there that grant-giving is impossible? Do NGOs submit only proposals that they know they can get money for, while donors stick with the same old English-speaking recipients that they know they can work with, and the same old kinds of projects that they know will be successful in their own limited terms and will appeal to the trustees? But an event like the 1998 miners' strike in the Jiu Valley, which quickly turned violent and threatened the very stability of the political system, shows that NGOs, with financial assistance and nudging from donors, must get to work correcting regional discrepancies. No civic organization was running any project in what was known to be the most volatile part of the country. Shaking the miners' conviction that they had a right to take by force what they considered their due would have been difficult, even perilous. But what are civic NGOs if not organizations *supposed* to work in such environments, and what are donors if not entities supposed to direct aid where it is most needed?

Another urgent issue is the self-sustainability of Romanian NGOs that used to receive or still do receive foreign funds. As discussed above, the large public donors, USAID and PHARE, have frozen grant-giving programs or gotten out of the business altogether. The abrupt break stranded immature civil society organizations that had been living from day to day (or rather, from small project to small project). No one was saying, and I could not discover, if the cutoff of funds was part of a deliberate strategy or was strictly due to bureaucratic imperatives and rhythms. And not even the operators of the grant-giving programs know what the programs' future will be. Under these conditions, the organizations' ability to keep themselves going financially is a matter of survival.

Donors' proposal guidelines and the applications submitted usually include several lines on the sustainability of the project and nothing on the sustainability of the organization. But whatever is said on the subject is generally calculated to make some bureaucrat happy. The truth is harsher. With the exceptions noted above, grants have been large enough only to sustain a project, not to build up an organization so that it can stand on its own, or to provide seed money, or to allow investment in profit-making ventures. In a shrinking transition economy where the private sector is struggling to survive, domestic corporate funding is hard to get and harder to live off. Since many NGOs are not deeply rooted in the community, expressing a common need and demand, they cannot hope for community support. And finally, all the free money since 1990 has raised expectations of staffs and clients of NGOs to unrealistic levels. Now that foreign funds have dried up, more and more NGO-trained staff are leaving for jobs in the public or private sector.

Looking to the Future

Our look into the future must begin with a brief look back. The enthusiastic rebirth of Romania's NGO sector in the early 1990s was followed by steady growth in both quantity and quality of NGOs, then by a phase in which the NGOs searched for an identity. As the decade closes, the sector has begun to both speak and set goals for itself in a coherent manner. Slowly, NGOs have become a player in Romanian society, but as yet they are a timid one, whose role is still unclear to many. Their role needs to be strengthened and built up.

Some may regard Romanian civil society in its present state as a dismal failure, just another service provider in thrall to the market. But one also sees positive signs cropping up. Organizers of the annual NGO conference in Romania, which for the first time in 1998 asked for a participation fee, express surprise that few of the "old-timers"—Western-funded NGOs—have shown up at recent events They are overrun instead by fresh new groups, mainly cultural or social-protection organizations, living on corporate donations, dues, and other domestic sources of funds. One finds out about a clinic and hospital for street children run by a church group and financed solely by the local church and the local Rotary club. About the application sent in to a funder by an eight-hundred-member children's association that sponsors weekly civic, religious, ecological, and leisure activities, which needed only a fax machine and had never received a grant or NGO management training. Examples abound around us. It is difficult to say to what extent foreign assistance, through initiatives for the development of civil society, has influenced these seemingly spontaneous apparitions. But probably it has helped—either indirectly, by providing an example or paving the way with the authorities, or directly, by offering technical assistance and specialized information.

Another healthy sign is that the old-timers among the civic movements are adapting. Pro-Democracy, one of the leading civic organizations in Romania, has decided to concentrate its programs in the small cities, closer to the community, moving away from large, impersonal cities and Parliament. Another group is thinking about becoming a political party and jumping into the fray, sick and tired, maybe, of being an outcast among NGOs because of its political stand.

Far more important, the NGOs that gather at the annual national NGO conference have identified their own weaknesses and are trying to address them. They see—correctly—a lack of capable internal governance within civil society groups and of minimal standards for governance as a major flaw, and have begun to remedy it with the creation of a committee of experts that will design self-regulating norms for NGOs. Other initiatives, such as legislation to curb fraud by shell NGOs, are being seriously considered by government officials.

The most important challenge, however, is self-sustainability, and the numbers there show promise. A comparison of sources of NGOs' funds in 1995 and in 1998, as highlighted in Table 1, indicates diversification of resources and a decreased reliance on foreign funding. The approximate amount of funds raised and allocated for the NGO sector in 1995 was about 435 billion Romanian lei (approximately $189.2 million), or .06 percent of GDP. The amount for 1998 is not yet available, but is expected to be larger.

At a time when foreign funding has been falling and the number of NGOs slowly increasing, NGOs have moved toward alternative sources of funds. These sources are, first, individual contributions and membership fees, and second, sponsorship and donations from local businesses. Although at first it may seem surprising, fees for services could not be expected to rise, since NGOs primarily serve impoverished, or at least economically disadvantaged, groups of people. Slightly disappointing is the relatively low increase in subsidies and fees for services from the government, despite increased collaboration between NGOs and the public sector. One can, however, expect an increase in this category, as Par-

Table 1. Funding Sources for Romanian NGOs

Sources	1995 % of total	1998 % of total
Foreign governmental, nongovernmental, and private funds	56%	36%
Donations and contributions of the population (including membership fees)	12%	28%
Fees for services	11%	12%
Sponsorships and donations from businesses	7%	13%
Subsidies and fees for services from governmental sector	5%	7%
Dividends	N/A	4%
Other sources	9%	N/A

liament recently approved legislation encouraging local government to contract work out to NGOs. The category of "Dividends" was, for the first time, large enough to warrant its own line, showing a mature strategic and economic sense at work in the sector.

The data also show that support from foreign donors, though much reduced since 1995, still accounted for the largest share of NGOs' revenue in 1998. The data all come from a period when the EU was a major actor. The sudden drop in funds available that has occurred with the EU's possibly permanent suspension of PHARE aid will have a severe impact on the NGO sector. In the present economic downturn, with small private companies going bankrupt by the hundreds every month and the standard of living falling, it is doubtful that the alternate suppliers will be able to fill the gap.

For the actors involved in developing civil society in Romania, much remains to be done. In my opinion, the driving force setting and structuring goals and methods for such development should be the Romanian NGOs. In spite of frequent dysfunction and confusion among Romanian NGOs, donors need to be more responsive to local conditions and demands. The bulk of the work must be done by the NGO sector. Although the sector may only be in its early adolescence, the more mature and influential NGOs should continue the attempts to discipline the sector from within and to educate the funding agencies, while looking to the needs of the community rather than those of bankrupt NGOs disconnected from the society they purportedly serve. The challenges the donor agencies face are difficult not so much operationally as morally. Donors' goal should be to look at themselves honestly and examine their effectiveness more than their efficiency. Good strategies and operating procedures will follow, as in any healthy organization.

Probably the toughest challenge lies with the administration in Romania, which has taken on the responsibility of creating a civil society that functions well. There is still a cleavage between the political sphere and the civil service, as well as between the civil service and its clients, including the private organizations. The long-expected civil service reform remains in the realm of endless changes of the organizational structure and downsizing of public institutions. Decentralization and governance reforms at the local level are progressing slowly and unevenly in the absence of effective incentives and the lack of capacity to fulfill their duties. The cultural barriers between the public sphere and the private are still a tough obstacle impeding the growth of necessary trust. I remain optimistic, however. Continuous change in the structure of ownership and the obvious political will to improve the allocation of resources and modernize society will yield their benefits, as history generally shows.

Another trap both donors and the Romanian government must avoid is narrowing the field of civil society development to NGO development. The educational system, the academic community, and the medieval, conservative Orthodox Church are all in varying states of reform and development, their determination to provide the support the community expects from them in a neck-and-neck competition with a worsening economy and the apathy and resentment that it breeds. But even the church has begun to venture out of its shell and involve itself more in the community and in national issues in a positive, constructive way. It has started a school for social workers, and priests are now encouraged to call on the community to work together. Academia, on the other hand, is living through a crisis. It is awake and dynamic, but brilliant students and professors leave the country in a veritable brain drain, driven out not so much by the poor living standards as by the lack of outlets for their intellectual endeavors in an obsolete civil service and a reduced private sector. This is alarming because the intelligentsia in Romania, probably more than NGOs, is the core of civil society and the leading support for democracy.

A final question: What can the civil society do for democracy? First, it can help Romanians survive through this depressed period, which is testing citizens' belief in democracy. Second, it can help educate citizens to accept the adventure of transition and to make informed political choices. Both are difficult tasks that Romanian civil society is only partly prepared to shoulder. In undertaking the first, it lacks the institutional capacity to process funds and projects that aim to provide social protection. A start has been made, and a number of organizations are involved in such projects. Still, as mentioned above, the worst-hit areas are the ones where civil society is less active. Action on the second task, which is the main role of civil society, is hampered by poor knowledge of the issues, by the cleavage and poor communication between civil society and the community, as well as by the loud populist roar of politicians. Right now it is a challenge mainly for the intelligentsia. Will intellectuals be willing to speak loud enough to be heard? Will they cast off their Olympian detachment, changing the syntax and semantics of their message so as to make it palatable to the people? They have the technology, the knowledge and sometimes even the resources, but do they have the will? The future will tell.

Notes

The views expressed in this chapter are the author's own; they do not reflect the views of the World Bank.

1. The Romanian revolution began with a minor riot in the western city of Timisoara on December 16, 1989. The brutal response of the army and the police sparked protests in many other towns and cities, including Bucharest, the capital. On December 22, Ceausescu, faced with a popular uprising, fled Bucharest when the army sided with the population. He and his wife were executed by an impromptu military tribunal on December 25. A group calling itself the Council on National Salvation announced that it was taking power, and by December 28 the situation had stabilized. About a thousand people had been killed or wounded in the street-fighting during Ceausescu's last days in power. Few of those responsible for the killing of Romanian protesters in December 1989 were brought to justice, a lapse that still rankles ten years later.

2. Between 1990 and 1992, 80 percent of Romania's ethnic Germans emigrated to Germany, leaving a much deplored vacuum in society. Whole villages or large parts of many towns were left empty. The example of the German community, with their emphasis on work ethic, community involvement, and associative initiatives had served as a competitive stimulus to the other ethnic com-

munities such as the Romanians and Hungarians. Anecdotal evidence points to the fact that their departure is deeply regretted by the autochthonous population.

3. A noteworthy exception was the Westminster Foundation, which financed political NGOs in 1993–94.

4. NGOs in the know took care not to do too well in the evaluation, which would have meant that they did not need assistance and so would have been refused funding.

5. European Commission, *La stratégie de pre-adhesion de l'Union Europeenne pour les pays associés d'Europe Centrale* (Brussels: European Commission, 1996).

6. These long delays in an environment that was rapidly changing led to situations in which the project objectives had become redundant by the time of contracting. This resulted in the recipients having to change the project objectives and modify implementation before even getting under way.

7. Unfortunately, the German Marshall Foundation has reduced its support for institution building of NGOs, reorienting aid toward think tanks, security issues, and the like.

Part Five

Latin America

9

Latin American Democratization: The Civil Society Puzzle

Michael Shifter

> In the case of a word like democracy, not only is there no agreed
> definition, but the attempt to make one is resisted from all sides. It
> is almost universally felt that when we call a country democratic
> we are praising it: consequently the defenders of every kind of re-
> gime claim that it is a democracy, and fear that they might have to
> stop using the word if it were tied down to any one meaning. Words
> of this kind are often used in a consciously dishonest way. That is,
> the person who uses them has his own private definition, but al-
> lows his hearer to think he means something quite different. . . .
> Other words used in variable meanings, in most cases more or less
> dishonestly, are: class, totalitarian, science, progressive, reaction-
> ary, bourgeois, equality.
> —George Orwell, "Politics and the English Language," 1946[1]

One suspects that if Orwell were here at the start of the new millennium,
he would be tempted to put "civil society" at the top of his list of manipulated terms. The term has gained broad appeal and currency in the
United States and around the world. Yet it is slippery, reflecting the pervasive conceptual confusion about the realms of society outside government and thus serves the purposes of analysts and activists who use it to
posture and drive home a political point.

In the context of Latin America, a variety of meanings can be dis-
cerned. Together, these constitute the pieces of what might be called the
"civil society puzzle." The pieces are in play simultaneously, and over-

lap and link up in complex ways. Laying them out, fitting them together—and noting the points of tension—can be instructive and can reduce future misuse. Three pieces deserve closer examination.

The first piece is the most wide-ranging notion of civil society. It refers to voluntary associations that are not part of the state or the market. In this regard, Latin America offers a particularly rich mix. Despite the central role of the state in the region's history, this broad universe of civil society is the product of a strong tradition, incorporating but going well beyond charitable institutions and organizations linked to the Catholic Church. It has evolved independent both of "waves" of democracy and of assistance programs carried out by international donors.

The second piece blends into, and is subsumed under, the first piece. Its temporal reference and political connotations are more specific. Civil society in this sense refers to the organizations involved in the global transformation that democratization has wrought over the past two decades. The opposition to, and ultimate collapse of, communism gave the concept of civil society resonance and weight. Unlike in Eastern Europe, where civil society groups defied regimes of the Left, activists in Latin America challenged military, authoritarian regimes of the Right. In the Western Hemisphere, the turn toward civilian, constitutional government actually preceded the end of the Cold War, making significant progress in the early 1980s. Opposition forces and social movements in more than a dozen countries—women's movements often prominent among them—demanded the restoration or construction of democratic politics and institutions.

The third piece, distinct from and even narrower than the second, has to do with the conception of civil society predominant among external actors seeking to promote democratic change. It concerns the programs that donors undertake in the name of strengthening civil society. These are programs, which though carried out under a general civil society rubric, are often intended to advance the public policy agenda of a specific issue such as human rights or of particular groups such as women or the indigenous people of a country or region.

How are civil society groups in Latin America perceived by donors and by Latin Americans themselves, and what assumptions or conceptual lenses are applied to understand this sector's role? In addition, why did civil society programs emerge when they did, how do they tend to operate, whom do they reach, what do they seek to accomplish, and what are the limitations on and possibilities of their efforts?

This chapter will analyze the three pieces in turn. It strives to impart greater conceptual clarity and analytical sharpness to the concept of "civil society," as used in aid circles. Sorting through and figuring out the "puzzle" will not only stimulate discussion among donors, recipients, and aspiring recipients but may also help shape donors' thinking and programming in this area. "Civil society" can be understood in its broadest and richest sense only by paying close attention to all three pieces and their interplay. Yet such an appreciation seldom informs democracy assistance efforts.

To keep the discussion manageable, the study focuses on the cases of Guatemala and Peru and on the programs of the United States Agency for International Development (USAID). The U.S. civil society assistance efforts in Guatemala and Peru are fairly typical of U.S. civil society aid around the region, and the political transitions in those countries are largely typical as well in regional terms. Some reference, however, will be made to other Latin American countries and donor organizations. The hope is that the study will be relevant for other societies, and other donor programs, involved in various ways in the democracy assistance enterprise.

Setting the Context

Compared to Latin America's long history of regular democratic breakdowns, democratically elected government has in recent decades had a remarkable run in Latin America. What Larry Diamond has called "electoral democracy"—"a civilian, constitutional system in which the legislative and chief executive offices are filled through regular, competitive, multiparty elections with universal suffrage"—has for the most part taken hold in the region.[2] Since the mid-1980s, interruptions of elected, civilian government have been rare. Although the twenty-first century opened with some troubling signs of democracy under strain (concentrated in several Andean countries), the overall trend has been positive. Accompanying benefits for citizens have included greater opportunity to express their ideas, channel their demands, and organize their interests.

Another characteristic of the region, however, is much less salutary. Despite the succession of democratically elected, constitutional governments, social and institutional conditions in Latin America remain dismal. The region is marked by the worst social inequality in the world, with notoriously low educational levels and a large underclass. In addition, many of the key institutions that performed vital functions in previous decades have lost much of their credibility and coherence. Political parties in many countries no longer command the allegiance and support they once did. Unions are substantially weaker. The Catholic Church has lost ground to Latin America's growing evangelical movement. Indeed, the region's institutional performance—in the governmental, private, and nongovernmental sectors—has been generally disappointing, failing to deal effectively with citizens' most pressing concerns, including unemployment and public safety.

In several important respects, the experiences of Guatemala and Peru exemplify sociological and political trends in the region, including the continual tension between democratic experimentation and antidemocratic legacies and the formidable challenge of building democracy in societies marked by sociopolitical marginalization of significant numbers of people. In Guatemala, the transition away from decades of repressive military rule to formal democratic rule took place in 1985. Despite President Jorge Serrano's attempt to suspend the constitution in May 1993, the country has had a fifteen-year run of elected civilian administrations. Nor do serious observers anticipate a reversal—a return to direct, military government—at least in the short term.

Though Peru's political history has generally been marked by a higher level of institutionalization than Guatemala's, the Andean country, too, has continually struggled to achieve orderly democratic rule, making some progress, only to sustain serious setbacks. Peru turned to democratic politics in 1980 after twelve prior years of military rule and frequent democratic breakdowns during the twentieth century. Twelve years later, in April 1992, the constitutional order was again interrupted. President Alberto Fujimori (succeeding where Serrano would fail in Guatemala) suspended the constitution, shut down Congress, and took control of the judiciary, claiming that the Shining Path insurgency and economic collapse made these steps necessary. Though the military exercises substantial influence over political affairs, voters legitimated Fujimori's rule in 1995 with his second resounding victory in national elections. Fujimori's bid for a third term in 2000 proved controversial, however. Despite serious questions about the regime's legitimacy due to a flawed electoral process, the Peruvian president appeared determined to remain in power.

Both societies are fragmented, and social exclusion, particularly among the large indigenous population in each country, is common. Though estimates vary considerably and arouse much debate, indigenous people make up roughly 60 percent of the population in Guatemala and nearly 40 percent in Peru. In both countries, the national government's presence in remote rural areas has been minimal, giving rise to widespread disenchantment and frustration there. A largely absent state is one of the most powerful explanations for the insurgencies that have afflicted both countries in recent years.

In Guatemala, the four-decade civil war ended in December 1996, within the framework of an internationally supervised peace agreement. The Guatemalan National Revolutionary Union (URNG) formed a legal political party which, though weaker than counterparts in neighboring El Salvador and Nicaragua, participates in the political process. In Peru, the more virulent Shining Path insurgency suffered a major blow in 1992 with the capture of many of its leaders. Though the group continues to operate in some areas, it has been crippled and no longer poses a major threat.

In both countries, the leading political parties and government institutions are fractured and weak. This is true particularly for Peru. Indeed, Peruvian parties have been in deep crisis for the past decade, and President Fujimori has preferred to preside over various inchoate movements that are constantly in flux. The chances for renewal or renovation of the country's political party system at this point seem slim.

Surveys show that most Guatemalans are disenchanted with their political parties, and their politicians as well. In the context of the peace accords, many observers have pointed to the Guatemalan government's inability to put ample international aid to good use. Indeed, the 1999 election of Alfonso Portillo of the right-wing opposition party, Guatemalan Republican Front (FRG), reflected the previous government's failure to deliver promised benefits to its citizens, which created a keen, widespread desire for change.

Despite the marginalization of the poor, recent political changes in both Peru and Guatemala seem to reveal a current running in the opposite direction. Guatemala has seen a demonstrable increase in participation among its indigenous population. Indigenous representation from several parties (though predominantly from the FRG) in the National Congress has risen substantially, to more than 10 percent since the mid-1990s. In municipal government, too, indigenous political figures are more prominent than ever before. The move toward a more inclusive society is one of the major objectives of the peace accords. Many regard it as the critical test of Guatemala's social progress.

In Peru as well, political participation is broadening. Fujimori is, after all, the child of Japanese immigrants, and projects a fresh image of the country, a departure from traditional, oligarchic rule. (Moreover, in early 2000, Fujimori's principal rival for the presidency was Alejandro Toledo, described in Peru as a *cholo*, or an urbanite of Indian descent.) The question of indigenous people is far less clear-cut than in Guatemala, since Peru's Aymaran and Quechuan peoples do not represent a self-conscious, politically identifiable group.[3] Nonetheless, Peru is opening up in this regard also.

In sum, Latin America—Guatemala and Peru in particular—offers a complex and varied political landscape. On the positive side, elections, whatever their flaws, have become nearly routine, acquiring a life of their own. And the political arena is somewhat more open than it was prior to the 1980s, less manifestly the preserve of a traditional elite. At the same time, however, political institutions are generally in disarray and often perform poorly. Political parties have been incapable of channeling and responding to public demands. Most citizens, as a result, sharply question them. And despite greater macroeconomic stability (in Peru particularly), broad social conditions have as yet shown little improvement.

The First Piece: A Wide Frame

For Michael Walzer, civil society refers to "the space of uncoerced human association and also the set of relational networks—formed for the sake of family, faith, interest, and ideology—that fill this space."[4] Applying this broad definition to Latin America past and present yields a plethora of groups and organizations that Walzer would say makes up the sector.

A number of scholars have attempted to develop useful taxonomies and systematic mappings of Latin America's civil society organizations. Recent historical studies have, for example, detailed the rich array of sports clubs, networks, community groups, professional associations, mutual aid societies, and the like that have long characterized the region and its public life.[5] More recently, Bruce Schearer and John Tomlinson of the Synergos Institute prepared for the Inter-American Development Bank a fairly comprehensive overview of civil society organizations in Latin America and the Caribbean. In their revealing profile of the 222,000 registered civil society organizations in Brazil, Schearer and Tomlinson report that most of the organizations can be divided among four categories: beneficent, religious, and welfare associations (23 percent); sports and recreation associations (20 percent); cultural, scientific, and educational associations (15 percent); and religious groups (13 percent). The authors maintain that the breakdown is typical of the civil society sector of other countries in the region as well. They stress that between half and three-quarters of the registered portion of the sector is made up of groups that are not nongovernmental organizations (NGOs), which they define as organizations "with some type of professional staff that conduct advocacy activities or provide development services."[6]

Drawing on case studies of Brazil, Argentina, Peru, and Colombia, Leilah Landim and Andres Thompson have produced a similarly wide-ranging overview of the "emerging non-profit or voluntary sector in Latin America" that emphasizes that sector's changing fortunes and different paths. They are especially sensitive to the various circumstances under which associations have surfaced and developed. Their approach highlights "the existence of a universe of non-profit organizations much broader than what is understood in Latin America by the term NGO." That universe experienced its sharpest growth in many Latin American countries in the latter nineteenth century and in the early twentieth century, spurred in some measure by the arrival of immigrants from Western and Eastern Europe. Many of the mutual-benefit societies, in Brazil especially, grew more politicized and class-oriented, siding with and aiding trade unions. During the same period, professional associations, such as the Brazilian Press Association, and employers associations developed as well.[7]

Perhaps the dominant and most tightly interwoven thread in Latin America's civil society tapestry has been religion, above all the Roman

Catholic Church. Although its strength today varies from country to country, the Catholic Church has shaped a large part of civil society. As Landim and Thompson point out, "The role of this institution—particularly by way of its orders like the Franciscans, Dominicans, Augustines and principally the Jesuits through the Company of Jesus as well as the Sisterhood of Saint Charity—was to be fundamental in cultivating any new spaces, initiatives and values which led to what we now call the philanthropic ventures of the colonial era. Educational, health and social welfare establishments were almost all the responsibility of the church practically until the mid-nineteenth century." Local elites carried out comparable efforts in the secular sphere, but those tended to be less significant in the voluntary sector than the church's activities.

More recently, observers have noted the decline in the Catholic Church's authority and number of adherents and the attendant expansion of evangelical churches throughout the region.[8] Indeed, the number of evangelicals in Latin America has grown from under 250,000 in 1900 to more than forty million in 1990, with more than sixty million projected for the year 2000.[9] In terms of percentage of the population, the phenomenon has been most pronounced in Guatemala, Peru, and Brazil. Between 1962 and 1982, the number of Protestants in Guatemala increased from 60,000 to more than 300,000 baptized adherents active in some 5,000 local organized churches belonging to over 200 autonomous church groups such as Jehovah's Witnesses, Mormons, and Church of Christ.[10] In Walzer's inclusive conception of civil society, this part of the country's social and institutional landscape is salient.

In the contemporary secular realm as well, in Peru, Guatemala, and many other Latin American countries, one often finds a dense social and associational life in poor urban areas. Throughout the region, a substantial portion of the labor force—in some countries, as much as 50 or 60 percent—works in the largely unregulated "informal sector." Many of the organizations that dominate the social life of the region's poor revolve around development, often with a focus on small-scale entrepreneurship. Associations made up of microenterprises—for example, so-called national development foundations—are especially prevalent in Latin America. Others are more community-based and mainly perform social roles. This broad spectrum of civil society includes associations of all kinds—many devoid of political purpose, others with a clear political agenda.

The Second Piece: Civil Society and Political Change

The second piece of the civil society puzzle highlights a more politicized sector. This is the sector that captured the attention of many analysts, and played a role in the democratization process in Latin America and throughout the world over the past several decades. The best-known counterparts of Latin America's highly politicized civil society groups were those of Eastern Europe in the 1980s and early 1990s, although the groups there challenged regimes of the Left, rather than of the Right as in Latin America.

A politicized conception of civil society is hardly new. It has, however, undergone profound changes, as the manifestations shifted from union-based activities to "new social movements" to more radical, indigenous forces that burst on the scene in such countries as Ecuador in the early twenty-first century. In addition, a key strand of politicized civil society has exercised important political influence in ways that have baffled pundits. Concentration on the second piece inclines one to overlook or belittle the often hidden significance of key social actors—including, for example, voluntary groupings of evangelical associations or informal sector networks—pressing their own way for political change. As explained further below, the cases of Peru, Guatemala, and, more recently, Venezuela underscore the importance of the political role of those actors, which so far has remained largely unexamined.

But in Latin America, the second piece is most commonly associated with the movement from authoritarian to democratic rule over the past several decades. While negotiations and pacts among elite sectors help account for the transformation, civil society's spurring of change "from below" was significant. During this period, the region's extremely varied "new social movements" were made up of groups and organizations that defended and advanced primarily gender and identity-based, rather than purely economic, interests. Prominent among these groups were women's, indigenous people's, and human rights organizations (such as the Mothers of the Plaza de Mayo in Argentina).

The phase was distinguished by a greater appreciation of political democracy—the formal and procedural aspects of political systems—than had existed before in the region. In part, the appreciation derived from the exhaustion and failure of a more traditional "leftist project," which became evident in the 1980s. But it was also bound up with the powerful reaction against authoritarian governments that was sweeping through Latin America.

In particular, repression in historically democratic countries like Chile and Uruguay helped foster commitment to the rule of law. Beginning in the mid-1970s, the repressive practices by military governments in the Southern Cone sparked cries to protect human rights and civil and political liberties seldom heard before in Latin America. In Chile, for example, the organizations working on behalf of, say, human rights or women's concerns developed greatly under the military regime of General Augusto Pinochet (1973–90). During the democratic transition of the late 1980s and early 1990s, however, many of these organizations were demobilized as nongovernmental leaders moved into government and other sectors, and what one analyst has characterized as a "conspiracy of consensus" prevailed. Indeed, the church-linked Vicariate of Solidarity—the most well known among the groups of Chile's, if not the region's, human rights movement and a symbol of opposition to the Pinochet dictatorship—closed down after the turn to civilian, constitutional government.

In Guatemala, development of a self-consciously politicized sector of civil society came relatively late. It was delayed and constrained by the intense civil war in the country, the military's significant role, and waves of political repression. A number of groups—including human rights organizations and indigenous people's associations—existed, but they were weak, often embattled, and maintained a low profile.

In the early 1990s, with the opening of political space and the marked move toward a peace settlement, Guatemala became more hospitable to the development of nongovernmental groups. David Holiday and Tania Palencia have described in detail the sector's growth and expansion, particularly the significant efforts of groups promoting human rights and women's and indigenous people's interests.[11] Perhaps the most widely recognized is the umbrella organization COPMAGUA (Coordination of Organizations of the Mayan People of Guatemala), a broad coalition that is playing a key role in the attempt to carry out the country's ambitious, wide-ranging peace accords.

The fledgling sector received a further boost from President Serrano's failed *autogolpe*, or self-coup of May 1993. Serrano's attempt to assume near-dictatorial powers rallied opposition to an already unpopular president and encouraged calls for greater political participation. What had been an assortment of dispersed groups began to come together and pull in the same direction; the Assembly of Civil Society became the recognized umbrella organization for the sector. Although private business, represented by the Coordinating Committee of Agricultural, Commercial, Industrial, and Financial Associations (CACIF), also played a major role in challenging and ultimately thwarting Serrano's unconstitutional actions,[12] it was not part of the broader assembly. That fact reflected one of the important cleavages among the groups committed to defending constitutional rule in Guatemala.

The politicized civil society sector in Peru developed and crystallized before its counterpart in Guatemala, in the late 1970s, toward the end of military rule. It was then, for example, that a cluster of women's groups— notably the Manuela Ramos Movement, Peru Mujer, and the Flora Tristan Center—emerged and began to press feminist demands. In addition, in the early 1980s, observing the harsh state response to the incipient Shining Path insurgency, human rights organizations such as the Legal Defense Institute began to document and denounce abuses and draw attention at home and abroad to the deteriorating situation. These were joined by a vibrant array of development-oriented NGOs that sought to promote higher levels of organization and greater community participation in poor areas, both rural and urban. Peru in the 1980s could point to a burgeoning, diverse nongovernmental sector.

Many of the sector's groups were sympathetic to some degree with what was then the most significant legal party of the Left in Latin America, the United Left. Some notion or expectation of fundamental social change propelled the emergent civil society. Still, although political representation increased somewhat, as Peruvian sociologist Nicolas Lynch has noted, the promising civil society organizations of the 1980s generally failed to translate those gains into coherent, effective, sustainable political roles.[13]

In the 1990s, many of the organizations, adapting to political realities, increasingly focused on resolving particular problems, often related to matters of public policy. They tended to oppose Fujimori's rule, not only the president's markedly neoliberal economic policies but his authoritarian proclivities, expressed most clearly in the 1992 self-coup that interrupted constitutional rule.

The changing ethos in Peru's nongovernmental realm exemplifies a regionwide trend. The prevailing notion in the 1980s was that politicized organizations combining in social movements would generate broad support and eventually lead to a more open, democratic political order. In the 1990s, disillusionment set in, and the theory of large-scale political transformation was jettisoned for the most part. Many of the movements gradually settled into sectors made up of nongovernmental groups representing and promoting particular interests. Over time, then, lofty ideas about transformation of the social and political order gave way to technocratic concern with solving particular problems and developing sound public policy. As the next section explains, that evolution has led to the third piece of the puzzle, the externally assisted portion of civil society.

To be sure, the slice of civil society that identified itself as explicitly political was not keen about Fujimori's programs and policies. Most Peruvians, however, supported the 1992 self-coup and, for most of the 1990s, Fujimori's rule in general; at times, popular approval was overwhelming.

In the 1990s, a new force coalesced in civil society and exercised its political voice. Less self-consciously political and less visible than the politicized segment of civil society prominent in the 1980s, with fewer international connections, this segment is made up of microenterprise associations, evangelical groups, cultural organizations, and the like. In the presidential election of 1990 and afterward, it resoundingly rejected the traditional political establishment and backed Fujimori's prescriptions for Peru, even when they flouted the constitution.

Fujimori's victory in 1990, with its landslide endorsement for the political neophyte and virtual unknown, was perhaps the most stunning electoral result of the twentieth century in Latin America. In the contest, civil society expressed itself politically—with a vengeance. Post-election studies showed that Fujimori successfully drew on the multilayered associational life in Peru, particularly on the highly organized evangelical movement and networks of microenterprise groups.[14] It was not, to be sure, the Peruvian state or the market that provided the organized pillars of Fujimori's support.

The results in 1990 dramatically illustrated the complex, fragmented nature of Peru, so poorly understood by observers. Indeed, in a revealing account, Peruvian journalist Jose Maria Salcedo reported that just a few days before Fujimori's unexpectedly strong showing in the first round, several of the country's leading analysts and activists not only failed to sense his impending triumph, but could not even identify who he was.[15] Acute, discerning, and committed to democratic politics, these prominent figures of Peru's better-known and widely recognized civil society were nonetheless caught entirely off guard.

Though not to the same degree, the results of Guatemala's December 1999 elections similarly upset the most conventional prognoses that prevailed not too long before the contest. In this case, Alfonso Portillo of the FRG was a known quantity, having competed in and lost the presidential election of 1995. Significantly, the FRG was founded by former military dictator Efrain Rios Montt, a self-avowed evangelical (as was former Guatemalan President Serrano). There is some evidence that Portillo's victory, consistent with broader political trends in Latin America, reflected public disenchantment with the status quo and a desire for greater economic and physical security. Portillo also did well among the voters of Guatemala's sizable evangelical community, presumably because of his association with Rios Montt.[16]

Perhaps Latin America's most compelling political figure at the start of the twenty-first century, Venezuelan President Hugo Chavez also benefitted from evangelicals' support in his 1998 election. To fortify his already substantial base, Chavez reached out to his country's evangelical community (estimated at roughly 5 percent of the population), concentrated in the shantytowns that dot the main urban centers.[17]

Within the second, politicized piece of civil society, then, one should distinguish between two segments made up of very different kinds of political actors. The first, dominant and more widely recognized, consists of political actors previously involved in various social movements who have settled into NGOs. The second segment, which includes the evangelical movement and microenterprise networks, is far less visible and much less studied, but it has helped shape countries' politics by delivering electoral results in Peru, Guatemala, and other Latin American nations.

The Third Piece: Externally Assisted Civil Society

These elements form the context within which a more familiar conception of civil society—the externally assisted portion of civil society, oriented more toward public policy—has taken hold. Though patterns and sequences vary greatly from country to country, today's Latin America is marked by the discrediting and exhaustion of a "leftist project"; a succession of civilian, constitutional governments; stubbornly acute social problems and the failure of institutions to deal adequately with them; and a proliferation of nongovernmental groups committed to generating better public policies in various public interest areas and advancing group interests. Whether such groups are viewed as temporarily supplanting traditional mechanisms of political representation (for example, political parties) or as more permanent features, they are typically regarded—at least by many Western analysts and donors—as contributing significantly to more participatory, responsible politics and the deepening of democracy.

A considerable number of those working in the externally assisted sector of civil society—many now in their forties and fifties—played important roles in the democratization in the region over the past several decades. In many cases these people have been travelers on a political and intellectual journey mirroring ones that have taken place in other countries around the world. But in Latin America this sector has also attracted a younger generation, its members now in their twenties and thirties. This cohort's route to a concern with public policy has been more direct than that of the previous generation. Young people in Peru, Guatemala, and other Latin American countries are often free of the ideological baggage and the legacy of political divisions that characterized their elders; most of their training has been in developing technical solutions for concrete institutional problems. Viewing themselves as institutional engineers, they strive to find precisely the right formula, the right reform. Despite their different political backgrounds and experiences, the two generations have come together and tend to identify themselves—and are identified by their counterparts in the external donor community—as "civil society" actors. At least within the optic of democratic development, foreign donors only rarely regard most community-based, voluntary groups in such terms.

Whatever their role or reputation, externally assisted civil society groups, operating independently of the state and the market, are now broadly accepted not only in Guatemala and Peru but throughout much of Latin America. At times, tension and mistrust, even hostility, mar relations between such groups and the state or the private sector; at other times, constructive collaboration is the rule. In any case, civil society has become part of the political discussion throughout the region, and also figures prominently on the hemispheric and international agendas.

The Aid Response

In the mid-1980s, the U.S. government began creating aid programs explicitly designed to support democracy abroad. The establishment of the quasi-governmental National Endowment for Democracy (NED) in 1984 was the first major step in this regard. In 1985, USAID established an office for democracy programs in its Latin American bureau. During the Cold War years, U.S. efforts, initially at least, sought to contain or combat forces perceived to bear traces of communism—in some measure, to provide ideological reinforcement for the military and political confrontation with the Soviet Union and its allies. In Central America, the political motives behind democracy aid were unmistakable. U.S.-funded projects attempted to strengthen the capacity and effectiveness of public institutions, especially those of the judiciary. The goal was to bolster governments under threat—in the cases of Guatemala and, especially, El Salvador, governments threatened by leftist guerrilla groups. The Reagan administration's idea was that the United States should help fortify democratically elected, civilian governments, even those credibly charged with committing human rights abuses.

The results of this largely top-down strategy were meager if not counterproductive, sometimes even pernicious. As some observers have noted, the principal problem was one of political will—governments lacked a commitment to serious reform in public sector institutions. Though they accepted USAID resources and went through the motions of fulfilling the agency's bureaucratic requirements, they evinced little interest in meeting meaningful criteria for democracy by making institutions more effective and responsive.[18]

The end of the Cold War, political change in the region, and some introspection and learning of lessons at USAID helped agency officials gain a greater appreciation of civil society's potential as a source of democratic progress. The early 1990s brought greater openness to experimentation with civil society groups. Former USAID administrator Brian Atwood sees the focus on civil society (which USAID describes as one of democracy's four "building blocks") as essential to constructing, strengthening, and deepening democracies in Latin America and around the world.[19] For USAID, civil society is the "nexus for participation in governance," which is, it says, essential in a democracy for "political expression and influencing government policy choices." The agency supports civil society organizations

> whose advocacy efforts give voice to citizens and expand their influence on the political process. Strengthening civil society is increasingly seen as a way to counterbalance the exercise of excessive authority by governments and economic and political elites, and as a way to encourage more open dialogue about public policy matters too often decided behind closed doors. A vibrant civil society can even provide recourse to justice through the work of human rights groups, especially in post-conflict situations.[20]

To be sure, USAID is mindful of civil society organizations "in the broadest sense," the wide-ranging associations that fit the description of the first piece of the puzzle. Still, the agency's Center for Democracy and Governance "makes a distinction between programming that supports civil society writ large and civil society programming that fits into a democracy strategy. The focus is not on encouraging the growth of civil society organizations for their own good, but on encouraging elements of civil society to play a role in promoting certain kinds of democratic change." Clearly, USAID's main emphasis is "organizations that enter the public policy arena, the so-called 'politically active' or advocacy civil society organizations."[21]

The sequence for civil society programming tends to begin with civic education and later turns to advocacy intended to advance public policy goals. In Guatemala, USAID's first civil society project (in civic education) was fraught with organizational difficulties. But the agency expanded its focus, directly funding several groups working on citizen advocacy and later, in 1997, launching a three-year, $5 million initiative called "Incidencia" (Advocacy). Working from an explicitly Washington-style model of public advocacy (and through Creative Associates, a Washington-based private consulting group), the program has given priority to five areas: human rights, concerns of indigenous peoples, women's issues, public security, and judicial reform.[22] Nearly all of USAID's civil society work falls under this umbrella program.

Civil society programming, however, constitutes only a small piece of USAID's democracy effort in Guatemala, the bulk of which continues to be directed to public institutions including the judiciary, National Congress, and police. The Guatemalan government subscribed to the agreements on basic reform that helped end the civil conflict and, despite a change in administration, is presumably committed to meeting the targets laid out in those agreements.

Perhaps the most controversial aspect of USAID's Incidencia program was the effort in mid-1998 of some recipient organizations to propose constitutional reforms pertaining to indigenous people's rights that went beyond the modest ideas the Guatemalan government favors. That effort created strain, since the government prefers civil society groups in roles that strengthen its capacity rather than challenge its positions.[23] The tension is inherent in the attempt to balance support for a government committed to reform with support for a vital sector engaged in advocacy.

Because of the situation in Peru, USAID's program there emphasizes support for an alternative civil society sector, one that sustains certain democratic values and gives citizens the opportunity to participate. According to USAID officials, the idea is less to influence government action (although there is some of that) than to assist a group of policy advocates and equip them to keep the government in check.[24] Apart from substantial funding for the quasi-governmental Human Rights Ombudsman's Office, USAID has, for political reasons, suspended direct support to public institutions under its democracy initiative.

Although for several years in the mid-1990s USAID provided two umbrella grants, to Catholic Relief Services and the Peruvian organization GRADE (Group of Analysis for Development), for human rights and governance projects respectively, since 1997 it has supplied direct support to groups working on such questions as legal defense of the unjustly detained, human rights education, alternative dispute resolution, and political participation by women. A project that seeks to solve common problems in unfamiliar ways, and to expand women's participation in politics, is carried out through the Manuela Ramos Movement, one of the country's leading feminist groups, formed in the late 1970s.[25]

Both Guatemala and Peru, along with many other Latin American countries, have a multiplicity of civil society programs. Many donors— private or public, national or multilateral, European, Canadian, or American—rank strengthening civil society as one of their highest priorities. Nowadays, it is hard to find a funder in the political development field that does not include this line of work. Frequently the reasoning is cast in terms similar to USAID's: to contribute to deepening democratization by increasing mechanisms of accountability, participation, and transparency.

Although USAID stresses evaluation of its programs, judging the success or failure of civil society efforts is difficult. Attitudinal surveys, however carefully conceived and designed, at best often offer only a rough approximation of a program's performance, given the problems of connecting attitudes to particular interventions of projects. What seems fairly clear is that a particular set of nongovernmental organizations working on a particular set of issues is getting stronger as a result of USAID support (and support from other donors). Whether such assistance has translated into broader-based, more significant, and sustainable NGOs is, however, another question.

Several innovative USAID-supported initiatives seem to point in promising directions. In Guatemala, Accion Ciudadana (Citizen Action) seeks to promote more structured work in different sectors and in the national legislature undertaken jointly by a variety of advocacy groups. The group serves as a clearinghouse for information about relevant legislative proposals and attempts to bridge the worlds of the Guatemalan Congress and Guatemalan NGOs.[26] In Peru, USAID has responded to the intense politicization of the judicial sector by supporting efforts such as APENAC (Peruvian Association of Negotiation, Arbitration, and Conciliation), which emphasizes the demand side of access to justice and offers alternative forms of conflict resolution. Such efforts, however effective, raise questions about surrendering to a judicial system that does not seem amenable to serious reform.[27]

In addition, some U.S.-supported projects to strengthen civil society have had impressive reach and demonstrably beneficial multiplier effects. Since 1993, the National Endowment for Democracy has supported a program carried out by the Myrna Mack Foundation in Guatemala that works with poor communities of indigenous people, training leaders in basic constitutional rights and responsibilities. An external evaluation commissioned by the NED praised the effort.[28] In Peru, Lima-based groups supported by USAID, such as the Legal Defense Institute and IPEDEHP (Peruvian Institute for Education in Human Rights and Peace), have carried out education and human rights training efforts in selected areas of the country, with selected sectors of the population. A 1998 study highlighted the important social and psychological benefits of such programs, including developing greater awareness of basic rights and community leadership skills.[29]

An examination of externally funded civil society programs in Guatemala and Peru reveals a marked emphasis on enhancing citizens' participation and improving public policy advocacy. Although it is unclear how close most programs come to accomplishing their objectives, serious studies show that well-conceived and well-structured programs can be valuable. Their potential for transforming society is, however, harder to establish.

Fitting the Pieces Together

Having reviewed three discrete pieces of the civil society puzzle, it is worth exploring how they fit together in Latin America.

In one crucial respect, the fit in Latin America between the third piece and the dominant segment of the second piece—the externally assisted part of civil society and the self-consciously politicized, democratically committed part—is better now than before the 1990s. In the 1980s (not to mention the 1960s), there was a sharp disjuncture between the notion of democracy that programs pushed and the concept of democracy to which most recipients subscribed. The tendency to impose external conceptions doomed many efforts.[30] Thomas Carothers has exposed the major flaws of public sector democracy programs in Central America in the 1980s that relied on government officials who showed scant commitment to the programs' objectives.[31]

The 1990s saw greater congruence between the public advocacy orientation of the politically engaged segment of civil society and the mental framework and values broadly shared by external donors. Such a fit increases programs' likelihood of success. Still, several officials from the Incidencia program in Guatemala have commented on how few organizations satisfy USAID's definition of "advocacy" centered around public policy. In fact, some of the country's more successful and well-known civil society organizations lack the institutionalized patterns of operation that the term implies, relying instead on particular individuals to effect change.[32]

Another constraint on the effectiveness of democracy assistance in Latin America has been donors lagging far behind changing political and institutional dynamics. In many cases, programs were delayed as political decisions were taken and bureaucratic machineries got in gear. Perhaps such delay is inevitable, reflecting standard bureaucratic cycles. Still, several Guatemalan recipients of USAID support in 1998 commented that the assistance would have been especially valuable five years earlier.[33] It is unclear to what extent the political and organizational rhythms in the region were in sync with the policy guidelines and priorities set by donor agencies.

Also related to questions of timing and fit, it is reasonable to ask whether donor agencies, especially USAID, may have perhaps learned the lesson of "political will" a bit too well. While it is true that the bulk of USAID funding is still directed to public sector institutions and not civil society organizations, the latter are drawing increasing attention and resources. With scarce, and declining, resources for its Latin American democracy program, the wisdom of USAID maintaining a balanced portfolio between public-sector and civil society institutions should at least be explored.

That is particularly the case since, because of democratization's progress in the region, political will in many public sector programs is presumably greater than it was ten or fifteen years ago. Attractive opportunities in the public sector may in fact have increased, as Judith Tendler and her colleagues found in northeast Brazil.[34] Chilean political analyst Norbert Lechner has also expressed concern about donors' excessive emphasis on civil society, since the overriding challenge of further democratization in Latin America is, in his view, to improve the functioning of public institutions.[35]

Finally comes the question of fit between the first and the third pieces of what has been described in this paper as the civil society puzzle. Whether because of a scarcity of funding for democracy programs or because donors prefer it, most of the civil society programs that donors fund, including USAID's, work with a relatively narrow segment of organizations—those that exhibit a self-conscious commitment to democratic change. Such organizations, moreover, typically have a decided public policy focus. The other, less visible and less recognized, segment of the second piece of the puzzle—the piece that is *broadly* political—

also tends to fall outside the boundaries of the externally assisted sector of civil society.

There are at least two difficulties with donors' preference for advocacy groups concentrating on public policy. The first is that it overlooks sectors that have proved in Latin America to be highly politically relevant. The diverse associations in both Guatemala and Peru have been critical in shaping the countries' politics, as the 1990 elections in Peru and 1999 elections in Guatemala amply demonstrated. The second difficulty is that donors that claim to be working with civil society (a common claim) may unconsciously ascribe to such organizations greater representativeness and legitimacy than are warranted. If not properly qualified and specified, the term contributes to a distorted impression and understanding of social reality—and, as a result, to distorted policies and programs intended to shape that reality.

Some analysts have pointed out the differences in the language used to describe the public policy-oriented conception of civil society and the broader, more all-encompassing notion of civil society.[36] In fragmented, ethnically divided countries like Guatemala and Peru, the lenses through which civil society is perceived and understood can have important implications. Although the third piece of the puzzle fits reasonably well with the second piece, external donors tend to make bold claims that imply a realm much broader than the narrow confines of public policy advocacy—the entire range of voluntary associations.

Policy Implications of Rethinking Civil Society

This examination of the three pieces of the civil society puzzle suggests considerably more caution, modesty, and honesty than are now typical for developers of assistance programs. To be sure, many of the programs of USAID and other donors appear to be carefully conceived and competently implemented. But in setting out the rationale for such programs, it is important that donors eschew exaggerated claims and be explicit about which sector or slice of civil society they are working with.

This discussion also argues for basing a civil society assistance effort on a careful assessment of the relative needs and opportunities both in civil society sectors and in the public sector. In some cases, it may make sense for donors to concentrate resources on reform in the public sector. It may be tempting to do otherwise—to include a piece of civil society assistance or public advocacy as part of a broader democracy strategy. But policy-makers and program designers must recognize tradeoffs and realize that political will is not restricted to the civil society sector. The challenge for them is to examine the particular circumstances of each case and figure out the proper balance of support for civil society and for the public sector.

Of course, large organizations such as USAID face considerable bureaucratic and political constraints. Strong reasons encourage development of programs across countries and regions—and some measure of global comparability. But if will and commitment are the keys to success, donors should attempt to go beyond the standard formulas for programs and concentrate on attractive opportunities, wherever they are. Indeed, one of the main implications of this analysis is that ignoring the first piece of the puzzle in developing civil society programs may be a mistake. To be sure, as USAID officials rightly argue, many donors (including the agency) work closely with a wider set of voluntary associations in development-related efforts in, say, health, education, or microenterprises. But such work falls outside the democracy program and does not have an explicitly, self-consciously political purpose. In dealing with the vast and variegated landscape that is Latin America's civil society, it is important that donors take better advantage of the array of opportunities and paths for advancing democratic politics.

In Guatemala, the Soros foundations network, which set up operations in August 1998, is exploring more wide-ranging programs in civil society development. Its officials are especially interested in Mayan organizations, which differ greatly from most of the nongovernmental groups in the country's advocacy and public policy-oriented sector, being more mass-based and less confined to the arena of public policy. The foundation does not, of course, face the constraints that USAID and other major donors deal with in developing their programs. Although it is too soon to judge whether the Soros Foundation will succeed in engaging with and supporting a wider sector of Guatemalan civil society, its current thinking points in that direction, and its efforts deserve close attention.[37]

In light of the political dynamics in Latin America, the argument for taking a somewhat broader view of civil society development—and adopting a more creative view of democratic politics—is compelling. In 2000, many of the approaches intended to improve public policy formulation and refine advocacy strategies do not appear to be taking hold. Poll after poll suggests a profound questioning of dominant paradigms of democracy, and a search for alternatives. Throughout the region, trends may be running in a different direction, presaging a wider repudiation of the political establishment. The less visible, but critical, segment of the second piece of the civil society puzzle—the broadly politicized sector—may have more weight and relevance than democracy promoters anticipated.

At the beginning of the new millennium, the donor community committed to strengthening civil society should do what it can to avoid the lag and lack of fit that characterized much of its work in the early 1990s. Circumstances call for a sophisticated assistance approach, a double-track focus on the possibilities and the limitations of working with the first and second pieces of the civil society puzzle.

The context also calls for sharper, more explicit, and more honest discourse on the use of the phrase "civil society." A serious rethinking of the term could, at a minimum, yield better and clearer communication, which, as Orwell knew, has a great deal to do with producing better politics, and better societies.

Notes

1. George Orwell, "Politics and the English Language: An Essay," *A Collection of Essays* (New York: Doubleday Anchor Books, 1954), p. 169.

2. Larry Diamond, *Developing Democracy* (Baltimore: Johns Hopkins University Press, 1999), p. 10. See also Jorge Dominguez, "Free Politics and Free Markets in Latin America," *Journal of Democracy*, vol. 9, no. 4 (1998), pp. 70–84; and Scott Mainwaring, "The Surprising Resilience of Elected Governments," *Journal of Democracy*, vol. 10, no. 3 (July 1999), pp. 101–14.

3. Carlos Ivan Degregori, "Ethnicity and Democratic Governability in Latin America: Reflections from Two Central Andean Countries," in Felipe Aguero and Jeffrey Stark, eds., *Fault Lines of Democracy in Post-Transition Latin America* (Miami: North-South Center Press, University of Miami, 1998), pp. 203–34.

4. Michael Walzer, "The Idea of Civil Society," *Kettering Review* (Winter 1997), p. 8.

5. See Carlos Forment, "Democracy in Spanish America: Civil Society and the Invention of Politics," unpublished book manuscript, 1999.

6. S. Bruce Shearer and John Tomlinson, "The Emerging Nature of Civil Society in Latin America and the Caribbean: An Overview," prepared for the Inter-American Development Bank (New York: The Synergos Institute, 1997), p. 13.

7. Leihla Landim and Andres Thompson, "Non-Governmental Organizations and Philanthropy in Latin America: An Overview," *Voluntas,* vol. 8, no. 4 (1997), pp. 337–50.

8. See, for example, David Stoll, *Is Latin America Turning Protestant? The Politics of Evangelical Growth* (Berkeley: University of California Press, 1990).

9. See Patrick Johnstone, *The Church is Bigger than You Think* (Great Britain: Christian Focus Publications, June 1998).

10. David Scotchmer, "Life of the Heart: A Maya Protestant Spirituality," in Gary H. Gossen, ed., *South America and Meso-American Native Spirituality: From the Cult of the Feathered Serpent to the Theology of Liberation* (New York: Crossroad, 1997), p. 503

11. See Tania Palencia Prado and David Holiday, *Towards a New Role for Civil Society in the Democratization of Guatemala* (Montreal: International Centre for Human Rights and Democratic Development, 1996).

12. See Rachel McCleary, "Guatemala's Postwar Prospects," *Journal of Democracy,* vol. 8, no. 2 (April 1997).

13. Nicolas Lynch, "New Citizens and Old Politics in Peru," *Constellations,* vol. 4, no. 1, (1997), pp. 124–39.

14. See Carlos Ivan Degregori and Romeo Grompone, *Elecciones 1990: Demonios y Redentores en el Nuevo Peru, Una Tragedia en Dos Vueltas* (Lima: IEP Ediciones, 1991).

15. See Jose Maria Salceda, *Tsunami Fujimori, La Republica* (Lima, 1990); see also Sally Bowen, *The Fujimori File* (Lima: Peru Monitor, 2000).

16. See *Guatemala's First Post-Peace Elections: Power Changing Hands?*, IRELA Briefing (Madrid: Institute for European-Latin American Relations, November 1999).

17. See Oxford Analytica Latin America Daily Brief, January 28, 2000.

18. Thomas Carothers, *In the Name of Democracy: U.S. Policy toward Latin America in the Reagan Years* (Berkeley: University of California Press, 1991), ch. 6.

19. Brian Atwood, "El Fortalecimiento de la Democracia Mediante la Sociedad Civil," *Prensa Libre* (Guatemala), February 24, 1998.

20. *Report on Assistance for Democracy Development,* Center for Democracy and Governance, U.S. Agency for International Development, 1998, p. 16.

21. Ibid.

22. See *Proyecto Incidencia, Ejercicio de Validacion y Analisis,* Creative Associates International, USAID/Guatemala, January 1998; Memoria del Seminario-Taller, Incidencia en Politicas Publicas desde la Sociedad Civil, Retos y

Perspectivas, Antigua, Guatemala, 1999; and Proyecto Incidencia, Action Plan, Guatemala City, 1999.

23. Author interview with Incidencia project members, Guatemala City, August 26, 1998.

24. Author interview with USAID official, Lima, July 15, 1998.

25. Author interviews with USAID officials and Manuela Ramos Movement staff, Lima, August 9, 1998.

26. Author interview with Accion Ciudadana staff, Guatemala City, August 27, 1998.

27. Author interview with APENAC staff, Lima, July 14, 1998.

28. Sally Yudelman and Lucy Conger, *The Paving Stones: An Evaluation of Latin American Civic Education Programs* (Washington, D.C.: National Endowment for Democracy, 1997), pp. 27–35.

29. See Marcia Bernbaum, "Entretejiendo Lazos de Amistad, Confianza y Compromiso Para Construir Democracia y Derechos Humanos En El Peru," unpublished report, October 1998.

30. See James A. Gardner, *Legal Imperialism: American Lawyers and Foreign Aid in Latin America* (Madison: University of Wisconsin Press, 1980).

31. See Carothers, *In the Name of Democracy,* ch. 6.

32. Author interview with Incidencia project members, Guatemala City, August 26, 1998.

33. Author interviews with USAID grant recipients, Guatemala City, August 27, 1998.

34. See Judith Tendler, *Good Government in the Tropics* (Baltimore: Johns Hopkins University Press, 1997).

35. See Norbert Lechner, "La problematica invocacion de la sociedad civil," *Espacios, Revista Centroamericana de Cultura Politica,* no. 4, April-June 1995.

36. See Jenny Pearce, "Perspectives in Paralysis: Discourses of Civil Society in Guatemala," paper presented at the Latin American Studies Association, Chicago, Illinois, 1998.

37. Author interview with Soros Foundation official, Guatemala City, August 28, 1998; see also Fundacion Soros-Guatemala, Discussion Paper, June 1998.

10

Civil Society Aid in Peru:
Reflections from Experience

Carlos Basombrío

FEW LATIN AMERICAN COUNTRIES have had long, consistent experiences with democracy. The United States was once one of the obstacles
to democracy in the region, siding with dictators to advance its own
economic and security interests. Since the resurgence of democracy in
the region and the end of the Cold War, however, the United States now
attempts to help the region's countries democratize and stay democratic.
One of the elements of this policy line are aid programs for democracy
building, something pursued not just by the United States but by other
governments and private donor organizations.

Since the early 1990s, the trend in external democracy aid has been
toward assistance for organizations in civil society, since working only
with governments, in Latin America and elsewhere, has proved frus-
trating and insufficient. The belief behind this new current of programs
is that a strong civil society makes democracy possible, or at least sustains it, while a weak one can lead to the rise of authoritarianism. The
difficulties lie in setting priorities, choosing partners carefully, and implementing projects in ways suited to local conditions. Democracy aid has
made a difference in Latin America, and the new emphasis on civil society has certainly been beneficial, but additional changes by donors could
better support democratization.

This chapter is written from the point of view of a recipient of such
aid, specifically Peru. What external aid accomplished and did not accomplish during the country's convulsive recent past sheds light on the

virtues and limitations of programs that assist civil society in the hope of advancing democracy.

Background of a Tragedy

For most of the twentieth century, the United States, the most powerful actor in what it considered its "backyard," maintained working relationships with or actively backed many of Latin America's dictators for political and economic reasons. That policy dovetailed with Washington's strategy during the Cold War years, when American officials saw most democratic movements in Latin America as being on the wrong side in the East-West conflict and regarded anticommunist dictators as necessary allies.

Only in the 1980s and 1990s did the climate for a more pro-democratic U.S. policy improve. Almost all the Latin American countries elected governments in the 1980s, and some put in place the bases for democratic institutions. With the end of the Cold War in 1989, the United States' support for democracy in the region, already visible, increased significantly.

The wave of civil society assistance that began to flow in the 1990s is not the first attempt by outside actors to help organizations in civil society gain political influence or promote change in their countries. What is new is that the strategy, once the province of leftists and progressives and of a limited circle of donor governments sympathetic to those political groups, is now official policy in Washington, and that Latin American governments say and behave as if such programs are good for their countries. The organizations of civil society find that they are no longer considered—or at least not nearly so much as formerly—enemies of stability but rather, sometimes to their amazement, politically desirable and essential to democracy.

Peru's political history has many similarities with and yet crucially differs from the histories of its neighbors, which makes it an interesting and perhaps illuminating case for study. Like most Latin American countries, Peru has experienced significant periods of military rule in the past hundred years with occasional efforts at elected civilian rule. And like most, it experienced a political opening and began to refashion itself as a democracy in the 1980s, with its opening coming somewhat earlier than most others, at the very start of the decade.

As elsewhere in the region, democratic institutions and practices had shallow roots in Peru; even the move to democracy in 1980 came about through undemocratic as well as democratic means. In the 1970s, the military-dominated, but left-leaning government imposed, with an almost complete disregard for democratic niceties, an ambitious project of social reform. By late in the decade, land reform, urbanization, improved access to education and information, and other fundamental changes led several sectors of society to pressure the government for basic rights, so preparing the ground for a more democratic Peru. The people's repudiation of the reformist military regime for its failure to manage the economy, as well as a new international climate favoring democracy, also contributed to the military's downfall and the reestablishment of democratic government.

But the chance to build a lasting democratic system slipped from Peruvians' grasp. The return of democracy coincided with the rise of one of the most fanatical revolutionary movements imaginable, *Sendero Luminoso* (Shining Path), a Maoist group that began a "popular war" against the state in the 1980s in a remote, impoverished area of the highlands. Between 1988 and 1993, widespread violence on the part of both insurgents and government forces, economic collapse, and general political mismanagement combined to wreck the democratic transition.

History, it turned out, carried much more weight than the recent democratic reforms. Fed by many Peruvians' anger over their grinding poverty and social marginalization, as well as by the mistakes the state made in its counterinsurgency campaign, the Shining Path soon became the most pressing of Peru's problems. Long-standing traditions of repression, exclusion, and distrust again came to the fore; the government and the armed forces saw peasants in affected areas and later entire regions as potential enemies and treated them accordingly. Gasoline poured on a small fire had the predictable results. Violence spread throughout the country and with it the state's "dirty war," which created a human rights crisis the likes of which Peru had never known under its military governments.

As if the political violence were not enough, in the late 1980s the economy collapsed, with the GNP plummeting 50 percent in a few years and inflation spiraling out of control. Voters turned to Alberto Fujimori in the 1990 presidential election. Two years later came the president's *autogolpe* (self-coup). Fujimori asserted that by suspending democracy he could conquer both the economic problems and the Shining Path—which he did, although mainly for reasons other than the authoritarian measures he instituted.

Thus Peru is the only Latin American country that went distinctly backward in democratic terms in the 1990s and it did so with the open support of most Peruvians. Some democratic rules have been reinstated since the *autogolpe*, mainly because of pressure from the international community, but the country continues under what is by and large an authoritarian regime.

Peru has some of the characteristics of democratic life—for instance, periodic elections and some freedom of the press—but there is no longer a real separation of powers, one of democracy's most vital elements. First, the judicial power has been compromised. Judges are temporary appointees beholden to the executive branch; the military plays a large role in court cases against civilians; the independent members of the Constitutional Court have been dismissed by the president; and the responsibilities of the Magistrates Council have been eliminated. As for Congress, the executive branch took away some of its key powers and now controls it. Finally, the electoral authorities serve at the pleasure of the president and no longer command wide legitimacy among the population. Strong and diverse political parties, never a mainstay of Peruvian society, have all but disappeared,[1] and social groups are generally weak. Moreover, the government allows the armed forces to participate openly in politics, and it has maneuvered to stay in power for longer than the law permits. Most Latin American countries have reached the point in democratization where the discussion is about how to strengthen weakened institutions, make democracy more accessible, and create mechanisms to ensure officials' accountability. In Peru, the problems of democracy are more elemental.

An Unusual Alliance

Before examining U.S. support for Peruvian civil society in the 1990s, it is important to outline the broader policy context of which that aid was a part. What is highly noteworthy—given the history of the U.S. role in the region—is that the United States government has, through both its aid programs and its diplomatic posture, been exerting pressure for democratization on a regime that has both destroyed a communist revolutionary movement and carried out economic reform measures almost fully in line with the "Washington consensus" favored by the International Monetary Fund (IMF), the World Bank, and the U.S. government.

The newly elected Fujimori government, trying to rebuild after the economic collapse, began implementing a strict economic adjustment plan and attempting to reintegrate Peru into the world economy. After years of nonpayment of debt and numerous international sanctions, Peru desperately needed certificates of good conduct that would give it renewed access to credit and make it attractive to foreign investment. The United States supported Fujimori's economic policies with economic aid and its influence in international financial organizations. At the same time that all this was going on, the seemingly unstoppable spread of civil violence in Peru legitimized, in most people's eyes, authoritarian measures, and the government soon resorted to open repression.

Despite this helpful posture on the economic front, the U.S. government, often in de facto common cause with Peruvian human rights groups, pro-democracy forces, and what remained of the independent Peruvian media, became the principal constraint on the hardening of the regime in Peru. Between 1991 and 1994, Washington placed the issues of democracy and human rights at the center of relations with Peru. It linked U.S. aid to the regime's protection of human rights and implementation of democratic policies. It conditioned efforts to reintegrate Peru into the world economy on improvements in Peru's human rights record. After examining information provided by the Peruvian human rights community, the State Department set forward a list of human rights cases that it insisted be resolved for U.S. cooperation with Peru to continue. The Peruvian government was evasive about the cases and rarely addressed the United States' specific demands. Its failure to act forced it to take on new financial commitments and face greater aid conditionality.

Washington's position became more explicit after the 1992 self-coup. If Fujimori was defeated in his bid to seize absolute power, it was not any weakness in his regime but rather pressure from abroad that stopped him. He did not reckon with the strength of the new international support for democracy, spearheaded by the United States and supported by many countries in Latin America and Western Europe. The rest of the decade in Peru would be marked by a dispute between pro-democracy forces, strongly supported by the United States, and *fujimorismo*, a political alliance of Fujimori, the military, and other key regime supporters that attempted to preserve the essence of the coup's project. During these years Washington suspended military aid, imposed further conditionality on other assistance projects, and sent a variety of observer missions to Peru. Successive ambassadors to Peru frequently and publicly voiced the views of Peruvian democracy and human rights organizations and turned attention to many cases of human rights abuse. Throughout this period, President Fujimori's approach was what might be called unwilling institutionalization—he clearly disdained the idea of institutional democracy as inefficient but needed for public relations purposes to give the impression that he cared about such things.

And All Its Contradictions

The value the United States has placed on democracy in its relations with Peru since the late 1980s has hardly been exempt from contradictions and fluctuation. To begin with, the Fujimori government is not a tinpot dictatorship supported solely by corrupt cronies and considered completely illegitimate by the populace. On the contrary, it was successful in several areas and had strong support from the business community and important sectors of the citizenry. Foreign pressure for democratization had and continues to have clear limitations. How harshly can the United States criticize Fujimori, and how much can it lean on his government, without rupturing ties that allow it sustained influence in the area of democratic reform and, perhaps more important to Washington, in other areas of U.S. interest?

In addition, contradictions spring from the fact that the agencies involved in formulating and implementing U.S. policy toward Peru— including the Department of State, the Pentagon, the Central Intelligence Agency, and the Drug Enforcement Administration—have different interests in Peru and different perceptions of Fujimori's value. While the State Department's emphasis on democracy—and, more recently, that of Congress, both the Senate and the House—is noteworthy, other U.S. agencies and interests struggle with the official policy of promoting democracy. Then, too, international financial organizations have their own views on the situation in Peru.

Since Fujimori's reelection in 1995, U.S. policy has changed. Although the issue of democratic governance has not disappeared from the bilateral agenda, it has faded. Fujimori's second term began with an appearance of legitimacy and legality, seemingly putting an end to the exceptional period that began in 1992. Even more important, however, are the requirements of counternarcotics strategy. Peru, along with Bolivia, Colombia, and, more recently, Mexico, is a key country in the flow of drugs into the United States. When counternarcotics efforts, primarily in Colombia but to some extent in Mexico, ran into difficulties, constituents worried about the use of illegal drugs in America had to be reassured. This led the United States to highlight Peruvian successes in the war on drugs, including a reduction in the acreage devoted to growing coca, aerial eradication of drug crops, and the capture of several important drug traffickers. But Washington's enthusiasm for Peruvian antidrug policy has grown increasingly hard to reconcile with the U.S. desire to promote democracy, given that the most criticized member of the Fujimori government, Vladimiro Montesinos, a man suspected of past criminal wrongdoing and little regard for human rights principles, appears to head Peruvian counternarcotics efforts.

The Evolution of Assistance

Such is the political context for U.S. democratization programs in Peru funded through the U.S. Agency for International Development (USAID). The USAID projects are far from being the only foreign-sponsored programs operating in the country that are intended to promote democracy, but they are the most relevant here given the focus of this book. Generally speaking, until the 1992 coup USAID concentrated its democracy-related aid on supporting state institutions, rather than civil society, seeking to make them more efficient and democratic.[2] Modernizing Peru's Congress was a priority; many other programs targeted the Ministry of Justice and the judicial branch. In general, institutional reform was rough sledding, due to a lack of seriousness about such reform on the part of the government. For example, USAID pushed the design and establishment of a National Registry of Detained Persons. Many of the abuses of and problems with detainees take place early in detention, and the idea was that having accurate information about detainees' location would deter further abuses. But it took USAID a long time to persuade the government to establish the registry, and then the authorities lacked the will to enforce registration of detainees, so it never became a useful tool.

After the *autogolpe*, USAID shifted the bulk of its democracy work from state institutions to support for civil society, in the hope of fostering reform from below. Although that shift corresponded to the broader rise of interest in civil society work within USAID in those years, it was accelerated by the deteriorating political climate. In the late 1990s, USAID virtually abandoned its collaboration with the state on democracy programs, with the significant exception of support for the Defensoría del Pueblo, the national ombudsman's office. The change was a bold one for USAID, as the agency opted for working with actors and on issues that directly oppose the Fujimori regime and its policies—and has kept a fairly high profile while doing so.

USAID has established contacts, which have evolved into structured pro-democracy programs, with well-regarded organizations in Peru's civil society. Among the most important new programs, several deal with human rights advocacy and reporting; others promote citizens' participation in public life, especially at the municipal level, including electoral participation; and still others have given significant support to groups that promote women's rights and involvement in politics.

What Civil Society?

The idea that effective democracy assistance requires involving actors from civil society is extraordinarily important, in my opinion. But taking the next step—deciding what constitutes civil society in a particular country and time, which actors are the most relevant, and whom to support—is not easy. As discussed in the introduction to this book, such decisions raise challenging questions about the separability of civil society from the political sphere and the market as well as the actual pro-democratic functions that different sectors of civil society perform. I seek to contribute to the discussion by identifying the sectors of civil society that might be relevant to the strengthening of democracy in Peru and how outside actors can make productive choices about which to support.

In Peru, unlike in Chile during its transition to democracy, it cannot be said that a vital civil society acts as a counterweight to an authoritarian regime. There is, in fact, a dearth of groups in Peru to which donors might reasonably channel democracy aid.

Let us begin with political parties and the range of civic organizations that parties can generate. Apart from the difficulties inherent in assisting a specific political movement,[3] the extreme weakness of Peruvian parties makes them poor recipients for democracy aid. Many Peruvians and outside observers view the parties as part of the problem rather than the solution.

Peruvian parties are weak partly because they have always been and partly because of more recent events. Many parties began as the personal vehicle for a *caudillo*, the Latin American version of a strongman, and never developed much organizationally. The most important party in Peru's history, the American Popular Revolutionary Alliance, governed between 1985 and 1990 under the leadership of Alan Garcia with catastrophic results, destroying decades of political capital. Most Peruvians think that political parties are to blame for what has happened to their country, and in some ways they are right. They abhor parties, favoring candidates clearly identified as independents, as evidenced most dramatically of course by Fujimori's election (as a political outsider) in 1990. Beyond all this, in recent years the discrediting of political parties and of politics in general seems an almost universal trend.

Donors could consider channeling support for democracy in Peru through business leaders and their associations. These are actors of great importance in the country's political life, with real influence over the national agenda. Historically, however, they have not viewed democracy as central to development. Instead, their acceptance or rejection of a regime has depended on their assessment of its ability to foster economic activity and opportunity.

A third possibility is support for what in Latin America have come to be known as "popular organizations"—associations that have grown out of the fight for social justice by the least privileged. In Peru and other countries, these include unions, farmers' organizations, community associations of various types, and organizations motivated by a specific identity that brings disadvantages or exclusion (such as women's organizations and groups based on ethnicity).

While Peru did not have a tradition of strong political parties, it was a Latin American paradigm for strong popular organizations, at least from the mid-1970s to the beginning of the 1980s. Democracy, however, was never a political issue for these organizations. Influenced primarily by leftist ideology, they regarded democracy as a hollow shell and sought mainly to address economic and social concerns. Despite that, they played an important, even decisive, role in determining the pace and quality of Peru's transition to democracy at the end of the 1970s through their reform impetus and ability to mobilize citizens.

The economic collapse and all its social consequences, combined with the corrosive effect of the violent conflict between Shining Path and the state, sabotaged many popular organizations along with Peruvian democracy. The unions, once the soul of the popular movement, saw their social and political power shattered. To give some idea of the magnitude of the change, if strikes were the unions' most feared weapon at the end of the 1970s, ten years later owners were encouraging them to strike, collapsed markets having made the bosses eager for a month when they would not have to pay salaries and would have a good excuse for additional layoffs. Shining Path's infiltration of some unions, though not on a large scale, also helped weaken and discredit the unions.

In the cities, where networks of popular organizations had thrived, economic crisis and harshly applied free market policies took their toll. In shantytowns where poverty and despair ruled, many residents interpreted market reform as: "Not everyone can survive, so do it yourself by any means, legal or not, moral or not, and to the hell with the others." Then Shining Path burst onto the scene and made a bid to control the remaining popular organizations through terror. In rural areas, peasants fled the spread of fighting, and those who stayed were unable to use their traditional organizations to control the violence.

Not all the news in those years was bad. Many organizations managed to survive and accomplish important things for their people. New organizations full of potential emerged from the ashes of the economy and civil violence. Among them were thousands of self-help economic "survival" organizations comprised of and led by women. Hundreds of thousands of peasants organized self-help groups to fight against the Shining Path. Although aiding such popular organizations carried many risks in terms of democratic development (given their often militarized nature) for donors, it offered interesting possibilities for developing citizenship in rural areas.

Popular organizations have now lost their shaping influence over society and politics in Peru. Many have preserved a strong local presence, but they are extremely fragile institutionally and few make the jump to a larger arena. Associations that grew out of these grassroots organizations and have incorporated a political dimension into their activities have not managed to turn themselves into effective institutions and more often than not do not have the resources to mobilize support nationally.[4]

So with Whom Should Donors Work?

In practice, when those who would offer democracy assistance define their priorities and identify possible recipients, they no longer face the wide world of civil society but a much narrower cross-section of actors. Generally speaking, what they are dealing with are nongovernmental advocacy organizations—human rights groups, pro-democracy associations, groups fostering electoral participation, women's rights organizations, groups that fight discrimination, and so on. Here are actors with great potential, yet also definite limitations.

There are many differences among advocacy NGOs but several traits are common:

- They have a pro-democracy agenda that includes a focus both on promoting free and fair elections and influencing policymaking.
- Their concern with democracy is not always explicitly or exclusively formulated as such but instead is often linked to their efforts in areas that affect democratization (for example, human rights, women's rights, and the rights of young people and ethnic minorities).
- They do not directly represent others. They are groups of people who have chosen to work for a specific cause but do not necessarily speak for the victims they hope to assist or for anyone else who may benefit—which does not mean, however, that they do not have strong links with these possible beneficiaries or that they cannot mobilize large volunteer networks.
- They offer proposals for the national policy issues and have the ability to push them. Their influence in public life comes from

their ability to reach specific sectors of the population directly, their access to the media and credibility among reporters, and their skill in articulating their ideas and proposals.

- They are not formally affiliated with political parties and do not always maintain cooperative ties, either on the local or the national level, with those so affiliated. That is especially true in Peru where the political parties exercise little political or moral leadership and on occasion have hindered more integrated visions for the solution of the country's problems.

- Finally, they are structured organizations that have been around a while and have compiled a track record. Typically they are made up of middle-class professionals with social commitment in their backgrounds; many members come from involvement with leftist ideology or the missionary work of Christian churches. The public views these organizations, both their individual members and as institutions, as legitimate. They have relatively solid institutional foundations with experienced managers and staff, modern accounting practices, and infrastructure that allow them to manage the increasingly complex requirements of funded projects.

Unexpected Crossroads

Let us follow the evolution of these actors in Peruvian civil society and see why they were ready to be found by donors interested in promoting civil society. International assistance channeled through organizations of civil society—more often than not nongovernmental organizations (NGOs)—began decades before the recent wave of such aid. The donors were primarily private organizations in Europe and North America. Although the projects supported are usually smaller than those that governments sponsor, the total investment is often significant.

The bulk of this assistance, it is true, goes to poverty relief and development programs (though the same must be said of aid from governments). But in both cases, sponsoring organizations have sought, perhaps not always successfully, to link a focus on basic needs to efforts to strengthen the beneficiaries' civic awareness and capacity—democracy-building, in other words. In addition, a smaller though still substantial portion of aid has for years been channeled into programs that promote women, youth, decentralization, public education, human rights, direct support for grassroots organizations, and other areas of concern.

Public and private donors now often explicitly emphasize democracy and civil society strengthening in the projects they sponsor. Prior to the mid-1980s, however, they did not; they aimed to raise awareness about civil rights and sociopolitical participation through "popular education." Although formulated in extremely general terms that were far from orthodox leftist proposals,[5] the empowerment of the people that these projects sought called for a sort of revolutionary change that would combine the political dimension of democracy with the social dimension.

During the 1980s, in part because of the evolution of political ideas in the wider world, a profound change began to unfold within civil society in Peru. It was accelerated by the horrors of the Shining Path's terror tactics and the harsh counterinsurgency measures that the Peruvian government used to combat it. Although civil society organizations did not abandon social exclusion as a topic of discussion or a motive for activism, they increasingly valued and promoted the democratization of politics. More important, they came to see political democratization as a prerequisite for achieving significant progress on the social and economic fronts. Paradoxically, during this same period, many members of political parties that had traditionally supported democracy became convinced of the need to exchange democracy for stability and security.

Since the end of the Cold War swept away most of the ideological suspicions that had exacerbated political differences between some donors and Peruvian civil society groups, and with the other relevant actors in Peru being so weak, democracy assistance in the 1990s has tended to go to groups already working on programs related to democracy. Thus a bridging of the traditional progressive sector and the Western democracy promoters has occurred, something unthinkable until recently in Latin America.

Visible Progress in a Stagnant Transition

One way to measure the success of cooperative efforts to strengthen democracy in Peru would be to examine how democratic the country is today. Peru is, to be sure, the most flagrant example of a stagnant transition in Latin America, or perhaps more accurately, an antitransition. And, in any case, many problems of democratic consolidation are far beyond the scope of NGOs. But even in a situation as trying as the one in Peru, NGOs there can point to several important, concrete results of their work.

Democratic change has numerous and interrelated causes, many of which work slowly, so credit for reforms can never be precisely assigned. The results of aid projects cannot be completely separated from those of other foreign policy instruments that donor countries employ. Nor can one assume that results are the outcome of recent actions. The gains from many years of effort by civil society must be factored in. With these caveats, I will briefly discuss six areas of positive change in Peru in which assistance has played an important, though not an exclusive, role.

Preserving Space for Democracy

First, and crucially, the civil society groups supported by international aid have helped preserve many fundamental liberties after the 1992 coup. These include the right to disagree with the regime's policies and actions and to present opposing opinions and freedom of association and organization. Human rights, though still far from perfect in Peru, are violated less often and less brutally than in the early 1990s. These achievements cannot be explained by the protections that state institutions offer (with the recent exception of the ombudsman's office) nor by the efforts of the political opposition, which have amounted to little. The political oxygen that keeps the hope of democracy alive is the product of the work of a variety of media groups and organizations from civil society, together with assistance from the international community.

Peru's human rights movement is a case in point. It has organizations in almost every corner of the country, working for a common cause, coordinating their policies and public statements. At critical moments the international community looked to the movement to keep the government from further misconduct, and its influence proved decisive. After the coup, Washington made it a non-negotiable condition for resuming financial aid that the Peruvian government hold "a regular dialogue with the human rights community." For several months, ministers and other high-ranking members of the least open and most authoritarian government in Peru's recent history sat down, against their will, with human rights representatives and "dialogued." If these meetings achieved nothing of substance, they nonetheless made clear what was expected of the authorities and what would happen if the regime insisted on poor human rights practices.

Solving Citizens' Problems

Like assistance from nongovernmental sources, the pro-democracy initiatives that U.S. and European government agencies have funded have often challenged Peruvian authorities and policies. They have focused on controversial topics ranging from displaced persons to the reconstruction of institutions in zones formerly under emergency law. I will highlight here one such problem they have taken on—that of innocent people accused of terrorism.

A few years ago, thousands languished in jail on unjust terrorism charges while the Peruvian state, and ordinary Peruvians, either ignored their plight or considered it an inevitable cost of peace. USAID has played a particularly important role in financing NGOs that work on this issue, and it has maintained a high profile while doing so. Through strategies that have included an intensive campaign to influence public opinion, the legal defense of thousands of people, demands for changes in the law, and the search for "heterodox" mechanisms to resolve cases with incontestable but badly flawed judicial decisions, these organizations have accomplished much. Thousands of innocent people have been released,[6] and some of the laws and procedures that allowed arbitrary detentions and sentences have been changed. Moreover, most people realize that the problem of the falsely accused extends beyond those currently in prison to the thousands of people who have capture orders pending against them and could eventually land in jail.

In addition to the concrete results of the direct assistance to thousands of people, such programs have helped advance democratization by pushing for changes intended to "normalize" penal laws passed during the period of violence and emergency and by highlighting the consequences of due process violations and judges' lack of autonomy.

Creating Social Networks

Not only state institutions are in ruins in Peru. The majority of organizations in civil society are also in disarray. But amid the chaos, international assistance has helped promote the creation of dynamic social networks that hold great potential.

Here are two examples. The first involves young people's participation in a monitoring effort, sponsored by the nongovernmental organization Transparencia, for the 1995 elections. The effort was the first visible sign that youth are taking an interest in public affairs. The second example is one of Peru's most successful networks, the human rights community, with thousands of "advocates" dedicated to the protection of human rights (including the National Coordinator for Human Rights and the Peruvian Institute for Education in Human Rights and Peace).

Increasing Women's Participation

The gender focus of many civil society programs, along with projects specifically designed to increase women's participation in social and political life, has helped produce important advances. An increased role for women in political life is now widely considered a legitimate issue for discussion and reform. More and more women in Peru, on both sides of the political spectrum, are taking up important political posts. Their assignments are not limited to so-called women's issues or family issues but span all areas of concern to the nation. In addition, civil society's efforts have spurred legislative action, including passage of a law that mandates that 25 percent of candidates on party lists in municipal and congressional elections be women. Political participation by women has grown in areas of the country where marginalization of women has been—and in many respects continues to be—most severe. Moreover, rising participation by women creates a more favorable climate for the idea that cultural change is important in strengthening democracy. People working for women's advancement are better able to bring machismo and domestic abuse out of the private sphere and help others see them as the sources and expressions of authoritarianism they are.

Legitimizing the Role of Civil Society

Another important effect of the democracy projects has been the legitimization of civil society's work in public life. This is partly due to the efforts of the individuals and organizations of civil society, backed by powerful, well-respected international entities, and partly to the weakness of other actors, especially the political opposition. Yet much depends on the organization in question. Many civil society organizations are known and perceived as legitimate at the local level; only a small number have an indisputably national presence.

Citizens need NGOs to help with the resolution of specific problems. At times that need exceeds what those organizations can provide, because of limits on their role and their resources. Many NGOs are also a source for ideas in their areas of specialization, and as such are regularly consulted by the media, the government, and foreign actors. In many cases state agencies ask them to collaborate on specific programs at the local level or in a particular sector. More generally, it is NGO work that has made the case for the importance of community participation in the design and execution of development projects.

Though much remains to be done, many Peruvians now believe it is possible to participate in public affairs and complement the proposals of the political parties while working to get the needs and concerns of the people onto the national agenda. They believe that their participation should not be narrowly ruled by the logic of the market—though this is a legitimate consideration—but should instead follow a professional and technocratically informed path that incorporates the civic values of broad participation and solidarity, values so easily forgotten in this day and age.

Pushing for the Transition to Democracy

Peru is nearing a decisive moment. In 2000 the country will hold congressional and presidential elections—the first after years of violence and crisis, authoritarianism and institutional collapse—that will mark a confrontation. On one side is a regime that hopes to continue running the country, counting on core support from a minority of Peruvians but above all on its almost complete control over the instruments of power, including the armed forces and the intelligence agencies. On the other side is a diffuse set of democratic forces, often at odds with each other, that will be attempting to turn the opportunity into an authentic transition to democracy. The outcome cannot be predicted, but I believe that the democrats could easily be frustrated by the government or that political change could become very difficult, perhaps even traumatic.

There are, nevertheless, some positive signs, compared to just a few years ago, which civil society has helped bring about and continues to support, with assistance from international donors. Peruvians' attitude toward the use of force to resolve problems has changed. Ideas such as ruthless behavior as a means to an end and contempt for dialogue and negotiation—regarded as necessities and even virtues as recently as a few years ago—have come into question. This cultural change is borne out by the work of NGOs at the local level and confirmed by all national public opinion polls.

Civil society has also contributed to the development of an agenda for democratic transition in Peru. Stepping into the vacuum left by the political parties, organizations in civil society have, in a multitude of ways, proposed themes for democratization and promoted discussion of them. Among the topics being talked about are new forms of political representation; the importance of the local arena; methods of decentralizing and monitoring government offices and citizen participation; guaranteeing the consolidation of peace through discussion of the causes and consequences of violence; resolution of human rights problems; novel ways of framing the responsibilities of state institutions; and alternatives in civilian-military relations and in national security. But if civil society's ability to propose and lobby for political changes is beneficial in that it fills a vacuum in the public debate, it also carries the risk of usurping and eventually replacing the country's political movements. That temptation it should resist.

Unfinished Themes

The Political Sensitivity of Foreign Aid

A leading concern in the NGO community has been the political sensitivity of aid from institutions with U.S. government ties, especially for work in controversial fields. One experience illustrates the point. In 1993 or thereabouts, USAID's general offer of aid to Peruvian human rights organizations sparked a debate among them over whether they should accept and, if so, under what terms.

They feared two things, one because of past experiences and the other looking ahead. Some recalled how, during the Cold War, USAID had linked its programs in various countries to actions and projects that worked against the cause of human rights and the strengthening of democracy. Others emphasized the political evolution of all the actors involved. The second fear was that the government and some media outlets would point to the aid as proof of foreign intervention in Peru's domestic affairs, thereby delegitimizing NGOs' participation in public life. After some soul-searching, the human rights organizations in Peru agreed to accept assistance, so long as USAID did not demand changes in the priorities of organizations receiving funding. To allay concerns about foreign interference, USAID developed a mechanism for indirect aid with resources channeled to an American NGO that set the parameters for the aid projects that would support the local NGOs.

Neither in this phase, however, or later, when aid went directly to local NGOs—with some fanfare[7]—did Peruvian officials raise any difficulties. Despite innumerable crises in relations between Lima and Washington, the authorities in Peru have never questioned such aid; indeed, they have never addressed the issue publicly, whether approvingly or disapprovingly. Fujimori's government avoids stirring up new conflicts that might jeopardize other programs that depend, directly or indirectly, on aid from the United States. As it turns out, the foreign aid awarded to human rights organizations has conferred added legitimacy on the causes those organizations promote.

Dependence on Foreign Aid

All democracy-building projects face the question of sustainability: would the initiatives continue if foreign aid became unavailable? Their answer, as of today, is that sustainability would be impossible to guarantee. While such programs are not costly, they help people who could never afford to pay for them, or they promote changes in policy and public opinion, which require specialized personnel and infrastructure not easy to come by.

The problem is not specific to democracy promotion. It bedevils the entire nongovernmental world in Peru, as in most developing countries. Private philanthropy is underdeveloped in Peru, and where it is a factor it concentrates on humanitarian work, cultural promotion, and educational development. Within the government, few have worked with the nongovernmental sector or have an interest in doing so. Any cooperation between the state and NGOs has been at the local level, especially in antipoverty programs, and is vulnerable to the ever-changing decisions of the authorities. As things stand, it is unthinkable that Lima would earmark public funds for democracy promotion.

The reality is that democracy projects rely on foreign funds. An abrupt change in donor agencies' priorities—a variable impossible for recipients to control—would close down projects, and there would be no way to restart them in the short term. Future relaunchings would depend primarily on the emergence in the government of decision-makers who valued the programs and could obtain funds for them.

The Temptation to Replace Politics

This chapter has emphasized the importance of the organizations of civil society. The weakness of political movements and parties has also been noted. The latter is not desirable; in all democratic countries, strong and vital political parties help sustain democratic life. One of the key challenges for Peru's transition to democracy is ensuring that the country has modern, democratic, institutionally developed and representative political parties.

In theory, everyone involved in democratization efforts accepts this thinking, but they do not always act like they do. When political parties were more powerful, politicians mainly sought to exploit the organizations of civil society or paid no attention to them. Now the tables have been turned, and there is a certain temptation for civil society to substitute for or simply ignore the political sphere.

The Material Foundation for Democracy

Democracy in the industrialized countries of North America and Europe rests on a foundation not only of a political culture that favors democratic governance but also of material conditions that make it possible. These include a large, educated middle class and income gaps that are not as abysmal as elsewhere. Governments can at least meet the most basic needs of the poorest citizens.

Although Peru cannot aspire to lay such a foundation now, democracy cannot be completely dissociated from the need to deal with the problems of poverty and extreme inequality in society when political and economic conditions are better. In fact, these problems pose the main challenge for democracy in Latin America today.

If donors wish to promote democracy in the region, their approach could benefit from a few alterations. First, they could help recipient countries alleviate poverty and inequality in education, housing, health, and opportunity. They must also ask if the democratization efforts carried out through assistance for civil society organizations are in accord with the economic policies that they encourage or demand of governments in recipient countries, which often include a reduced state and fewer government services. A second area of possible change in democracy aid is more concrete and might result in more immediate progress. Donors must link democratization projects more closely to those under way in the field of development. Each type of program has its objectives, but greater coordination can and should be attempted.

Notes

1. In the 1980s, Peru's political environment was divided, in essence, into thirds: the Center-Right of Popular Action and the Popular Christian Party, which shared power between 1980 and 1985; the Center (the American Popular Revolutionary Alliance, in power between 1985 and 1990); and the Left (United Left), which had a strong presence in parliament and in municipal government. Yet in the 1995 national elections the three combined were unable to obtain 10 percent of the vote. Currently there is no sign that the trend might be reversing or that new, genuine political parties might be developing.

2. For a more detailed analysis of the evolution of USAID programs in Peru, see Michael Shifter's chapter in this book.

3. The German political party foundations and other groups established by major European political parties to support like-minded parties worldwide can provide aid without worrying so much about charges of unfair partisanship, due to little legacy of European intervention in Peruvian politics. And the problematic state of Peruvian parties has led even these foundations to rethink their funding.

4. Once on the campaign trail, leaders of organizations that in theory represent hundreds of thousands of people receive few votes. In other Latin American countries—Ecuador, Guatemala, and, to a lesser extent, Bolivia, Mexico, and even Colombia—indigenous organizations have a vitality and an ability to project their ideas that their Peruvian counterparts have never had.

5. If in the early stages of their development (until the late 1970s, roughly) Peruvian NGOs had received support from the leftist parties, in the 1980s the NGOs quickly distanced themselves from the parties, often developing strategies and ideas that conflicted strongly with those of the Left. In the 1990s, the political parties virtually disappeared, and this source of tension faded.

6. Despite the obstacles the regime places in the way of human rights lawyers, more than one thousand people have been freed after a court trial, and the Ad Hoc Commission, created by the government in response to public pressure, has released nearly five hundred others. Several hundred cases are still pending.

7. The majority of donor institutions manage their relations with their local recipients in private. In the case of USAID, however, every new program or renewal is announced to the media and a contract is signed in a public ceremony in the presence of the U.S. ambassador, with full public disclosure about the amount and destination of the funds.

Part Six

Conclusion

11

Toward Civil Society Realism

Marina Ottaway and Thomas Carothers

THE PROMOTION OF CIVIL SOCIETY has become a major element of the burgeoning universe of international democracy assistance. When they began trying to support the "Third Wave" of democracy around the world in the late 1980s and early 1990s, most democracy promoters focused on fostering free and fair elections and reforming state institutions. In the mid-1990s, however, they embraced civil society development as a necessary part of democracy promotion and launched hundreds, even thousands, of projects under that rubric. Enthusiasm for civil society programming is now common among international actors involved in democracy aid, including bilateral aid agencies, international institutions, and private foundations.

The idea that an active civil society is central to a thriving democracy is a classical one, but relatively untested as a developmental credo. Innumerable studies, from de Tocqueville on, have shown that "government by the people" means more than participation in elections; it requires sustained effort by organized groups to influence government decisions. The current discourse on democracy goes even further, treading in uncharted territory. "The people" are seen as participating in two distinct capacities: as "political society," when they organize into political parties that seek to win elections and thus to gain control over a country's institutions; and as "civil society," when they come together in a variety of civic organizations that do not aspire to the commanding heights of power but seek nonetheless to help determine what government does by educating citizens about their rights and lobbying for policy reforms assumed to be democratic. The new discourse on democracy casts civil society as the virtuous incarnation of "the people," the necessary watchdog over democracy's more dangerous side represented by political parties and even democratically elected institutions.

The concept of the virtuous civil society has long coexisted uneasily with doubts about the ability of democratic governments to stand up to special interest groups and lobbyists. Special interest groups and lobbies have a well-established place in the political game, at least in the United States, but have not usually been seen as particularly virtuous. On the contrary, they have often been regarded as unduly powerful, distorting for their own purposes the workings of elected, representative institutions. But the nongovernmental organizations, or NGOs, that came to be favored in the civil society promotion arena in the 1990s do not see themselves, nor are they seen by promoters of civil society, as special interest groups. They seek to influence government, the NGOs claim, not on behalf of special interests but on behalf of civil society at large. Thus they have a special right to be listened to and occupy a special place in the political system apart from those of other organizations attempting to influence government policy.

The assertiveness of NGOs that view themselves as representatives of good civil society and its defenders against ever-problematic political society is a relatively new phenomenon even in mature democracies. In the United States, government agencies are still learning to cope with increasingly assertive NGOs claiming a special right to be heard; international organizations, particularly the United Nations, are seeking to define the appropriate forms of NGO participation in their meetings and deliberations. But even as established democracies struggle at home to define the role of the new civil society and its NGOs as against that of elected, representative institutions, they are engaged in promoting that new civil society abroad.

The chapters in this collection analyze the first generation of aid programs explicitly aimed at promoting civil society under a pro-democracy rubric. This generation of assistance efforts has flourished in a short time span, yet is already entering a period of self-examination and possible modifications. The chapters vary considerably in their findings, reflecting the diversity of the regions under study, the diversity of the authors themselves, and the complexity of the subject matter. Nevertheless, taken together they shed light on the core questions motivating this volume, relating to the nature and validity of donors' assumptions about civil society and its role in democratization, the impact of aid to civil society, and lessons learned about methods of implementation. This chapter summarizes those conclusions.

Equating NGOs with Civil Society

A central assumption of civil society aid carried out under the auspices of democracy promotion is that advocacy NGOs are a critical segment, perhaps *the* critical segment, of civil society, at least with regard to democratization. That assumption stems from the belief that the advocacy function of those groups necessarily engages key democratic processes—such as representing interests, challenging the state, and fostering citizens' participation—in ways that other kinds of civil society activities do not. It also reflects the more mundane fact that it is much easier for donors to assist professionalized NGOs than most of the other kinds of groups that make up civil society in developing and transitional countries, such as religious organizations, ethnic associations, and informal community groups.

As the studies in this volume make clear, however, the assumption of NGOs' centrality is questionable. Other kinds of civil society groups frequently drive political change, eclipsing what is often the circumscribed role of policy or advocacy NGOs. In South Africa, as both Christopher Landsberg and Marina Ottaway emphasize, a social movement, rather than advocacy NGOs, brought down apartheid. Mustapha Kamel Al-Sayyid makes the point that, in Egypt, traditional professional associations—which U.S. aid providers exclude from civil society aid programs—are major players in the struggles over political liberalization. In Latin America, as both Carlos Basombrío and Michael Shifter note, the profound struggles of the 1980s against dictatorship and repression were conducted by many social and political forces very different from the technocratic advocacy NGO donors would favor in the 1990s. And in the Philippines, Bangladesh, and elsewhere in Asia, Mary Racelis and Stephen Golub argue, citizens' groups focused on socioeconomic issues are having major effects on long-term processes of societal change.

Donors' tendency to think of NGOs as the heart of civil society is part and parcel of their ahistorical approach in this domain. When Western democracy promoters embraced the notion of civil society aid in the early 1990s, they often assumed that since the countries in which they were working had few organizations of the type donors designate "civil society organizations"—that is, Westernized advocacy NGOs—they had little civil society of any kind. In fact, as the chapters in the volume highlight, in all the regions under study (with the exception of some Eastern European countries coming out of communism), civil society was already very much present when donors launched their aid efforts for it. Programs have been built on top of or alongside existing civil society, which includes localistic, politically disengaged groups; traditionalistic, often religion-oriented, associations; politicized populist organizations; and extensive citizen networks dealing with socioeconomic issues. Correspondingly, the course and eventual success of the programs for civil society have had much to do with the extent to which programs have constructively melded with existing forms of civil society.

In the future, it is essential that providers of civil society aid abandon their notion that civil society is mostly about NGOs and instead strive to understand how civil society is already structured in each recipient country and assist it accordingly.

The Mirage of Apolitical Engagement

A second assumption underlying civil society aid is that of apolitical engagement. By fostering nonpartisan civic advocacy by NGOs, the assumption runs, donors can affect the political development of recipient countries without ever directly intervening in politics. Appealing as it sounds, the idea does not hold up in practice. On the ground, civil society aid is constantly confronting political issues large and small, as highlighted in the book's five chapters devoted to case studies of a country. In Egypt, the NGO domain is marked by significant political and religious loyalties, and U.S. choices about which organizations to support are fraught with political considerations. The U.S. government supports the principle of civil society development, but avoids aiding groups in civil society whose leaders may not be sympathetic to Washington's policies in the Middle East. Egyptians perceive the civil society aid that is meted out as one more element of America's projection of its political preferences and interests onto the Egyptian scene.

In Peru, as in other Latin American countries such as Guatemala and El Salvador, Washington funds many projects in intensely politicized NGO communities, often supporting progressive groups that a decade before it would have shunned (and that would not have dreamed of accepting its money). In Peru, these groups have been deeply involved in the struggle against President Alberto Fujimori's continued authoritarian rule.

In Romania, aid to NGOs in the first half of the 1990s was one of the principal channels through which Washington supported people and groups it hoped would oppose the former communists in government and help the opposition to victory. After the defeat of incumbent Ion Iliescu in the 1996 presidential election, many activists in Romanian civil society, and their backers in the United States and elsewhere, openly took credit.

Much of the extensive international support for civil society's development in South Africa in the 1980s and early 1990s was highly political—at root, its goal was to help drive the South African government out of power. Since the 1994 elections and the transition from apartheid, U.S. civil society assistance has found itself part of different but equally complex political struggles. The Mandela government at times criticized the United States for supporting groups unfriendly to the government.

Finally, in the Philippines, the NGO community has long played a significant political role—helping bring down the Marcos regime, challenging and helping define national political agendas under presidents Aquino, Ramos, and Estrada, and taking sides in the 1998 presidential elections to support Estrada over Ramos. Thus U.S. and other international aid for Philippine NGOs has inevitably been directly related to political currents and choices.

That the NGO sectors of transitional countries—and, by extension, the aid programs that support them—are often directly involved in partisan politics and open political struggle is not a flaw or a confusion of purpose. It is a normal feature of civil society in a democracy. To cite just one parallel example from the United States, the AFL-CIO—part of civil society—regularly engages in partisan politics such as fund-raising for favored candidates and parties. The point is that some donors' belief that civil society promotion allows them to foster democratization without actually being political, or partisan, is an illusion. Many aid groups involved in promoting democracy steer clear of political party work, insisting that they do not want to do anything too political. They turn instead to civil society work, thinking it will provide them a nonpolitical means of encouraging political change. Recipients, however, with good reason, often perceive such donor institutions as highly political despite their protestations of political neutrality.

The Question of Impact

Following Imco Brouwer's scheme, we will review the impact of a civil society-based approach to democracy promotion at three levels: 1) at the microlevel—whether civil society programs have met their immediate objective of setting up and strengthening NGOs; 2) at the mesolevel—whether more and stronger advocacy NGOs amount to a stronger civil society; and 3) at the macrolevel—whether a stronger civil society has actually helped produce greater political liberalization or democratization. The success imputed to aid can vary considerably depending on the level of analysis and the measurements used.

Microlevel

At the microlevel, the impact of civil society assistance has been nothing short of dramatic. Funding from donor governments and foundations in the past ten years has created and kept alive thousands of NGOs in the assisted countries. Furthermore, in many countries in the five regions studied, few NGOs existed until recently. In most countries, including many under heavy state control, citizens have in recent decades organized to achieve common goals. The associations they have formed have ranged from informal, community-based groups with purposes from mutual aid to entertainment, to broad-based movements espousing nationalist or, often, socialist ideologies. In their own ways, many of these organizations have sought to influence the government or at least make up for its failures; they were civil society organizations with public-minded rather than private goals. However, until the past ten or fifteen years, most of those organizations were not NGOs. This is hardly surprising, since the NGO explosion is a phenomenon of the late twentieth century even in established democracies. Civil society assistance thus not only increased dramatically the number of organizations operating in recipient countries but also introduced NGOs as a pervasive associational form, marking a departure from the past.

For example, as Kevin Quigley argues in his chapter, in Eastern Europe after the revolutions of 1989, citizens associated civil society with highly successful mass movements such as Solidarity in Poland or Civic Forum in Czechoslovakia, and nobody was giving much thought to NGOs. Yet within a few years there were tens of thousands of NGOs in Eastern Europe. Similarly, in civil societies in Latin America, a significant shift occurred over a decade, with the traditional left-wing popular movements that Washington regarded with suspicion shrinking or disappearing, to be replaced by the many NGOs supported by the U.S. government and other international actors that were springing up. Similar changes took place in the Middle East and Africa, although the lower level of economic development in those regions limited the growth of NGOs to more modest numbers.

Although largely new to recipient countries in all regions, the donors' definition of civil society as NGOs was readily accepted everywhere. Two factors helped NGOs become the preferred form of civil society organization: first, and probably more important, the availability of donor financing for that type of organization; and second, the attractive employment opportunities NGOs offer for members of educated elites displaced by political change as well as by economic crisis and restructuring. We do not want to imply that leaders and personnel of donor-funded NGOs have no commitment to democracy or human rights, or that they do not have a sincere desire to help their countries become democratic. The commitment and courage of civil activists struggling to create political space and use it productively in difficult transitions have often been notable. Nonetheless, many activists' decision to channel their work through the organizational form of NGOs was clearly shaped by donors' preference for such organizations and by the attractive working conditions such jobs often offered. In many countries undergoing political transitions, the rapid expansion of the NGO sector created important opportunities for young people who wanted to get involved in public affairs but were shut out of or skeptical of political parties or the state. Through NGO work, they have gained training in organization, civic activism, and leadership that they can take to other domains or build on in civil society.

Since the explosion of NGOs was supply-driven to a significant degree, the large number of "democracy NGOs" does not necessarily indicate that that organizational form is particularly well suited to the needs and requirements of the countries where they emerge. Indeed, the contributors to this volume concur in their judgment that the overwhelming majority of NGOs in their particular parts of the world would be unsustainable without funding from donors (although one contributor, Golub, asserts that we should focus on the sustainability of NGO impact rather than the sustainability of the organizations themselves). Some of the studies, above all Dan Petrescu's on Romania and Al-Sayyid's on Egypt, turn up evidence that the organizations of civil society that manage to attract local funding and become self-supporting tend to be either service-delivery organizations, as opposed to policy-oriented ones, or associations that protect the corporate interests of their members, such as the Egyptian professional syndicates and labor unions and business organizations everywhere.

In short, civil society assistance has been enormously influential over the past ten years. It has been responsible for the emergence of NGOs in all regions of the world—indeed, for implanting the idea that NGOs are the model of what civil society should be in democratic countries. That the NGOs are highly dependent on donor support, however, should raise serious concerns about the long-term impact of civil society assistance even at the microlevel. At the very least, the number of democracy NGOs can be expected to decrease drastically where donor support declines and eventually to stabilize at much lower levels, the surviving NGOs becoming capable of raising inside the country the funds they need. If that happens, donor assistance will leave a lasting legacy, though perhaps not a dramatic one.

Mesolevel

The question of whether civil society is stronger and plays a more important role in the political life of the country as a result of assistance from donors—the mesolevel—is much more complicated. In many countries, new advocacy NGOs have engaged national and local governments on numerous public interest policy questions—police abuse, women's rights, the environment, corruption, transparency—and prompted useful reforms. Success on the advocacy front varies considerably. The contributors writing on Africa and the Middle East report that NGOs have discouragingly little effect on policy processes. Those reporting on Latin

America, Asia, and Eastern Europe are more positive. Basombrío makes clear that, harassed and circumscribed as they are by the Fujimori government, Peruvian NGOs have been essential in forcing the government to engage on issues of human rights. Quigley and Petrescu report that Eastern European NGOs' impact on policy has fallen short of donors' inflated expectations, but also note some successes. Racelis finds that NGOs play a major policy role in the Philippines, a role Golub underscores in his analysis of that country, and finds at least some evidence of it in several other Asian countries.

Although donor-supported advocacy NGOs influence policy in some places, their ability to represent citizens' interests often remains weak. Donors hope that NGOs will be a means of aggregating citizens' interests and serve as a two-way conveyor belt between states and citizens. Yet the policy work many advocacy NGOs engage in—at least the elite NGOs often favored by Western democracy promoters—is carried out on behalf of citizens with whom the NGOs often have little real contact. Thus policy impact per se is not equivalent to the broader goals of interest representation and broader citizen participation.

The distance separating many advocacy NGOs from their own societies is often related to the kind of people who gravitate to the NGO sector and to the nature of technocratic policy advocacy work. Yet it also stems from those NGOs' dependence on donors. The survival of the advocacy NGOs in the short run often depends more on their ability to talk to and engage the donors than their ability to talk to and engage their fellow citizens. Donors' preferences lead NGOs to use certain kinds of language and organize around issues that may appear abstract or remote to their countrymen. Both Landsberg and Ottaway, for example, note that the groups organizing around concrete, immediate grievances built constituencies more easily than those seeking to organize around donors' favored ideals, including democracy. The tendency for NGOs to speak the language of donors so as to ensure their funding is understandable, but makes it difficult for them to attract a large domestic constituency, which undermines their viability in the long run.

NGOs that promote women's rights are a major exception, in that this issue not only attracts donor funding but can also gain widespread grassroots support. Our research in several countries, including Nepal, Zambia, and Uganda, indicates that women's NGOs are among the most successful in connecting to local constituencies. While many NGOs, and not only women's NGOs, are undoubtedly good at attracting donor support while building strong ties to their constituencies, the emergence of so-called organizations of civil society that are isolated from the society surrounding them is one of the paradoxical consequences of civil society assistance.

As mentioned above, both Golub and Racelis conclude that civil society in the Philippines is a major force for both economic change and democracy, and thus believe that donor funding has contributed very significantly to the development of a strong civil society in that country. There are, as Racelis points out, many reasons for the unusual strength of civil society in the Philippines, including the long history of citizens' groups there and the extraordinary role those organizations played in the restoration of democracy after the ouster of President Ferdinand Marcos. But another reason is that the focus of most NGOs in the Philippines is not the promotion of a formal democratic system but the participation of citizens in promoting economic development and tackling the social problems that affect them directly. Democratic participation is thus not an abstraction but a means to an end that is directly important to the lives of people. Democratic participation becomes an extension of such efforts to improve one's life chances.

It is impossible to extrapolate general conclusions from the example of the Philippines, where the role of NGOs appears to be unique. The experience of that country, however, raises important questions. Has democracy assistance, for example, focused excessively on organizations that promote democracy for democracy's sake, rather than on organizations that promote grassroots involvement in the solution of socioeconomic problems? And would the cause of democracy be better advanced by organizations that mobilize their members not around the ideal of democracy but around the protection of their own interests? On the second question, the example of South Africa is also relevant: the organizations that finally forced the white government to accept the transition from apartheid initially mobilized their members not around the issues of human rights and democracy but around mundane, concrete issues such as rent payment and electricity rates.

Macrolevel

Assessing the impact of civil society assistance on overall political change in recipient countries is even more difficult, and the analysis that the chapters in this volume provide is not a sufficient basis for a definitive answer. First, the status of civil society is only one of many factors that contribute to the success or failure of democratization. Even when most effective, civil society assistance alone could not be expected to bring about a highly undemocratic system's transformation into a democracy. Donors understand that, and thus divide their democracy aid portfolios among various priorities besides development of civil society, including free and fair elections and democratic state institutions. Second, the importance of civil society organizations, as opposed to political parties, varies considerably even among established democracies. In European countries, for example, civil society organizations have historically tended to work through the political parties and to affect their internal processes, rather than to influence directly the operation of government institutions. In other words, many democratic systems are based on a strong political society but a relatively weak, and subordinate, civil society.

In the regions under study here, the effects of civil society assistance on overall democratization vary somewhat, but the evidence fairly consistently indicates that such assistance alone is unlikely to be a major factor. In Egypt and Palestine, nondemocratic leaders negate most of the aid's prodemocratic potential. In both places, burgeoning Western support for civil society throughout the 1990s corresponded with stagnation or even backsliding on political liberalization. In Romania, NGO activists find themselves frustrated by the inability of the credible new NGO sector to ameliorate the extremely weak performance of a series of Romanian governments and citizens' concomitant loss of faith in democracy. In South Africa, as mentioned previously, it was a broad social movement, not advocacy NGOs, that led the way in the fight against apartheid. In the post-apartheid era, the NGO advocacy sector has not become a major force in the country's new political life. In Peru, advocacy NGOs have been on the front lines of struggle against Fujimori, but they are scarcely alone; political opposition figures, concerned foreign governments, and international institutions are all involved. Even in the Philippines, the powerful NGO sector that helped bring down President Marcos in the mid-1980s has recently been running up against limits on its ability to counteract the shortcomings of democracy under a president inclined toward populist sloganeering.

Although it cannot on its own ensure democracy, a strong civil society clearly can contribute by increasing the pluralism of the political system. Interest groups that are not organized formally as political parties and do not aspire to a state role can affect government decisions nonetheless. In countries where civil society is organized, more demands are likely to be heard, and more interest groups can have their say. But the evidence from the chapters in this volume, while far from conclusive, raises doubts about the contribution to pluralism of the type of civil society that democracy assistance engenders. It appears that NGO-oriented democracy assistance promotes a pluralism that is more organizational than political. The policy followed by many donors, of promoting large numbers of NGOs through numerous small grants while at the same time promoting a narrow range of types and orientations of NGOs, has led to civil societies that are much less pluralistic than the numbers suggest. That is the conclusion Quigley reaches looking at Eastern Europe and Ottaway looking at Africa. Civil society organizations supported by donors tend to resemble each other greatly in political orientation, the character of their personnel, and demands, and thus fail to reflect the full range of interests in the society.

Furthermore, donors have their own political interests and biases, which lead them to exclude certain kinds of political organization from civil society assistance. During the Cold War, left-of-center citizens' organizations got no aid from the United States or some other nations, even when the groups played a major role in bringing about political change that moved their country closer to democracy. Basombrío and Shifter point out that during the Cold War, important popular organizations in Latin America were excluded from U.S. assistance because of leftist leanings common to popular organizations at the time. Brouwer and Al-Sayyid show Egypt and Palestine facing a similar problem today, since Islamist organizations are automatically excluded from receiving civil society aid, even if the focus of their activities is charitable and developmental rather than political.

Certainly it would be difficult for the United States or any other democratic country to assist and work closely with organizations that embrace ideologies that are, according to the Western definition, antidemocratic. But when such groups have a large popular following and large numbers of local actors see them as legitimate, their exclusion can also have a negative impact on democratization. Historically, in many democratic countries, it was organizations with large popular followings and socialist or populist orientations, such as labor unions, that transformed democracy from competition among elites to a process in which the entire population is involved.[1] In many countries, the cost of designing the civil society component of democracy programs primarily around organizations that explicitly focus on democracy may contribute to the elitist character of civil society organizations and, depriving them of mass support, condemn them to ineffectiveness. This is not an easy dilemma for donors to resolve, but the way in which it is tackled may determine whether civil society assistance contributes to democratization or simply to the multiplication of new organizations.

Problems of Implementation

Civil society assistance requires close collaboration among organizations that vary greatly in size, work style, and requirements. Relations between them are inevitably difficult. On one side are donor agencies—relatively large institutions, usually quite bureaucratic. Furthermore, although donor organizations strive to influence policies and conditions in other countries, they are accountable or responsible not to the citizens and governments of the targeted societies but to those of their home state. On the other side, the NGOs that are the beneficiaries of civil society assistance tend to be small startup organizations with entrepreneurial leaders and very small staffs; they often carry the imprint of the founder's style, and thus are often idiosyncratic. Donors have strict accounting requirements and formal systems for approving projects and grants, and they must satisfy their own criteria for accountability and evaluation. Recipient NGOs have trouble developing the expertise to meet those requirements; left to their own devices, they tend toward what was known in apartheid-era South Africa as "struggle accounting," a loose system of financial control that donors accepted from organizations operating under the precarious conditions of the antiapartheid struggle but one that they reject in most cases.

The mismatch between donors and recipients creates many problems in implementation. NGOs scrambling to work in highly fluid political environments complain that donors' operational rigidity often makes it hard to seize opportunities and respond to new challenges. They argue that some donors' unwillingness to cede real control over the nature and direction of NGO activities to the NGOs themselves impedes the development of trust. And they assert that many donors' persistent tendency to define programs' priorities in advance leads to activities that do not correspond to the realities or requirements of the recipient societies. Petrescu and Quigley detail the many shortcomings in implementation of USAID's flagship program for civil society support in Eastern Europe, the Democracy Network Program. Golub goes even deeper in his critique of USAID's methods of implementation, tracing the problem to causes ranging from an overreliance on Western consultants to a rigid administrative project cycle to a numbers-oriented, inflexible evaluation system. It is clear from most of the chapters here that much improvement is needed in this area. Private foundations are somewhat better situated than government agencies to deal with such problems, because they can be more flexible in their rules and can take risks with their funds that government agencies cannot take with taxpayers' money.[2]

Cumbersome grant-making procedures and reporting requirements do more than overload lightly staffed NGOs; they also teach the organizations to speak a language that is not that of their societies but that of the donors. Donors have set up training programs to teach NGOs that language in many countries and regions, as the chapters indicate. Use of the language helps in relations with donors but can complicate relations with the NGOs' own societies, creating suspicion and making the organizations an easy target for the scorn of hostile governments. Racelis, Petrescu, and Golub point out that NGOs are often told not only how to write their proposals but also what to ask for. In our own research, the similarity among the statements of goals issued by NGOs around the world confirms the existence of a universal NGO language that owes nothing to the specific problems or cultural traits of individual countries. To what extent, then, can NGOs still be considered to represent genuine needs and demands rather than outsiders' view of what is good for the society? The more successful some training programs are from donors' point of view, the more they risk creating a barrier between NGOs and society.

Other choices donors make in administering civil society assistance also affect the relationship between NGOs and their society. One is the choice of intermediaries on which large agencies depend when assisting local NGOs. USAID relies on American NGOs and contractors to provide technical assistance and sometimes to oversee the actual giving of grants; the European Union in Eastern Europe chose instead to develop a network of local Civil Society Development Foundations, through which it funded local NGOs. While the staying power of these EU-sponsored civil society foundations is not yet established, they are in a much better starting place than large U.S. contractors.

The problems of implementation are significant but also largely remediable, though change is always difficult given the internal bureaucratic imperatives of funders. Donors must redouble their emphasis on achieving in practice what are usually a well-rehearsed set of hortatory principles: flexibility, local control, responsiveness to local conditions, risk-taking, and the like. Generally a positive evolution is discernible. The shortcomings in implementation are beginning to be addressed, in large part because advocacy NGOs on the receiving end have started to use their advocacy skills to press for change in the organizations that support them.

But other fundamental problems in the implementation of civil society assistance cannot be easily solved or even ameliorated, and are likely to remain a problem. In particular, clashes between a donor country's interest in promoting democracy and its other foreign policy interests are difficult to avoid. The Middle East offers abundant examples, as Al-Sayyid and Brouwer show, but it is not unique. The United States' commitment to democratization and thus to civil society promotion in that region is counterbalanced by its commitment to maintain friendly relations with the moderate Arab autocrats who support the Arab-Israeli peace process and by its desire to maintain ready access to some of the world's major oil reserves. In this sensitive environment, U.S. policymakers become acutely aware of the potentially destabilizing effect of strong civil society organizations. Officials are particularly cautious in their choice of groups eligible for assistance, which lessens the impact of programs.

Looking Ahead

In the 1990s a first generation of civil society aid was carried out across the developing and post-communist worlds. During that decade, the idea of civil society promotion took hold throughout the international aid community, huge numbers of civil society programs were launched, and NGOs multiplied dramatically in dozens of aid-receiving countries.

With the new century under way, donors are asking themselves what that first generation of civil society aid accomplished and how they should move forward.

The aid has clearly helped implant in many countries the important idea that civil society has a rightful role in governance. The aid has unquestionably helped along or even spurred NGO booms in numerous transitional countries. Some of the new NGOs have had a positive effect on policy, provided vital socioeconomic services, and served as a training ground for thousands of civic activities. It is now also clear, however, that development of NGOs does not equal development of civil society. In many transitional countries with hundreds or even thousands of NGOs, basic features of civic democratic life—widespread participation by citizens, solid public belief in democracy, dynamic patterns of accountability and interaction between the state and the society—are still woefully absent.

The next generation of civil society aid has not yet taken shape. Many donors are disinclined to go on increasing their support for NGOs, uncertain both about the value of continuing on the same path and, at least in some countries, about whether significant opportunities remain for new NGO programs. Moreover, there is no guarantee that all or most of the accomplishments of the past ten years will survive. The new world of advocacy NGOs in many countries is a fragile one, and its vulnerability will become increasingly evident as more countries graduate from shrinking development assistance programs and as new humanitarian crises cry for aid.

The uncertain state of the "Third Wave" of democracy raises deeper concerns about the appropriate direction and shape of civil society aid. The first generation of civil society programs was built on the early-1990s vision of a broad, rapid wave of democratization around the world, in which rapidly expanding NGO sectors would take their place in the processes of democratization. Yet only a small number of countries—approximately a dozen relatively affluent countries in Central Europe, East Asia, and the Southern Cone of Latin America—have accomplished transitions of that sort.

The great majority of the roughly one hundred countries in Latin America, Africa, Eastern Europe, the former Soviet Union, Asia, and the Middle East that experienced political openings in the 1980s or early 1990s and were labeled by the international community as "in democratic transition" are in fact hovering in a gray zone somewhere between democracy and dictatorship. They are semi-authoritarian, or at best hyphenated democracies of one kind or another—electoral democracies, delegative democracies, illiberal democracies, partial democracies. They have democratic forms, but the democratic substance is limited. In such countries, the optimal or even possible roles for nascent civil society vary. In some, civil society groups struggle just to help preserve a modicum of political space. In others, such as Venezuela, Ecuador, and Bolivia, civil society is part of the rise of new forms of populist (and sometimes antidemocratic) reaction to poorly functioning democratic systems. Undoubtedly the roles of civil society in the new transitional gray zone will be as diverse as the partial democracies that make up that zone. What is certain is that roles will not conform neatly to the idealized view of civil society as a zone of virtuous civic engagement that animated donors' initial rush into the domain.

In short, donors seeking to carry forward their commitment to civil society promotion have no well-marked path ahead. They should instead build on some of the basic lessons that have emerged from recent experience. First, they should give serious, sustained attention to the sustainability of their support. That does not mean simply helping NGOs figure out how to generate resources from their own societies. It also means opening up debate on whether the Western model of professionalized NGOs is broadly appropriate in developing countries, given the relatively high costs of many such organizations relative to the local economies, and discussion of alternatives that might fit better in the host societies.

Second, donors must take seriously the challenge of improving their basic methods of implementation for civil society aid. The shortcomings of method—including bureaucratic rigidity, aversion to risk, and the imposition of external priorities and approaches—are now well known, yet many donors have not attacked the problems. The push for greater accountability in countries that receive aid must be matched by greater accountability of aid providers, especially when it comes to the societies they are to assist.

Third, aid providers should continue to expand the range of organizations they seek to assist in civil society programs. When it has occurred, the extension of aid from public interest advocacy NGOs to NGOs concentrating on socioeconomic issues has often been useful. Donors must concentrate more on spurring NGOs to work in conjunction with other sectors of civil society and on extending their own civil society aid to groups other than NGOs.

Finally, it is high time for democracy promoters to jettison the notion that the many political transitions under way around the world are best understood as passages along a predictable sequence of stages from political opening through to democratic consolidation. Where transitions have been fairly successful, advocacy NGOs may indeed play a role in improving government policies. But in countries where political space is shrinking, NGOs may be most effective as the new dissidents, keeping alive the vision of democracy. Donors must recognize the profound heterogeneity of attempted transitions and try to understand the forms and roles of civil society, and of civil society aid, in light of it. Only thus can they match the praiseworthy motivation of trying to foster what ultimately can be a crucial part of democratic societies with aid efforts worthy of that complex task.

Notes

1. See Dietrich Ruschemeyer, Evelyne Huber Stephens, and John D. Stephens, *Capitalist Development and Democracy* (Chicago: University of Chicago Press, 1992).

2. On the differences between public and private methods of aid-giving, see Thomas Carothers, "Aiding Post-Communist Societies: A Better Way?" *Problems of Post-Communism*, September-October 1996, pp. 15–24.

Bibliography

This list focuses on writings about civil society aid rather than civil society and NGOs generally. It is primarily made up of secondary sources and includes only a small number of the numerous documents produced by USAID and other aid organizations on their civil society programs.

Abramson, David M. "A Critical Look at NGOs and Civil Society as Means to an End in Uzbekistan," *Human Development*, vol. 58, no. 3 (Fall 1999): 240–51.

Albright, Madeleine. *Focus on the Issues: Strengthening Civil Society and the Rule of Law*. Washington, D.C.: U.S. Dept. of State, 2000.

Arruda, Marcos. *NGOs and the World Bank: Possibilities and Limits of Collaboration*. Geneva: NGO Working Group on the World Bank, 1993.

Bebbington, Anthony, and Roger Riddell. "The Direct Funding of Southern NGOs by Donors: New Agendas and Old Problems," *Journal of International Development*, vol. 7, no. 6 (1995): 879–93.

Bebbington, Anthony, et al. *Non-Governmental Organizations and the State in Latin America*. New York: Routledge, 1993.

Bernard, Amanda, et al. *Civil Society and International Development*. Paris: OECD, Development Centre, 1998.

Bernbaum, Marcia, and Guillermo Marquez. *Final Evaluation of USAID/ DR Strengthening Civil Society Activity*, USAID Document no. PD-ABN-518. Santo Domingo: USAID Mission to Dominican Republic, December 1, 1996.

Bhat, M. K. *Life Goes On—Sustainability of Community Development Programs and the Withdrawal of NGO Support: An Enquiry into Expectations and Implications*. London: Center for Innovation in Voluntary Action and Bangalore Consultancy Office, 1999.

Biekart, Kees. *The Politics of Civil Society Building: European Private Aid Agencies and Democratic Transitions in Central America*. Amsterdam: Transnational Institute, 1999.

Blair, Harry. "Donors, Democratisation and Civil Society: Relating Theory to Practice," in David Hulme and Michael Edwards, eds., *NGOs, States and Donors: Too Close for Comfort?* New York: St. Martin's Press, 1997: 23–42.

Blair, Harry, and John Booth, et al. *Civil Society and Democratic Development in El Salvador: A CDIE Assessment*, USAID Document no. PN-ABU-449. Washington, D.C.: USAID, March 1, 1995.

Blair, Harry, and Joel Jutkowitz. *Civil Society and Democratic Development in Bangladesh*, USAID Working Paper no. 212. Washington, D.C.: USAID Center for Development Information and Evaluation, 1994.

Bratton, Michael. "Non-Governmental Organizations in Africa: Can They Influence Public Policy?" *Development and Change*, vol. 21 (1990): 87–118.

Brown, David. *Report on Southern NGO Capacity Building Issues as Observed by Nine NGO Support Organizations*. Boston: Institute for Development Research, 1997.

Burma Center Netherlands and Transnational Institute. *Strengthening Civil Society in Burma: Possibilities and Dilemmas for International NGOs*. Chiang Mai, Thailand: Silkworm Books, 1999.

Carothers, Thomas. *Aiding Democracy Abroad: The Learning Curve*. Washington, D.C.: Carnegie Endowment for International Peace, 1999.

———. "Think Again: Civil Society," *Foreign Policy*, no. 117 (Winter 1999/2000): 18–29.

———. "Western Civil-Society Aid to Eastern Europe and the Former Soviet Union," *East European Constitutional Review*, vol. 8, no. 4 (Fall 1999): 54–62.

Chandler, David. "Democratization in Bosnia: The Limits of Civil Society Building Strategies," *Democratization*, vol. 5, no. 4 (Winter 1998): 78–102.

Clark, John D. *Civil Society Participation in World Bank Country Assistance Strategies: Lessons from Experience, FY 97–98*. Washington, D.C.: World Bank, 1998.

Clayton, Andrew, ed. *NGOs, Civil Society and the State: Building Democracy in Transitional Societies.* Chippenham: INTRAC, 1996.

Cohen, John M. "Foreign Advisors and Capacity Building: The Case of Kenya," *Public Administration and Development,* vol. 12 (1992): 493–510.

Conroy, Michael E., Douglas L. Murray, and Peter M. Rosset. *A Cautionary Tale: Failed U.S. Development Policy in Central America.* Boulder: Lynne Rienner, 1996.

Diamond, Larry. *Promoting Democracy in the 1990s: Actors and Instruments, Issues and Imperatives.* New York: Carnegie Corporation of New York, 1995.

Draimin, Tim. *Strengthening Civil Society: The Role of Southern Foundations.* New York: Synergos Institute, 1999.

Dulany, Peggy. *How Community Development Foundations Can Help Strengthen Civil Society.* New York: Synergos Institute, 1993.

Eade, Deborah. *Development, NGOs, and Civil Society.* Oxford: Oxfam, 2000.

Edwards, Michael, and David Hulme. *Beyond the Magic Bullet: NGO Performance and Accountability in the Post-Cold War World.* Hartford, Conn.: Kumarian Press, 1996.

Ekiert, Grzegorz. *Civil Society from Abroad: The Role of Foreign Assistance in the Democratization of Poland.* Cambridge, Mass.: Weatherhead Center for International Affairs, Harvard University, 2000.

Figueredo, Roberto, Rhys Payne, et al. *Strengthening NGOs for Democratization and Sustainable Development in Morocco: An NGO Assessment,* USAID Document no. PN-ABY-781. Washington, D.C.: USAID Center for Democracy and Governance, February 1996.

Fine, Robert, and Shirin Rai, eds. "Special Issue: Civil Society: Democratic Perspectives," *Democratization,* vol. 4, no. 1 (Spring 1997).

Foley, Michael. "Laying the Groundwork: The Struggle for Civil Society in El Salvador," *Journal of Interamerican Studies and World Affairs,* vol. 38, no. 1 (Spring 1996): 67–104.

Foley, Michael W., and Bob Edwards. "The Paradox of Civil Society," *Journal of Democracy,* vol. 7, no. 3 (July 1996): 38–52.

Fowler, Alan. "Building Partnerships between Northern and Southern Development NGOs: Issues for the Nineties," *Development,* no. 1 (1992): 16–23.

——. "Non-governmental Organizations as Agents of Democratization: An African Perspective," *Journal of International Development,* vol. 5, no. 3 (1993): 325–39.

————. "The Role of NGOs in Changing State-Society Relations: Perspectives from Eastern and Southern Africa," *Development Policy Review*, vol. 9 (1991): 53–84.

Fox, Leslie. *Strengthening Civil Society Financing in Development: The Role of Official Development Assistance.* Washington, D.C.: Overseas Development Council and Synergos Institute, 1995.

Fox, Leslie, and Bruce Schearer, eds. *Sustaining Civil Society: Strategies for Resource Mobilization.* Washington, D.C.: CIVICUS, 1997.

Freres, Christian L. *The European Union's Civil Society Co-operation with Latin America.* Madrid: AIETI, 1998.

Gasparini, Alberto and Vladimir Yadov, eds. *Social Actors and Designing the Civil Society of Eastern Europe.* Greenwich, Conn.: JAI Press, 1995.

Gregorio-Medel, Angelita, Ana Maria O. Clamor, and Sixdon C. Macasaet. *Coalition Assessment: USAID Civil Society Program* [Philippines], USAID Document no. PN-ACF-110. Washington, D.C.: USAID Center for Democracy and Governance, April 1998.

Hadenius, Axel, and Fredrik Uggla. "Making Civil Society Work, Promoting Democratic Development: What Can States and Donors Do?" *World Development*, vol. 24, no. 10 (October 1996): 1621–40.

Hafez, Kai. *The Role of NGOs in the Development of Civil Society, Europe and the Arab Countries: Proceedings of a Seminar Held in Amman, Jordan on December 6–7, 1997.* Vienna: Bruno Kreisky Forum, 1999.

Hansen, Gary. *Constituencies for Reform: Strategic Approaches for Donor-Supported Civic Advocacy Programs,* USAID Program and Operations Assessment Report no. 12, USAID Document no. PN-ABS-544. Washington, D.C.: USAID Center for Development Information and Evaluation, February 1996.

Hansen, Gary, and Michael Calavan. *The Development of Civil Society in Thailand: Donor Approaches and Issues,* USAID Working Paper, no. 210. Washington, D.C.: USAID Center for Development Information and Evaluation, 1994.

Hately, Lynne, and Kamal Malhotra. *Between Rhetoric and Reality: Essay on Partnership in Development.* Ottawa: North-South Institute, 1997.

Haynes, Jeff. *Democracy and Civil Society in the Third World.* Malden, Mass.: Polity Press, 1997.

Hearn, Julie. *Foreign Aid, Democratisation, and Civil Society in Africa: A Study of South Africa, Ghana, and Uganda.* Brighton, UK: Institute of Development Studies, University of Sussex, 1999.

———. "The NGO-isation of Kenyan Society: USAID & the Restructuring of Health Care," *Review of African Political Economy*, vol. 25, no. 75 (March 1998): 89–100.

Heilman, Lawrence C., and Frank R. Pavich. *Final Report: Audit Evaluation and Project Support Fund-Independent Mid-Term Evaluation of the Democracy Network Program, Project No. 180-0249.83, Cooperation Agreement No. DHR-0032-A-00-5017,* USAID Document no. PD-ABP-229. Washington, D.C.: Management Systems International and USAID Center for Democracy and Governance, April 27, 1997.

Helmich, Henny and Jos Lemmers. "Civil Society and International Cooperation," *Development*, no. 1 (1998).

Hernandez, Ricardo. "IDB-Civil Society Consultation in Mexico," *The Other Side of Mexico*, no. 45 (March-April 1996).

Heyzer, Noeleen, James V. Riker, and Antonio B. Quizon, eds. *Government-NGO Relations in Asia: Prospects and Challenges for People-Centered Development*. New York: St. Martin's Press, 1995.

Holloway, Richard. "The Unit of Development is the Organization, Not the Project: Strategies and Structures for Sustaining the Work of Southern NGOs." Paper prepared for Johns Hopkins University New Directions Workshop. Washington, D.C., 1997.

Howes, Mick. "Linking Paradigms and Practice: Key Issues in Appraisal, Monitoring and Evaluation of British NGO Projects," *Journal of International Development*, vol. 4, no. 4 (1992): 375–96.

Hudock, Ann C. *NGOs and Civil Society: Democracy by Proxy?* Malden, Mass.: Polity Press, 1999.

———. "Sustaining Southern NGOs in Resource-Dependent Environments," *Journal of International Development*, vol. 7, no. 4 (1995): 653–67.

Hulme, David, and Michael Edwards, eds. *NGOs, States and Donors: Too Close for Comfort?* New York: St. Martin's Press, 1997.

Hyden, Goran. "The Role of Aid and Research in the Political Restructuring of Africa," in R. C. Crook and A. M. Jerve, eds., *Government and Participation: Institutional Development, Decentralization and Democracy in the Third World*. Bergen: Chr. Michelsen Institute, Dept. of Social Science and Development, 1991: 133–58.

Ibrahim, Saad Eddin. *Nurturing Civil Society at the World Bank: An Assessment of Staff Attitudes at the World Bank*. Washington, D.C.: The World Bank, 1998.

Institute of Development Studies. *Summary Report of the Workshop on Civil Society and Foreign Aid.* Workshop held at University of Sussex, June 6–7, 1996.

INTRAC. *Direct Funding from a Southern Perspective: Strengthening Civil Society?* Oxford: INTRAC, 1998.

Johnson, R. W. "Destroying South Africa's Democracy: USAID, the Ford Foundation, and Civil Society," *The National Interest* (Fall 1998): 19–28.

Johnston, Michael. "Fighting Systemic Corruption: Social Foundations for Institutional Reform," *European Journal of Development Research,* vol. 10, no. 1 (June 1998): 85–104.

Jutkowitz, Joel, Robert Asselin, and Stephen M. Brager. *Final Report: Evaluation of USAID Supported Civil Society of CSOs [Civil Society Organizations] in Nicaragua,* USAID Document no. XD-ABQ-661-A. Washington, D.C.: Development Associates, April 1999.

Keengwe, Maina. *NGO Roles and Relationships: Partnership Dilemmas for International and Local NGOs (in Kenya).* London: International Institute for Environment and Development, 1998.

Kilby, Patrick. "Human Rights, Aid and Civil Society," *Development Bulletin-Australian Development Studies,* vol. 34, no. 2 (August 1995): 30.

Kothari, Smitu. "Inclusive, Just, Plural, Dynamic: Building a Civil Society in the Third World," *Development in Practice,* vol. 9, no. 3 (May 1999): 246–60.

Macdonald, Laura. "Globalising Civil Society: Interpreting International NGOs in Central America," *Millennium: A Journal of International Studies,* vol. 23, no. 2 (1994): 267–85.

———. "A Mixed Blessing: The NGO Boom in Latin America," *NACLA Report on the Americas,* vol. 28, no. 5 (March 1, 1995): 30.

———. *Supporting Civil Society: The Political Role of Non-Governmental Organizations in Central America.* New York: St. Martin's Press, 1997.

Marcussen, Henrik Secher. "NGOs, the State and Civil Society," *Review of African Political Economy,* no. 23 (1996): 405–23.

Mendelson, Sarah E. *Democracy and NGO Strategies in Post-Communist Societies.* Washington, D.C.: Carnegie Endowment for International Peace, 2000.

Monshipouri, Mahmood. "Promoting Civil Society and Human Rights in the Third World: Global Changes, Setbacks, and Opportunities," *Journal of Third World Spectrum,* no. 3 (Spring 1996): 1–27.

Ndegwa, Stephen N. "Civil Society and Political Change in Africa: The Case of Non-Governmental Organizations in Kenya," *International Journal of Comparative Sociology*, vol. 35, no. 1/2 (January 1994): 19–36.

———. *The Two Faces of Civil Society: NGOs and Politics in Africa*. Hartford, Conn.: Kumarian Press, 1996.

O'Brien, David, and Luciano Catenacci. "Towards a Framework for Local Democracy in a War-Torn Society: The Lessons of Selected Foreign Assistance Programmes in El Salvador," *Democratization*, vol. 3, no. 4 (Winter 1996): 435–58.

Oloka-Onyango, J., and J. J. Barya. "Civil Society and the Political Economy of Foreign Aid in Uganda," *Democratization*, vol. 4, no. 2 (Summer 1997): 113–38.

Ottaway, Marina, and Theresa Chung. "Debating Democracy Assistance: Toward a New Paradigm," *Journal of Democracy*, vol. 10, no. 4 (October 1999): 99–113.

Pankhurst, Donna. "Striving for 'Real' Civil Society: The Roles of International Donors and Civil Society in Zimbabwe," *Global Society*, vol. 12 (May 1998): 197–219.

Pearce, Jenny. "Building Civil Society from the Outside: The Problematic Democratisation of Central America," *Global Society*, vol. 12 (May 1998): 177–96.

———. "NGOs and Social Change: Agents or Facilitators?" *Development in Practice*, vol. 3, no. 3 (October 1993): 222–23.

Peterson, Lisa. "Consolidating Democracy: Lessons We Are Learning From the Results of USAID Democratic Governance Programs in Africa." Presented April 23–25, 1996, Johannesburg.

Phillips, Ann L. "Exporting Democracy: German Political Foundations in Central-East Europe," *Democratization*, vol. 6, no. 2 (Summer 1999): 70–98.

Porter, Doug, and Patrick Kilby. "Strengthening the Role of Civil Society in Development? A Precariously Balanced Answer," *Australian Journal of International Affairs*, vol. 50, no. 1 (1996): 31–42

Quigley, Kevin F. F. *For Democracy's Sake: Foundations and Democracy Assistance in Central Europe*. Baltimore: Johns Hopkins University Press, 1997.

——— "Towards Consolidating Democracy: The Paradoxical Role of Democracy Groups in Thailand," *Democratization*, vol. 3, no. 3 (Autumn 1996): 264–86.

Reilly, Charles A., ed. *New Paths to Democratic Development in Latin America: The Rise of NGO-Municipal Collaboration*. Boulder: Lynne Rienner, 1995.

Renshaw, Laura Roper. "Strengthening Civil Society: The Role of NGOs," *Development*, no. 4 (1994): 46–49.

Robinson, Mark. "Strengthening Civil Society in Africa: The Role of Foreign Political Aid," *Institute of Development Studies (IDS) Bulletin*, vol. 26, no. 2 (April 1, 1995): 70.

———. *Strengthening Civil Society through Foreign Political Aid*. ESCOR Research Report, no. R6234. Sussex, U.K.: Institute of Development Studies, September 1996.

Roche, Chris. "NGOs, Civil Society and the State: Building Democracy in Transitional Countries," *Development in Practice*, vol. 6, no. 3 (August 1996): 270.

Sampson, Steven. "The Social Life of Projects: Importing Civil Society to Albania," in Chris Hann and Elizabeth Dunn, eds., *Civil Society: Challenging Western Models*. New York: Routledge, 1996: 121–42.

Siegel, Daniel David, and Jenny Yancey. *The Rebirth of Civil Society: The Development of the Nonprofit Sector in East Central Europe and the Role of Western Assistance*. New York: Rockefeller Brothers Fund, 1992.

Stamberg, Lou, et al. *USAID Support for NGO Capacity-Building: Approaches, Examples, Mechanisms*, USAID Document no. PN-ACE-381. Washington, D.C.: USAID Center for Democracy and Governance, July 1998.

Stiles, Kendall W. "Civil Society Empowerment and Multilateral Donors: International Institutions and New International Norms," *Global Governance*, vol. 4 (April-June 1998): 199–216.

Sullivan, Denis J. "NGOs in Palestine: Agents of Development and Foundation of Civil Society," *Journal of Palestine Studies*, vol. 25, no. 3 (1996): 93–100.

Swilling, Mark. "Political Transition, Development and the Role of Civil Society," *Africa Insight*, vol. 20, no. 3 (1990): 151–68.

Turner, J. Michael, and Yolanda Comedy. *Support to Decentralization and Civil Society in Mozambique*, USAID Document no. PN-ABX-969. Washington, D.C.: Management Systems International and USAID Center for Democracy and Governance, September 1995.

Tvedt, Terje. *Angels of Mercy or Development Diplomats? NGOs & Foreign Aid*. Trenton, N.J.: Africa World Press, 1998.

USAID. *Civil Society and Democratic Development in Kenya: A CDIE Assessment,* USAID Working Paper no. 213, USAID Document no. PN-ABX-8883. Washington, D.C.: USAID Center for Development Information and Evaluation, 1994.

———. *Consultancy on NGO Sustainability: USAID/South Africa Policy, Guidance and Training,* USAID Document no. PD-ABS-008. Macro International and USAID Mission to South Africa, February 1999.

———. *Developing the Civil Society in Romania,* USAID Document no. PN-ABY-808. International Foundation for Electoral Systems, USAID Bureau for Europe and the New Independent States, and USAID Mission to Romania, 1994.

———. *Engaging Civil Society and Governments on the Greater Horn of Africa,* Participation Forum no. 18, USAID Document no. PN-ACB-018. Washington, D.C.: USAID Bureau for Policy and Program Coordination, April 25, 1996.

———. *Lessons in Implementation: The NGO Story—Building Civil Society in Central and Eastern Europe and the New Independent States,* USAID Document no. PN-ACA-941. Washington, D.C.: USAID Office of Democracy and Governance, October 1999.

U.S. General Accounting Office, National Security and International Affairs Division. *Promoting Democracy: Progress Report on U.S. Democratic Development Assistance to Russia,* USAID Document no. PC-AAA-687. February 1996.

Van Rooy, Alison, ed. *Civil Society and the Aid Industry.* London: Earthscan Publications, 1998.

Wedel, Janine R. *Collision and Collusion: The Strange Case of Western Aid to Eastern Europe, 1989–1998.* Basingstoke: Macmillan, 1998.

White, Gordon. "Civil Society, Democratization and Development (I): Clearing the Analytical Ground," *Democratization,* vol. 1, no. 3 (Autumn 1994): 375–90.

———. "Civil Society, Democratization and Development (II): Two Country Cases," *Democratization,* vol. 2, no. 2 (Summer 1995): 56–84.

White, Jenny. "Civic Culture and Islam in Urban Turkey," in Chris Hann and Elizabeth Dunn, eds., *Civil Society: Challenging Western Models.* New York: Routledge, 1996: 143–54.

World Bank. "Cooperation between the World Bank and NGOs," *Transnational Associations* (November/December 1998): 284–96.

Index

legal reform in Eastern Europe,
199–200
political conditions affecting aid
in Eastern Europe, 205
Romanian, 219–221, 226–227
significance of, 14–15, 100, 219
USAID perspective, 148–149
See also specific country

Mahfouz, Naguib, 68
Mandela, Nelson, 86, 94, 116
Marshall Foundation, 240 n.7
Marxist thought, 167, 168, 169, 171
Meciar, Vladimir, 193
Media institutions
aid for investigative reporting,
139–140
democracy promotion by, 157
in Eastern Europe, 215 n.18
in Egypt, 25, 26, 67–68
in Philippines, 179
Middle East, 15, 307. *See also specific
country*
Military institutions
in Egypt, 24–25
in Guatemala, 246
in Latin America, 252
in Peru, 246
in South Africa, 105
Moi, Daniel arap, 95–96
Montesinos, Vladimiro, 275
Montt, Efrain Rios, 255
Morocco, 21
Mubarak, Hosni, 24, 27, 54
Museveni, Yoweri, 92
Muslim Brotherhood, 24, 26, 29, 53,
55–56, 65

Nasser, Gamel Abdel, 54, 55
National Democratic Institute,
225, 229

National Democratic Institute for
International Affairs, 35, 37
National Endowment for
Democracy, 37, 38, 224, 257, 260
Nepal, 142–143, 150, 301
Netherlands, 119, 120
New Civic Forum, 37
Noble, Lela Garner, 182
Nongovernmental organizations
in Africa, 81, 82–83
aid rationale, 37
aid to South Africa, 89–90,
116, 125
alternative funding mechanisms,
185, 209, 218, 236–237
in antidemocratic regimes, 91
in Arab countries, 22
in Asia, 139–141, 156, 157
assertiveness of, in political
process, 294
in building civil society, 210–211
in Cambodia, 144–145
characteristics of advocacy
groups, 279–280
decline of leftist activism and, 42,
290 n.5
degree of political liberalization
and effectiveness of, 91–93
democracy promotion by, 13,
181–182, 183–184, 206–207,
282, 295
donor relations, 305–306
in Eastern Europe
aid outcomes, 205–209
conceptualization of, 196
Democracy Network program,
201–203
European Union aid to, 203–204
improving aid to, 209–213
U.S. expectations for democratic
transition, 195–196

Contributors

MUSTAPHA KAMEL AL-SAYYID is professor of political science and director of the Center for Developing Countries Studies at Cairo University, Egypt. He is the author of several books and many articles in Arabic, English, and French on Egyptian and Arab politics, civil society, and democratization in the Arab world and on the political economy of development.

CARLOS BASOMBRÍO is director of the Legal Defense Institute in Lima, Peru. He has written widely on human rights and democracy issues in Latin America and has been a visiting fellow at the Woodrow Wilson International Center for Scholars in Washington, D.C.

IMCO BROUWER is research associate and coordinator of the Mediterranean Programme of the Robert Schuman Centre for Advanced Studies at the European University Institute, Florence, Italy. He is a member of the research team of a project at the European University Institute on Western democracy promotion in Central and Eastern Europe and the Middle East and North Africa.

THOMAS CAROTHERS is vice president for studies and co-director of the Democracy and Rule of Law Project at the Carnegie Endowment for International Peace in Washington, D.C. He has worked on democracy aid programs in many countries for a variety of organizations and has written extensively on democracy aid, including *Aiding Democracy Abroad: The Learning Curve* (Carnegie Endowment, 1999).

STEPHEN J. GOLUB, an Open Society Institute research fellow, teaches international development at the Boalt Hall Law School in Berkeley, California. He directed a recent Ford Foundation review of its law programs around the world and coedited the resulting book, *Many Roads to Justice* (Ford Foundation, 2000). He heads an Asian Development Bank study of how disadvantaged populations' use of law improves governance and alleviates poverty.

CHRISTOPHER LANDSBERG lectures in the department of international relations, University of the Witwatersrand, South Africa. He is currently establishing a Foreign Policy Studies Unit at Wits. He was formerly deputy director of the Centre for Policy Studies in Johannesburg and has been a Hamburg Visiting Fellow at the Center for International Security and Cooperation at Stanford University. He has published extensively on South African foreign policy and international relations.

MARINA OTTAWAY is senior associate and co-director of the Democracy and Rule of Law Project at the Carnegie Endowment for International Peace in Washington, D.C. She has taught at many universities including Georgetown University, Johns Hopkins University, University of Zambia, University of Addis Ababa, and the American University in Cairo. She is the author of numerous books on African and comparative politics including *Africa's New Leaders: Democracy or State Reconstruction?* (Carnegie Endowment, 1999).

DAN PETRESCU is external affairs officer in the World Bank mission in Bucharest, Romania. He has broad experience in civic activism in Romania since 1989, including work as the director of Centras, a Romanian civic education organization. He has been a Humphrey Fellow at the University of Minnesota.

KEVIN F. F. QUIGLEY is executive director of the Global Alliance for Workers and Communities. Previously he was director of public policy at the Pew Charitable Trusts, where he administered civil society assistance projects in Eastern Europe. He is the author of numerous publications on civil society and political development, including *For Democracy's Sake: Foundations and Democracy Assistance in Central Europe* (Woodrow Wilson Center, 1997).

MARY RACELIS is director of the Institute of Philippine Culture and professor of sociology at the Ateneo de Manila University. She is active in Philippine NGO circles and chairs the board of the Community Organizers Multiversity. She previously headed the Ford Foundation office in Manila and was UNICEF regional director for eastern and southern Africa in Nairobi. She has written extensively on urban poverty, participation, NGOs, civil society, gender, and social change.

MICHAEL SHIFTER is senior fellow at the Inter-American Dialogue in Washington, D.C. He has worked on western hemisphere issues in Washington and Latin America for several organizations, including the Ford Foundation, the Inter-American Foundation, and the National Endowment for Democracy. He teaches Latin American politics at Georgetown University's School of Foreign Service and writes frequently on Latin American politics.

THE CARNEGIE ENDOWMENT FOR INTERNATIONAL PEACE is a private, nonprofit organization dedicated to advancing cooperation between nations and promoting active international engagement by the United States. Founded in 1910, its work is nonpartisan and dedicated to achieving practical results. Through research, publishing, convening and, on occasion, creating new institutions and international networks, Endowment associates shape fresh policy approaches. Their interests span geographic regions and the relations between governments, business, international organizations, and civil society, focusing on the economic, political, and technological forces driving global change. Through its Carnegie Moscow Center, the Endowment helps to develop a tradition of public policy analysis in the states of the former Soviet Union and to improve relations between Russia and the United States. The Endowment publishes *Foreign Policy*, one of the world's leading journals of international politics and economics, which reaches readers in more than 120 countries and in several languages.